CW01018663

ANALYSING
FORMULA 1

To Rosemary, to Nigel, to Simon, without whom…

First published in January 2008

A catalogue record for this book is available from the British Library

ISBN 978 1 84425 447 7

Library of Congress control no. 2007940704

Published by Haynes Publishing,
Sparkford, Yeovil, Somerset BA22 7JJ, UK
Tel: 01963 442030 Fax: 01963 440001
Int. tel: +44 1963 442030
Int. fax: +44 1963 440001
E-mail: sales@haynes.co.uk
Website: www.haynes.co.uk

Edited by Quentin Spurring
Graphics by Rob Loxston
Design by Lee Parsons and Richard Parsons

All photographs are courtesy of LAT Photographic except the following:
Singapore GP PTE: 115
sutton-images.com: 128, 228
Getty Images: 210

Haynes North America Inc., 861 Lawrence Drive,
Newbury Park, California 91320, USA

Printed and bound in Britain by J. H. Haynes & Co. Ltd,
Sparkford, Yeovil, Somerset BA22 7JJ, UK

ANALYSING
FORMULA 1

Innovative insights into winners and winning in Grand Prix racing since 1950

Roger Smith

Contents

Monza, 1957.
Stirling Moss
shows to
advantage the
classic, flowing
lines of the
Vanwall.

Man and boy, I have lived and breathed Grand Prix motor racing these past 50 years. As a baby-boomer, I was at a formative age in 1957, unconsciously on the lookout for some interest or activity to fire my imagination. The name 'Vanwall' still sends a shiver down my spine. In the hands of Stirling Moss and Tony Brooks, at last here was the motor racing success story the British public had been craving.

The news media of the time seems comparatively primitive relative to the digital, satellite and internet driven communications today's 11-year-olds take for granted. Nevertheless, somehow a combination of newspaper headlines and snatches from the wireless must have reached me, even in the relatively isolated environment of preparatory school at Ascot (next to the racecourse).

Let's face it – post-war Britain had had a lot to endure in general and in the world of motor racing in particular. The former axis powers seemed to be having the better of it during the 1950s, economically and on the race track. Alfa Romeo, Maserati and Ferrari represented Italy, and the Silver Arrows, sweeping all before, showed Germany to be still über alles, at least technically. By contrast, the embarrassment of the BRM misadventure and the mediocrity of Connaught created more pain than not participating at all (England footballers, please note).

On the driver front, the 1950s were little better, at least to begin with. Farina and Ascari seemed to be the only ones able to present a realistic challenge to the prowess of Fangio. Until, that is, Hawthorn, Moss and later Collins began to emerge as genuine contenders. But somehow success for British drivers in Ferraris, Maseratis and Mercedes did not quite capture the public's imagination as much as success for British cars would have done. Or better still, British cars with British drivers.

And this was the heady cocktail for the 1957 season. No wonder the newspaper headlines screamed, and loud enough to even catch my attention, tucked away in leafy Ascot.

Anyway, I was hooked, although I did not realise it right away. I still have my model Vanwall from those days – a prized possession. An unusual die-cast replica, large, about eight inches long. More a Burago than a Dinky toy, not perfect but capturing those classic, flowing Frank Costin lines. On the underside it reads: Vanwall. The famous British racing car. Grand Prix winner. And then in smaller lettering, but proudly: Made in Gt Britain. Sadly, the manufacturer's name is not given, but the existence of such a model, thus inscribed, perhaps captures the patriotic joy of the era brought by the success of Tony Vandervell's team.

In my lifelong love affair with Grand Prix racing, I count myself most fortunate on at least two counts. First, my chosen passion happens to be a sport that has grown bigger and stronger and better over the years. In those early seasons of the Formula One World Championship, who could have imagined that in the comfort of one's own living room would be the means to watch live, colour broadcasts of all the races each year, with on-car footage and instant action reply, and fully interactive digital still to come. Second, I was born, through a happy chance, here in Gt Britain (sic), which has become the centre of the Grand Prix racing universe.

I challenge anyone who avidly follows a sport not to be affected by at least a tinge of patriotism mixed up with the pleasure of the sport itself. Watching a master at work defies all national boundaries. But if the master happens to come from your own stamping ground – well, for me anyway, it certainly adds to the emotion and excitement.

Today I can revel in the prowess of Fernando or Kimi without feeling I am being disloyal to Lewis. But it has not always been that way, particularly in those early days. Therefore, due to the wonderful succession of British drivers, manufacturers and champions, I have been granted much added pleasure to my own 'beautiful game'.

I hope this book introduces a few more youngsters to the magic of Formula One and ensures that this wonderful sport's rich heritage is kept alive to future generations. For those already smitten, by the final page I hope you will have found something new to wonder or argue about.

From Hawthorn
to Hamilton.
Lewis is the
latest in a long
line of British
winners since
Mike Hawthorn
opened the
account in 1953.
Montréal, 2007.

Roger Smith

To compete at world-class level is a remarkable achievement in any theatre of sport. It means that an individual or a team has won through at local, regional and national stages and reached the standard of excellence necessary to compete in the world arena. It is a lifetime opportunity, and to fulfil it – actually to be crowned as the champion of the world – is an astounding feat, the ultimate accolade. In the chosen sporting discipline, that person or team has successfully completed the preordained series of tests and, in so doing, has outperformed everyone else on the planet!

Golf, tennis, boxing, cricket, even snooker and darts have their World Championships, or rankings, to determine who is the numero uno. But, at first sight, the Olympic Games and the football World Cup tower above all other events which may genuinely be classified as having world championship status.

Why? It has much to do with the far-reaching number of nations which participate in these two great sporting extravaganzas. But there is a second factor setting these two events apart. It is the immensity of the worldwide television audience they each command.

It may seem hard to accept at face value but, alongside the Olympics and the Jules Rimet Trophy, there is a third sport which attracts the attention of an equally impressive global TV audience. The only difference is that it reaches almost a billion TV viewers each and every year, as opposed to the four-year cycle of those other two world sporting fests.

That sport is Grand Prix motor racing: to give it its formal title, the FIA Formula One World Championship.

What are the seeds of its massive popularity? Formula One encapsulates – absolutely – three innate passions of humanity: its love affair with the car; its obsession with speed; and, above all, its will to win. Add to this a large helping of glamour, its worldwide dimension and the intrigue of power politics, and it is not difficult to appreciate why Formula One is such an intoxicating concoction for so many. Global warming may determine that the days for the internal combustion engine – the technological gemstone at the very heart of Formula One – are numbered. Nevertheless, it is a certainty that, as long as humanity has cause to travel in overland vehicles, there will always be someone devising a sport around it to discover who can travel fastest. And at the pinnacle of that sport will be Formula One… Where there is Formula One, there will be a World Champion.

Setting aside the two elements necessary to any thriving professional sport – a governing body and a financial infrastructure – there are three essential ingredients which make up Grand Prix racing: sublime drivers; great cars; glorious circuits. Thirty-seven nations have been represented by drivers starting Grands Prix and, despite its European origins, half of these have been born beyond that continent. As many as 16 countries have been represented by the cars that have rolled onto the starting grids – a surprising number, when the technical and financial barriers to entry are so prohibitive. As for the circuits, 26 nations across six continents have staged World Championship races.

On 21 October 2007 at Interlagos in Brazil, Kimi Räikkönen became the 29th Formula 1 driver to be crowned World Champion.

The FIA World Championship of Drivers began in 1950. It has always been based on a system of points, awarded and accumulated in relation to results achieved in a series of races in any given year. The driver with the most points is crowned champion. In 1958, a corresponding Constructors' Championship was added, broadly run on similar lines. This development acknowledged the obvious: Grand Prix racing is a human and a technological sport; it is rare that a great driver can prosper without a great car, or vice versa. Grand Prix racing truly unites human sporting endeavour with human technological excellence – a heady fusion.

In this opening chapter, the spotlight is trained on the drivers and the Drivers' championship. The Constructors' championship is explored in depth in Chapter 6.

Across 58 seasons of the F1 Drivers' Championship, 29 drivers have become World Champions. Almost half of these have achieved this remarkable feat more than once. Indeed, between them, these 14 multiple World Champions have accumulated 43 championships, leaving just 15 others.

Alberto Ascari was the first back-to-back champion in 1952–53, and his feat has been emulated by Juan Manuel Fangio, Jack Brabham, Alain Prost, Ayrton Senna, Michael Schumacher and Fernando Alonso. Only Schumacher and Fangio have won more than two in a row, Fangio four consecutively from 1954–57 and, more than 40 years later,

Schumacher's astonishing opening to the new millennium with five on the trot (2000–04).

Such sustained dominance marks out an exceptional kind of sportsman or team. Not only do they reach the top, but they have the staying power to remain there. In any avenue of sport, the bringing together of all the ingredients which create a successful championship season is challenging and complex. To achieve that fusion repeatedly is very special and suggests that true champions, or 'champion champions', should be judged on their longevity and endurance, such as Pete Sampras in tennis, or Jack Nicklaus in golf.

The dismal showing by Schumacher and Ferrari over the course of the 2005 season may have provided a certain relief to many Formula One followers suffering from a monotony which had set in. But their relative failure brought into sharp relief the magnitude of the collective achievement over the preceding seasons. Correspondingly, the ensuing fall from grace of England's 2003 World Cup winning rugby team, along with the triumphant 2005 Ashes winning cricket team, shows that these two squads, and their team entourage, did indeed have a championship within them, but not a period of prolonged dominance. They could raise themselves once, but not sustain it. Neither could be called a 'champion champion'.

Graphic 1.1 identifies the 14 multiple Grand Prix champions and, even within such a formidable list – that

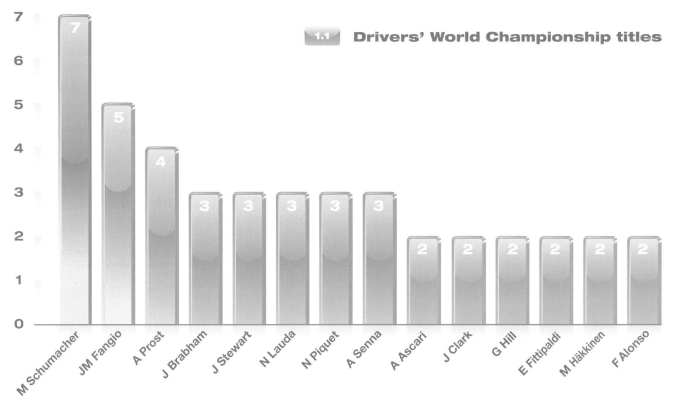

1.1 Drivers' World Championship titles

special breed who have achieved the ultimate accolade more than once – the arrangement of the information tends to establish a new pecking order for the six double champions, five triple champions and the three on the top of the pile who won 16 titles between them: Schumacher, Fangio and Prost.

For many years, it seemed inconceivable that Fangio's five titles could ever be equalled, let alone surpassed. By the same token, now that Schumacher has raised the bar to new heights, it is unimaginable that his feat will ever be replicated.

Additional perspective is needed to relate these two outstanding achievements made more than 40 years apart. By today's standards, Fangio's career was short. He had only seven active seasons, during which he delivered five championships, retiring at the age of 47.

Schumacher, on the other hand, on his retirement at the age of almost 38, had participated for more than twice as long, a further nine years – 16 seasons in total – to accumulate his seven world crowns. The ratio of seasons to championships is 71 percent for Fangio, 41 percent for Schumacher and, for the record, 31 percent for Prost, who retired at the age of 38 after 13 active seasons.

There are numerous caveats which might further qualify these bald statistics, but the most remarkable single number is the duration of Schumacher's career. The distinction with that of Fangio is largely a function of their relative ages but, by comparison with certain others, it lends weight to the grisly fact that the careers of some of the greatest Formula One champions were curtailed when they were in their prime, due to death or injury. This invites the speculation as to who, if their driving careers had not regrettably remained unfinished, had further championships within them: Ascari and Rindt, quite possibly; Clark and Senna, almost certainly.

In the case of Senna, whose career overlapped that of Schumacher, it seems reasonable to surmise that he may have landed three more titles over 1994-95-96, two of which subsequently belonged to Schumacher. But that is not how it was!

With his second title in 2006, Fernando Alonso became the latest driver to join a very select group of multiple World Champions.

Championship showdowns

Sometimes a particular driver/car combination has crushed the competition to such a degree that championship success becomes a foregone conclusion. Such runaway champions rarely make for an exciting championship. Just like a boxer winning with a knock-out blow in the final round of the contest, the ideal scenario is for the Drivers' title to be resolved in the final race of the series. Various mechanisms, such as dropping scores, have been used in an attempt to realise this desired outcome, and with some success. Twenty-four of the 58 championship titles have gone 'down to the wire'. And eight championships have been decided by one point – or even less!

Such was the 2007 championship battle. It went down to the wire and was decided by a single point. But additionally there was a three-way shoot-out for the title – a comparative rarity. As they prepared for the showdown in Brazil, one of the contenders was the reigning double World Champion, Fernando Alonso. On the brink of severing ties with McLaren after a fractious relationship had developed with team boss Ron Dennis, Alonso was attempting to appear philosophical in the face of championship defeat by his upstart team-mate at McLaren. The second contender, quite extraordinarily, was that team-mate, 22-year-old Lewis Hamilton, who in his maiden Grand Prix season led the championship throughout the summer and into the final round. And there in Brazil, with a sublime lap, he had placed his car on the front row ahead of his two championship rivals. The third contender, but a full seven points adrift and therefore the rank outsider, especially from P3 on the grid, was the driver who appeared to have left his mid-season charge for the championship a fraction too late, Ferrari's Kimi Räikkönen.

But, incredibly, this enthralling three-way shoot-out did contain the unexpected twist; it was the long-shot, Räikkönen, who triumphed, having made up a seemingly impossible 17-point deficit on Hamilton in the final two championship rounds.

The finale itself was won at the very first corner. The performance off the grid by the two Ferrari drivers in Brazil was truly stunning. It was akin to observing a smash-and-grab raid: hard to believe what was happening; all over in the blink of an eye, with the McLaren drivers left like dazed

Brazil 2007. The first three-way shoot-out for 21 years produced a result as unexpected as in 1986. Here the three protagonists jostle for position behind leader Massa.

onlookers as the pair of scarlet getaway cars fled into the distance. But even then it wasn't done. Not, that is, until lap 7, when McLaren's phenomenal 2007 reliability also deserted the team, leaving Hamilton powerless (in every sense) for a crucial 30 seconds.

For those who had expected the favourite, Lewis Hamilton, simply to stroll to an unprecedented rookie title, the feeling of incredulity at the outcome of the 2007 championship decider must have lasted for more than a passing moment. And for those with long memories it would have been peculiarly reminiscent of another occasion when the last race appeared to be a foregone conclusion for a title favourite: the previous three-way shoot-out that occurred 21 years earlier. Coincidentally, there were also some uncanny parallels between 1986 and 2007...

The cast of characters in 1986 included a British favourite, the reigning World Champion and a pair of warring team-mates! And the outcome? It was just as hard to swallow, perhaps more so since the startling turn of events took place towards the end of the race rather than soon after the start.

In 1986, Nigel Mansell entered the final round in Australia as the championship leader and hot favourite for the title. He was six points clear of World Champion Alain Prost, driving for McLaren, and another point up on his Williams team-mate Nelson Piquet. Even if one of the other two won the race, all Nigel needed to do was collect two points and his very first championship would be in the bag. And fully deserved it would have been, Mansell's tally of five race wins having been one up on Piquet and two up on Prost.

Following a strong start to the season, Prost still lay second in the points table entering this final round, but he was well aware that the car of the moment was increasingly the Williams-Honda, which had already racked up nine victories that year. The Frenchman had to win but would find that hard, especially from P4 on the grid. The Williams twins had locked out the front row with Mansell on pole. Piquet, lining up beside him, had to ruefully contemplate championship defeat by this upstart team-mate. Instead of riding shotgun as a trusty number two to a double World Champion, Mansell had turned out to be not only very quick but also a prodigious winner in his own right – sound familiar?

With fewer than 20 laps remaining, Mansell was handily positioned in third place, on target for the title. In what has become an iconic Grand Prix moment, captured on television across the world, a sudden twitch and a shower of sparks from the left rear of his car signalled the end of Mansell's championship dream. The tyre had delaminated, bucking Nigel's Williams-Honda into a yawing series of tail flicks as the driver fought for control, his stricken car leaving a trail of sparks as the wheel hub and skid block scoured the track surface.

After such catastrophic tyre failure, the Williams team had little choice other than to bring Piquet in for fresh rubber, handing the race and the title to an incredulous Alain Prost, even on the winner's podium still appearing slightly dazed if eminently happy by this extraordinary change in fortunes.

Twenty-one seasons later, also from the top step of the podium, Kimi Räikkönen, in a rare moment of joy for such an undemonstrative character, revealed his inner emotions as

THREE-WAY CHAMPIONSHIP SHOWDOWNS						
*Excl. Indy 500	*Rounds	Penultimate			Finale	Position
1950	6	Fangio	26	30	Farina	Up 2
		Fagioli	24	27	Fangio	
		Farina	22	24	Fagioli	
1951	7	Fangio	27	31	Fangio	No change
		Ascari	25	25	Ascari	
		González	21	24	González	
1959	6	Brabham	31	31	Brabham	No change
		Moss	25.5	27	Brooks	
		Brooks	23	25.5	Moss	
1964	10	G Hill	39	40	Surtees	Up 1
		Surtees	34	39	G Hill	
		Clark	30	32	Clark	
1968	12	G Hill	39	48	G Hill	No change
		Stewart	36	36	Stewart	
		Hulme	33	33	Hulme	
1974	15	Fittipaldi	52	55	Fittipaldi	No change
		Regazzoni	52	52	Regazzoni	
		Scheckter	45	45	Scheckter	
1981	15	Reutemann	49	50	Piquet	Up 1
		Piquet	48	49	Reutemann	
		Laffite	43	46	Jones	
1983	15	Prost	57	59	Piquet	Up 1
		Piquet	55	57	Prost	
		Arnoux	49	49	Arnoux	
1986	16	Mansell	70	72	Prost	Up 1
		Prost	64	70	Mansell	
		Piquet	63	69	Piquet	
2007	17	Hamilton	107	110	Räikkönen	Up 2
		Alonso	103	109	Hamilton	
		Räikkönen	100	109	Alonso	

he smiled with unabated pleasure at the way the seemingly impossible had come about. A glance at the accompanying table shows that his is just one of ten championships to have been won after a three-way showdown. Before Brazil Kimi might have taken heart from the fact that, marginally, the underdog has prevailed more often over the favourite. There again, he might have been daunted by the knowledge that only once before, way back in 1950, at the beginning of time for the Drivers' championship, has the third favourite come from behind to snatch the prize.

For very many reasons, 2007 was a very special championship year.

Beaten champions

Any points-based system, however well conceived, can occasionally produce eccentricities, and the Drivers' World Championship has had its share. Although down-to-the-wire champions and runaway champions form the two extremes, there is a third and perhaps more controversial category which is also the most emotive.

This third category is sometimes paradoxically labelled 'beaten champions', referring to the 11 occasions on which a rival has won more races than the champion in their championship year. As winning is everything in Formula One, it is somewhat incongruous that the championship points system rewards losers so generously. This keeps the title battle alive for longer, but can result in the possibility of a less than worthy champion. Thankfully, a Formula One World Champion has never been crowned having not won a race at all, but on two occasions, in 1958 and 1982, just one victory sufficed.

The 1980s stand out as having by far the highest incidence of 'beaten champions', the reasons for which will be fully explored in later chapters. It is notable that Prost was the beneficiary twice, as well as losing out on two other occasions. This might suggest that the rub of the green tends to even these things out, although Clark and Mansell may have been unconvinced by this point of view. Certainly few would begrudge a Formula One Champion his hard-won title, but somehow a title seems a little less convincing when it results from consistent points finishes rather than Grand Prix victories. Fortunately, this has not happened since 1989, but very recently, in 2005, the prospect of this possible outcome concerned the 24-year-old and newly crowned Fernando Alonso.

"We are the champions, we are the champions!" Fernando's unmistakable voice reached TV viewers around the world shortly after he crossed the line to win the Chinese Grand Prix in grand style. Even allowing for the distortion on his radio, the new World Champion's singing was unlikely to bring him a parallel pop music

career, yet his musical celebration was just one of many signs of genuine elation. Why did he seem even more euphoric than when he had clinched the 2005 Drivers' title, three weeks and three races previously in Brazil? Was it because he had made amends for Kimi Räikkönen's humiliation of Renault seven days before in Japan? Was it clinching the Constructors' title? Or just the end of a long, hard season? All of these, certainly, but the true explanation was something much deeper in his psyche. Alonso had got a monkey off his back, and one which had really been needling him.

Yes, he was World Champion, the youngest ever, but he had got it into his head that he did not want to emulate eight of his illustrious predecessors, namely

Year	Champion	Wins	Rival	Wins	Points Margin
1958	Mike Hawthorn	1	Moss	4	1
1964	John Surtees	2	Clark	3	1
1967	Denny Hulme	2	Clark	4	5
1977	Niki Lauda	3	Andretti	4	17
1979	Jody Scheckter	3	Jones	4	4
1982	Keke Rosberg	1	Watson	2	5
1983	Nelson Piquet	3	Prost	4	2
1984	Niki Lauda	5	Prost	7	0.5
1986	Alain Prost	4	Mansell	5	2
1987	Nelson Piquet	3	Mansell	6	12
1989	Alain Prost	4	Senna	6	26

Mike Hawthorn, John Surtees, Denny Hulme, Niki Lauda (twice), Jody Scheckter, Keke Rosberg, Nelson Piquet (twice) and Prost (twice). They each shared something in common which some believe dulled the sparkle of their achievement. They were all 'beaten champions'.

With McLaren and Räikkönen in the ascendancy in the latter part of the 2005 season, popular opinion was growing that, perhaps this year, the best car and the best driver had not won the crown. Somehow there was a question mark hanging over Alonso's accomplishment – the feeling that, in a sport which is all about speed, boring old reliability had won over raw pace. The tortoise had beaten the hare.

You could see young Alonso trying to deal with it in Japan, as Räikkönen suffered his fourth engine failure (and consequent 10-place grid penalty) of the season. Why else would he bother to point out that Räikkönen's problem was actually a manifestation of the Finn's good fortune: "Kimi has been lucky… Of the four or five engine problems he has had, they have always been very close

to the race… If they had happened during the race before or on the (following) Sunday, then he would have had 30 or 40 fewer points…"

Alonso had a point, but only within the context of the artificiality of the current 'long-life' engine rule. Not so long ago, an engine failure in qualifying or practice meant bolting in a replacement and going racing.

He was at it again on the Friday in China: "I'm just extremely happy to win the championship with the second quickest car. It doesn't happen very often, but I did it. McLaren are much stronger, so I'm more than happy." Here was someone in denial that he could win on Sunday, still with the mindset that, if that was to be the outcome, he had to take every opportunity to state his case against being branded the tortoise to Räikkönen's hare.

As it transpired, in that final race in China, Alonso beat Räikkönen into second place by four seconds, and the rivals ended the season with seven race wins apiece – as opposed to 8–6 to Räikkönen. No wonder Fernando broke into song on his slowing down lap.

A World Championship title eluded Stirling Moss, most cruelly during his 'Battle of Britain' with Mike Hawthorn in 1958. Here his Vanwall leads the eventual champion's Ferrari at Monaco that year.

A long with age and gender, great attention in sport is paid to nationality. Whether it is your national football team at the World Cup or the winning of individual gold medals in Olympic track and field, everyone loves to be patriotic. They want to see our boys and girls doing their stuff by beating opposition from other countries.

With the ritual playing of national anthems and raising of national flags at the post-race podium ceremony, Grand Prix racing is no different. Indeed, Nazi Germany made it hyper-nationalistic in the 1930s, when the silver Mercedes and Auto Union teams symbolised Deutschland Uber Alles. National colours were actually allocated to countries by the world governing body (see panel).

The multinational composition of team personnel, along with sponsorship logos emblazoned on cars, has perhaps made Grand Prix a little less partial these days. In any case, watching a master at work defies all national boundaries, as exemplified by Senna's passionate following in Japan. Nevertheless, many drivers like to include some national reference in their helmet design and there remains the overarching influence of team partisanship. Grandstands across the world can be a sea of Italian red for Ferrari, or an ocean of Renault blue for France. However, since Alonso's emergence as a championship contender, it has been the explosion of interest in Grand Prix racing in Spain that verifies that nationalism is alive and well in almost every part of our globe. Why was it that in 2005, TV ratings rose sharply in Spain and France, while taking the diametrically opposite direction in Germany and Italy?

The graphics neatly summarise the state of the nations. The first graph (1.2) shows the Drivers' Champions by nation, the second (1.3) the number of Drivers' Championships.

When Fangio decided to retire in May 1958, he commented that his awareness of a passing era was depicted by the increasing presence of mid-engined cars painted green. He was referring, of course, to the emergence of British cars and drivers. By the late 1950s, Britain had usurped all other European nations in terms of both numbers and success. Vanwall, BRM, Cooper, Lotus... Moss, Hawthorn, Collins, Brooks. These were the names that pioneered a lengthy period of British supremacy in Grand Prix racing, and laid the foundations that still place Britain at the heart of Formula One 50 years later.

To substantiate that claim, it is not necessary to search for British World Champions. After all, although Lewis Hamilton came close in 2007, there has not been one since Damon Hill a decade ago. For the evidence, look no further than the fact that seven of the 11 Formula One teams are based in Britain, and the other four employ many British personnel. If more proof is needed, Max Mosley, the president of the FIA, and Bernie Ecclestone, the CEO of Formula One Management, are two 'Brits' who effectively run the whole show!

 Argentina Blue & yellow, black

 Japan White, red disc

 Australia Green & gold, blue

 Malaysia Yellow & white

 Austria Blue, silver stripe

 Mexico Gold, blue band

 Belgium Yellow

 Monaco White, red band

 Brazil Light yellow & green

 Netherlands Orange

 Canada Red, white stripe

 New Zealand Green & silver

 Chile Red, blue & white

 Poland White & red

 CzechRepublic White, blue & red

 Portugal Red & white

 Denmark Silver-grey, red stripe

  South Africa Gold & green

 Finland White, blue stripes

  Spain Yellow & red

 France Blue

 Germany White (silver)

 Sweden Blue & yellow, blue bands

 Great Britain Green

 Switzerland White & red

  Hungary White, green & red

  Thailand Light blue, yellow band

 Ireland Green, orange band

 Uruguay Light blue, red band

 Italy Red

 USA White, blue stripes

 Venezuela White, green stripe

 Venezuela White, green stripe

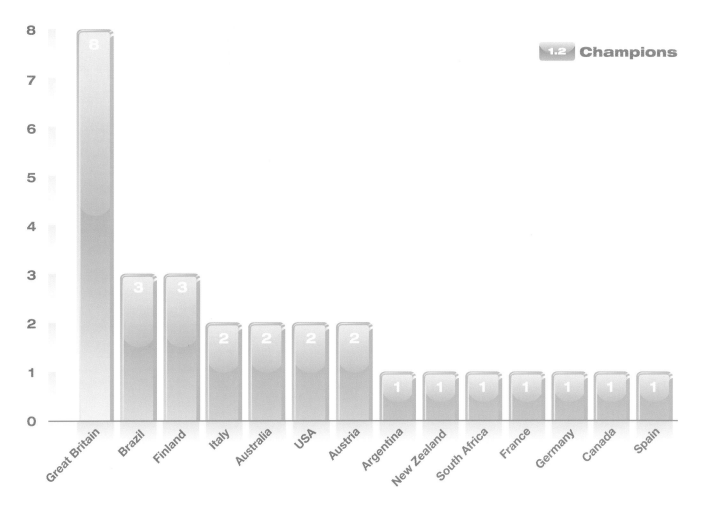

It is open to discussion to what extent the substantial British involvement in Formula One has led to more British champions than any other nationality. As many Brits have participated in Grand Prix racing as Italians and Frenchmen put together. Even so, despite the presence of Ferrari in Maranello, Italy has produced only two champions from 15 Grand Prix winners, and not one for more than 50 years. As for France, despite the Elf driver-sponsorship scheme which promoted many young French drivers to Grand Prix status in the 1970s and 1980s, Prost remains the only champion from as many as 12 French winners of Grands Prix.

After Britain, two nations record the most champions. One is Brazil: the country which stands astride the football World Cup is also a runner-up in Formula One – the sport with their second most passionate national following. The pressure on Rubens Barrichello and Felipe Massa from their homeland must feel palpable at times...

With the addition of Fangio's five titles, South America is right up there in producing some of the greatest Grand Prix drivers over the decades, the Brazilians in particular having honed their skills in British Formula 3. There are also seven champions from the English-speaking nations of Australia, New Zealand and South Africa who owed their success, at least in part, to their British connections. So, to a much lesser degree, did three North American champions, two from the USA and one from Canada.

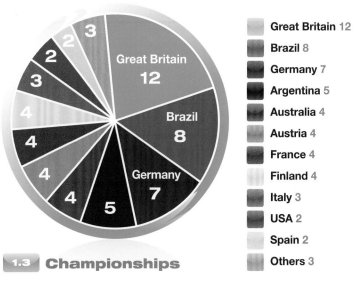

1.3 Championships

Great Britain	12
Brazil	8
Germany	7
Argentina	5
Australia	4
Austria	4
France	4
Finland	4
Italy	3
USA	2
Spain	2
Others	3

But there is another country which has just been elevated alongside Brazil to equal second place in the nations' league table of champions. Kimi Räikkönen, 'The Iceman', became Finland's third World Champion in 25 years, a record made even more exceptional by the fact that this country, situated on the Arctic Circle, has a comparatively tiny population. It must be something in the water...iced water.

That age-old problem

There is a fascination with age when sporting performances are compared across the decades. In most sporting arenas, youth seems constantly to challenge maturity and the 'youngest ever' mantle is normally worn proudly by the latest bright young thing: the youngest ever Wimbledon champion, the youngest ever footballer to play for his country, and so on.

It is now widely acknowledged that the modern Grand Prix driver is truly an athlete, and needs to be in peak mental and physical condition in order to retain concentration and motor-neuron alacrity, to absorb high temperatures and crushing g-forces, and to improve the chance of survival and recovery in the event of trauma.

Boris Becker, the youngest ever Wimbledon champion at the age of 17 years and 228 days, is proof enough that the exceptional teenager has the strength, fitness and athleticism to participate in the highest echelons of sport. In the early 1950s, 'men of steel' were required to drive Grand Prix racing cars for three hours or more, but it is difficult to imagine today's youthful Grand Prix pilots thriving in such circumstances. Yet, in this age of the personal trainer, fitness programmes and dietary regimes,

In his rookie season, Lewis Hamilton matched Jacques Villeneuve's record of four victories and became the youngest driver to lead the World Championship.

let alone personal managers, mentors and psychiatrists, one can only conclude that they would have coped equally well, quite probably better.

As for driving talent, that natural and invisible ingredient which separates the great from the average, this can burgeon at an indecently young age and, in the modern world, expresses itself most often through the highly competitive sport of karting.

Karting has long been regarded as the nursery slope for top-level motor sport. Since the 1980s, the majority of Formula One champions have served their apprenticeship in karts – Damon Hill is a recent if rare exception to that rule. Indeed, karting even features at the prestigious end-of-year celebration, the Autosport Awards, when the good and the great of motor sport gather to pay homage to winners, winning and success, the key motivations of sporting endeavour. The youngest award recipient, barely able to reach the microphone, is normally around 10 years old, has beaten allcomers to some cadet kart championship title, and is on the threshold of being offered a manufacturer driver programme. This is where precocious talent is identified,

LEWIS HAMILTON'S CAREER TIME-LINE				
Age	Year	Category	Series	Result
10	1995	Karting	British - Cadet	Champion
11	1996	Karting	McLaren Mercedes Champion of the Future - Cadet	Champion
12	1997	Karting	McLaren Mercedes Champion of the Future - Junior Yamaha	Champion
13	1998	Karting	McLaren Mercedes Champion of the Future - Junior ICA	Runner-up
14	1999	Karting	JICA	Runner-up
15	2000	Karting	Formula A	World No 1
16	2001	Formula Renault	Winter Series	5th
17	2002	Formula Renault	UK	3rd
18	2003	Formula Renault	UK	Champion
19	2004	Formula 3	Euro Series	5th
20	2005	Formula 3	Euro Series	Champion
21	2006	GP2	GP2 Series	Champion
22	2007	Formula One	World Championship	Runner-up

sponsored and groomed through the lower racing formulae in order to reach Formula One stardom and deliver winners' titles to their corporate masters.

The highest-profile example of this process is Lewis Hamilton, his meteoric career having been nurtured in exactly this way by McLaren and Mercedes-Benz (see panel). Despite Hamilton's impressive curriculum vitae, his closely managed and staged career development has meant that he did not have the opportunity to better Mike Thackwell's long-standing record as the youngest driver to start a Grand Prix. Back in 1980, aged 19 years and 159 days, Thackwell blasted his Tyrrell from the Montréal grid, but raced only as far as the first corner, where a clash with his team-mate eliminated both on the spot. Making a rather more auspicious debut than Thackwell was a driver who in 2007 did set an age-related record. Sebastian Vettel, substituting for Robert Kubica after the Pole's terrifying accident in Canada, brought his Sauber BMW home in eighth place in the US Grand Prix at Indianapolis. At 19 years and 349 days, he had already become only the sixth driver under the age of 20 to have started a Grand Prix, but by winning one championship point the young German also beat Jenson Button's equivalent benchmark established in 2000.

Record books also needed to be consulted when 22-year-old Lewis Hamilton won only his sixth Grand Prix. Did this remarkable achievement also represent a new age record over the incumbent? No. In 2003, just 26 days after his 22nd birthday, a certain Fernando Alonso became the youngest Grand Prix winner, beating the record set by Bruce McLaren 43 years before.

In sharp contrast, the oldest winner of a World Championship event has been Luigi Fagioli, who, at the age of 53, was credited with a shared victory when Fangio took over his team-mate's Alfa Romeo to win the 1951 French Grand Prix. And for the record, the oldest driver to participate in the World Championship was Louis Chiron: born in Monte Carlo in 1899, he raced a Lancia D50 into sixth place there in 1955 at an age almost three times that of Thackwell on his debut.

When the Drivers' Championship began in 1950, the average age of the starting grid was almost 41 (Graphic 1.4). This came down quite rapidly until 1960 and then remained stuck around 30-31 years, only dropping below 30 for the first time in 1994. From there a more distinct downward trend became discernible, although the average has never fallen below 28 because many teams continue to blend youthful talent with proven experience. As drivers such as Rubens Barrichello (debut 1993) and David Coulthard (debut 1994) demonstrate, a career lasting 15 years or more is possible in Grand Prix racing today, as long as a driver can maintain motivation and continue delivering.

Graphic 1.4 also shows that there have been seven 'youngest champions' since the inception of the Drivers' Championship in 1950. The first to win the title, Giuseppe

At Indianapolis in 2007, Sebastian Vettel became only the sixth driver aged under 20 to start a Grand Prix.

Farina, was almost 44. This, of course, was an anomaly resulting from pre-war cars and drivers largely populating the grids in the formative years of the new Formula One. In 1952, with Alberto Ascari's first title, the average age of the champion plummeted by 10 years, but at 34 his was still an age when the thoughts of many of today's drivers might be turning towards retirement, voluntary or otherwise...

Following Ascari's twin crowns, Fangio's run of championships ended in 1957, when the great man was 46. It was not until 1958 that someone who could be described as a genuine post-war driver first won the title. Mike Hawthorn's Grand Prix career began in 1952 and, along with Stirling Moss, Pete Collins, Tony Brooks, Stuart Lewis-Evans and others, he represented the influx of much-needed young blood into the sport as its popularity grew steadily throughout the 1950s.

Even so, at 29, Hawthorn was no spring chicken, and within five years Jim Clark had knocked another couple of years off the 'youngest' accolade. Of the next six champions who followed Clark, three were older (John Surtees, Jack Brabham and Graham Hill), and the others won their only or initial title at a later age (Denny Hulme, Jackie Stewart and Jochen Rindt). It was not until 1972 that a new and significant benchmark was made.

Emerson Fittipaldi won his first title at the comparatively tender age of 25 years 270 days. Thrust into the responsibility of Lotus team leader in 1970, following the death of Rindt, Fittipaldi won first time out in this new leadership role, in only his fourth Grand Prix start. And for that same team, in only his third active season, he took the Drivers' title.

Fittipaldi's achievement is remarkable for the fact that over 30 years would pass before his record was bettered. Over that lengthy period, and despite the emergence of such all-time greats as Alain Prost, Ayrton Senna and Michael Schumacher, not one of them won their first race or reached champion status at an earlier age. Also, because these three (and others such as Niki Lauda and Nelson Piquet) were multiple champions, Fittipaldi's record remained safe for longer.

Until 2005, that is, when Fernando Alonso, already the youngest ever Grand Prix winner, knocked 18 months off Fittipaldi's record, leaving it standing at 24 years and 57 days – close to half the age of Fangio when he won his fifth and final title.

Naturally, if events in Brazil 2007 had taken a different course, the first rookie World Champion would have also become the youngest title winner. And for one more year at least, he still can!

By winning the 1972 title, Emerson Fittipaldi became the youngest World Champion, a distinction he held for more than 30 years. At Brands Hatch he won an epic duel with Jacky Ickx (seen here) and Jackie Stewart.

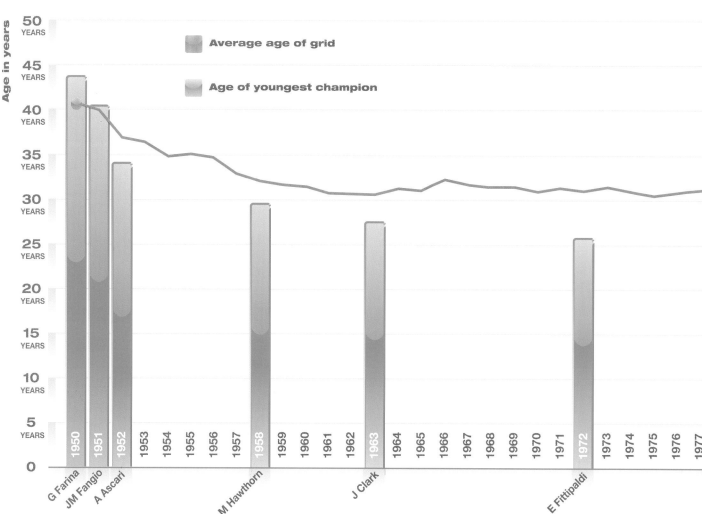

1978	1979	1980	1981	1982	1983	1984	1985	1986	1987	1988	1989	1990	1991	1992	1993	1994	1995	1996	1997	1998	1999	2000	2001	2002	2003	2004	2005	2006	2007

F Alonso

A long with age, there is another time-related statistic which generates much discussion. This is the swiftness by which a certain achievement landmark is reached. In Button's case, it was the number of races it would take him to receive the chequered flag for the first time…

How long does it take for cream to rise to the surface, for the champion to emerge from the pack? Graphic 1.5 suggests that there is no set norm. It plots both the number of races and the number of seasons that each of the 29 Formula One Champions has taken to win his first title. Once the first three named are acknowledged, but eliminated as the result of somewhat artificial circumstances, the eye is drawn to the other end of the scale. There sits 2007 World Champion Kimi Räikkönen, alongside his compatriot Mika Häkkinen, both late developers it appears. But the daddy of them all is Nigel Mansell, who took 13 seasons and 176 races before he landed his one and only title. Jenson Button

and others can take heed – and encouragement!

The tale of Mansell's championship is one of self-belief, determination and stamina. It illustrates how easy it is for opportunities to slip away, for things to go wrong. It demonstrates the importance for all the ingredients making up a championship season to come together, and the need to keep them together until the job is done. It confirms just how difficult the task is to achieve just the once, let alone numerous times. The reality is that, with Williams, Mansell could quite easily have been a four-time World Champion (in 1986–87, and 1991–92).

Mansell made his Grand Prix debut in 1980, the first of five fallow years with Lotus. The great Colin Chapman had belief in Mansell, and his mentor's death was naturally a massive setback in the latter part of his Lotus period. When Mansell clouted the barrier at Monaco, losing control on a wet track surface while leading the 1984 Grand Prix, many will have doubted that he would ever win a race, let alone a championship.

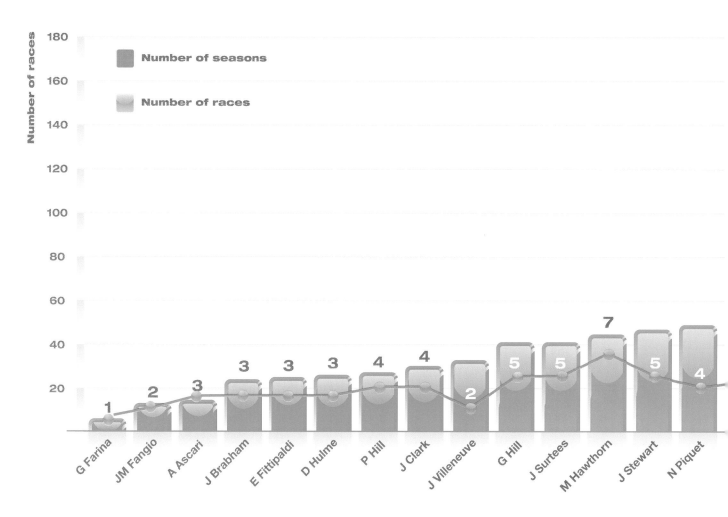

A switch to Williams for 1985 changed everything. Powered by Honda engines, the potential of the Mansell/Williams package was immediately apparent. His very first victory came towards the end of the season, in his 72nd Grand Prix start. That first success was like uncorking champagne. Mansell became a prolific winner, amassing 31 Grand Prix victories – the fourth highest all-time total.

In both of the next two seasons, Mansell was a strong contender for World Championship honours, competing with Senna, Prost and Piquet. As described earlier, on the threshold of victory the 1986 title was cruelly snatched from his grasp. Surely, things would work out differently 12 months later, wouldn't they?

For 1987, Mansell reached the penultimate round in Japan on a winning roll which might well have led to championship success, particularly in view of the fact that Nelson Piquet, his team-mate and championship-leading rival, added no further points to his total in those final two races. In the event, it was immaterial. An accident in practice ended Mansell's season, and his hopes.

After a spell at Ferrari, 'Il Leone', as the tifosi had nicknamed him in homage to his courageous approach to racing, returned to Williams with the promise of another genuine crack at that elusive title. Williams, now with Renault power, had designed and developed a car that took the application of electronic control mechanisms to new heights in the areas of suspension, gearbox and traction. In 1992, a 'B' version of the magnificent, Adrian Newey designed Williams FW14, which many consider to be the most technologically sophisticated car of all time relative to its opposition, combined reliability with dominant performance to realise Mansell's lifelong ambition. It could have (maybe should have) happened 12 months earlier, but poor early-season reliability gave Senna, McLaren and Honda far too much of a head start. On that occasion, although Mansell was a genuine contender, the title was not truly warranted.

As Lewis Hamilton has already learned to his cost, the Mansell story says much about the capriciousness between championship success and failure. His 13-year quest is in sharp contrast to Jacques Villeneuve, whose achievement – claiming the championship crown in only his second full season – must be placed on a very special pedestal.

Each championship has its own characteristics, and what this chapter discloses is that it is not only the racing, but often also the fight for the championship itself, which provides the most compulsive elements of F1. The championship is the glue binding together a series of races, many filled with excitement, some not so. But with each twist and turn in the points table, every one makes its special contribution to the ongoing Formula One World Championship story.

1.5 Time taken to first championship

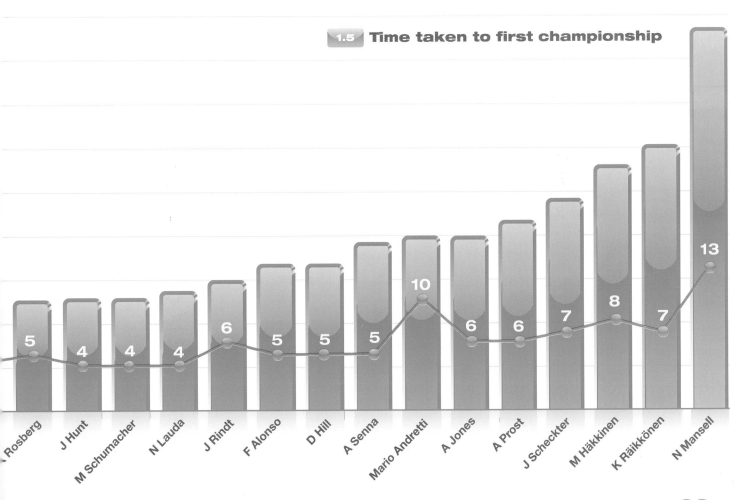

Rosberg	J Hunt	M Schumacher	N Lauda	J Rindt	F Alonso	D Hill	A Senna	Mario Andretti	A Jones	A Prost	J Scheckter	M Häkkinen	K Räikkönen	N Mansell
5	4	4	4	6	5	5	5	10	6	6	7	8	7	13

As has been seen, from time to time the World Championship points system – any points system – will produce champions who are not even the most successful drivers in their years of triumph, let alone the most deserving. So what? Good luck to them! They have (usually) played by the pre-ordained rules and come out on top of the pile. But, although championships add excitement and interest, it is for this reason that they should not form the basis by which excellence and mediocrity are distinguished. A measure besides championships and championship points must be found to separate the good from the great. In Grand Prix racing, that criterion is elegantly simple: winning races.

That is, after all, the rationale for the Grand Prix race – an event that normally reaches its climax as the victor crosses the finish-line and then, ushered to the top step of the podium, receives the crowd's acclaim and adulation. Yes, there can be many types of victories: the richly deserved or the fortuitous; the exciting or the dull; the farcical, even the tragic. Whichever, on that particular day, from all those who powered away from the starting grid together, one driver has completed the set distance at the fastest speed and is thus declared winner. Between 1950 and 2007, a total of 774 races have been won from a pool of 624 drivers making 17,499 Grand Prix starts.

Hungary, 2004. By taking his 12th victory from 13 starts that season, Michael Schumacher rewrote the record books and brought new meaning to the term 'serial winner'.

nd yet, despite the significant number of drivers and the vast number of attempts they have made to win a Grand Prix across those 58 years, a mere 88 have actually taken the chequered flag (Graphic 2.1). This remarkable statistic is not only a measure of the difficulty of winning in Formula One. It also signals what an outstanding accomplishment it is for those comparative few who have achieved such a feat… possibly comparable with winning an Olympic medal.

2.1 ### Just 88 winners in 58 years

Formula One World Championship: 1950-2007 (excl. Indy 500)

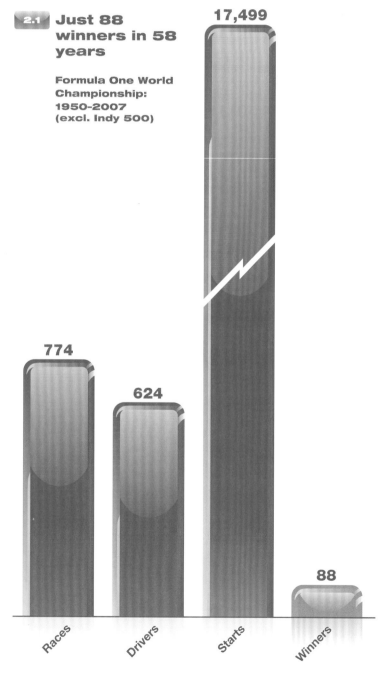

774
Races

624
Drivers

17,499
Starts

88
Winners

To emphasise the point, it means that there are drivers who have made hundreds of attempts to win that elusive first Grand Prix – but have failed despite considerable talent. At the very top of this list are Andrea de Cesaris, with 208 Grand Prix starts without a win, Martin Brundle with 158, and Derek Warwick with 147.

How can it be possible that Martin Brundle failed to win a Grand Prix, let alone a World Championship, despite nearly – and perhaps that's the point – despite nearly beating the great Ayrton Senna to the British Formula 3 title in 1983?

The following season, they both graduated to Formula One, Brundle joining Tyrrell, and Senna Toleman. Brundle's points finish on debut and second place at Detroit (the eighth round) was an impressive enough start to any Formula One career. Senna achieved similar performance milestones during the first half of the season. Did it all go wrong for Brundle, therefore, at the ninth championship race in Dallas when he received severe injuries due, by his own admission, to a self-induced practice accident?

Brundle recalled: "I went out, and it was almost a question of not whether I would be on pole, but by how much. On my first flying lap, I hit the wall and smashed up my feet. I think Ken [Tyrrell] could see I was going to do that. I had come from winning in F3, to finishing fifth in Brazil, to standing on the podium in Detroit – to ending up in hospital."

The circumstances of this accident are germane. Brundle and his team-mate (and fellow Grand Prix debutant), the highly rated Stefan Bellof, were driving naturally aspirated Tyrrells when turbo engines had become the required power source. Senna's Toleman-Hart was turbocharged, as indeed was the entire grid by the end of that season. Opportunities for Brundle and Bellof would come at the street circuits – Monaco, Detroit and Dallas – where the nimble properties of the Tyrrell-Ford DFV V8 could be fully exploited. At Monaco (the sixth round), Bellof qualified 20th and last. In attempting to emulate his team-mate, Brundle crashed heavily.

"I came through the chicane leading to the harbour front faster than I had done before," said Brundle. "The lap was near inch-perfect. The chicane was bloody near flat-out in our car, which meant arriving into the left-hander at Tabac at some staggering speed. The brake pedal went all soggy. I'd touched a kerb somewhere and got a bit of knock-off on a pad."

So Brundle failed to qualify, whereas Bellof finished a strong third behind Alain Prost and Senna, catching them both in the rain-shortened race. At the next street circuit, in Detroit, the tables were turned. Brundle finished strongly, snapping at the tail of winner Nelson Piquet's Brabham-BMW turbo as they crossed the finish-line, while Bellof crashed out at half-distance.

Brundle: "On the very next lap, he crashed. It was as if he needed to prove he was faster than me. Anyway, I now had fresh tyres and I just charged. I was absolutely flying."

The performance of the Tyrrell was indeed astonishing, and it would transpire that it was partly due to the adoption of underhand methods for which, shortly after the Dallas race, the whole Tyrrell team would be disqualified from the championship for that season.

As life itself, Formula One is full of the 'what-ifs', 'nearlys' and 'what-might-have-beens', as the Brundle anecdote serves to illustrate. It also hints at the difficulties of reaching the top, let alone remaining there, and suggests that many elements need to be brought together simultaneously. Chance may have some small part to play but, rather than a slice of luck, success will have far more to do with qualities such as vision, determination, attitude, judgement, and plain hard work – all mixed together with a vital ingredient called talent.

And, speaking of luck, remember that, ironically, it was Senna and Bellof who were each to die behind the wheel.

Detroit, 1984. Martin Brundle, in his first season, finished just one second behind winner Nelson Piquet – he never came closer to victory in a further 10 seasons.

There are winners... and there are winners

n Formula One, then, just becoming a race winner warrants high praise. But deeper analysis of how the 774 Grand Prix wins are distributed across our 88 winning drivers reveals something even more extraordinary. At one end of the scale, one driver – Michael Schumacher – accounts for more than 90 wins (Graphic 2.2). At the other, it requires the combined total of virtually 50 drivers to account for a similar win tally.

Such a phenomenon is known as the Pareto Principle (or the 80:20 Rule). This rule may be observed in many walks of life, particularly wealth, whereby a significant majority is concentrated into the hands of a relatively small minority, broadly in the ratio 80:20. In the case of Grand Prix racing (Graphic 2.3), just 27 drivers – 31 percent of all race winners – account for 76 percent of all race wins!

Naturally, these top 27 are all multiple Grand Prix winners, having each won 10 or more races (see Graphic 2.4). Are these 27 our 'serial winners'? Moreover, with more wins than any other, does this make Schumacher the greatest driver of all time?

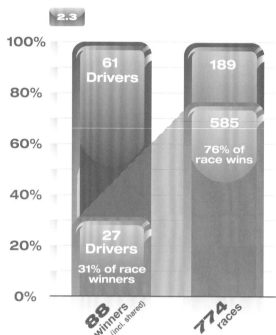

2.3

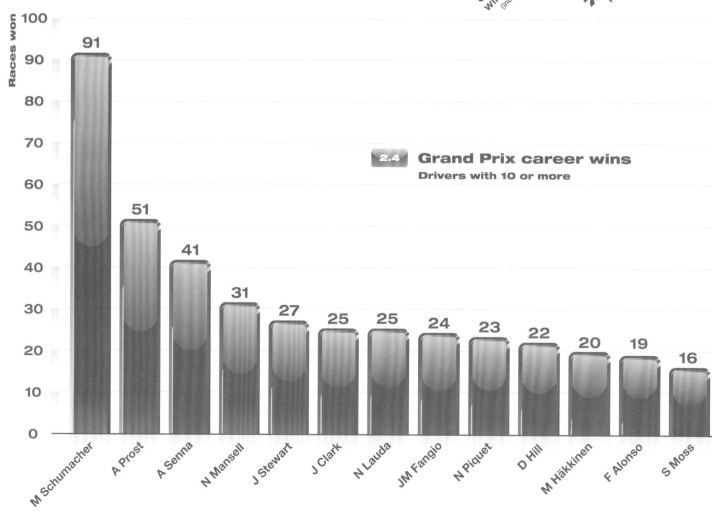

2.4 **Grand Prix career wins**
Drivers with 10 or more

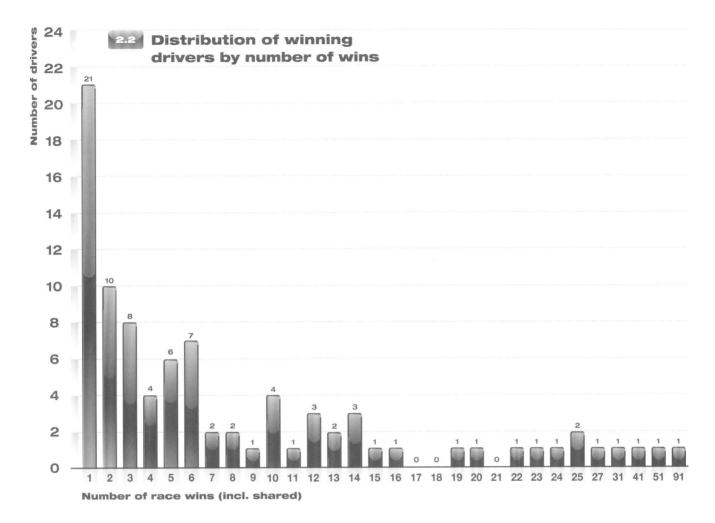

2.2 **Distribution of winning drivers by number of wins**

Number of drivers (y-axis): 0, 2, 4, 6, 8, 10, 12, 14, 16, 18, 20, 22, 24

Number of race wins (incl. shared) (x-axis): 1=21, 2=10, 3=8, 4=4, 5=6, 6=7, 7=2, 8=2, 9=1, 10=4, 11=1, 12=3, 13=2, 14=3, 15=1, 16=1, 17=0, 18=0, 19=1, 20=1, 21=0, 22=1, 23=1, 24=1, 25=2, 27=1, 31=1, 41=1, 51=1, 91=1

The answer is a categorical 'no' to both questions, although Schumacher's statistics are simply incredible. It is hard to believe that he ended up just nine short of a century of victories, and one short of the combined total of the next two on the winners' list, no less than Prost and Senna. Will Schumacher's tally of 91 wins ever be surpassed? Of today's drivers, Fernando Alonso comes nearest, with 19 race wins. He has a long, long way to go to even get close!

But absolutes are just one measure. The full comprehension of winning requires more analysis, further qualification. Schumacher's remarkable haul of wins was generated from an inordinately long career, over 16 seasons. His total of 249 Grand Prix starts is behind only Rubens Barrichello and Riccardo Patrese's record 256.

To achieve his phenomenal 91 victories, Schumacher also took part in 158 races in which other drivers were the winners. To place a win record into perspective, and to be able to relate it to another, it is generally accepted that the number of starts is applied to create a ratio normally referred to as 'strike rate'.

So, wins as a percentage of starts = strike rate.

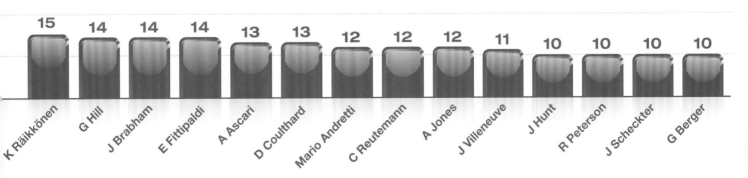

K Räikkönen 15, G Hill 14, J Brabham 14, E Fittipaldi 14, A Ascari 13, D Coulthard 13, Mario Andretti 12, C Reutemann 12, A Jones 12, J Villeneuve 11, J Hunt 10, R Peterson 10, J Scheckter 10, G Berger 10

nce drivers' strike rates are superimposed on the win counts (Graphic 2.5), a very different picture of their relative success emerges. Juan Fangio stands out with a rate of almost one win in every two starts (47 percent) whereas, at the other extreme, Gerhard Berger's total of 10 wins was accumulated at a rate of one in every 20 starts (5 percent). Wonderful though Berger's achievement is – ranking equal 23rd on our all-time list of Grand Prix winners – he patently could not be considered a 'serial winner' with an average, based on today's 17 to 18 races per year, of around one win per season.

In sharp contrast, in a season of similar duration, Fangio's strike rate would have taken him to the chequered flag between eight and nine times, and achieve this average each and every season he raced. He was truly a 'serial winner'.

But is the percent strike rate a sound indicator? The calculation assumes a direct correlation between winning and the opportunity to win for a given driver. For example, if Stirling Moss (24 percent strike rate from 66 races) had made the same number of starts as Prost (26 percent strike rate from 199 races), his tally of 16 wins would have climbed close to Prost's 51 wins.

It is impossible to speculate over the Moss/Prost scenario, but in his first 66 starts – equivalent to Moss's complete career – Prost won 12 times, suggesting the hypothesis to be a reasonable one.

Additionally, there are two other abundant winners with a similar 1 in 4 career strike rate – Jackie Stewart and Senna. Stewart again bears out the validity of the correlation, winning 14 times in his first 66 races, just two short of Moss and two more than Prost. With his prolific McLaren period yet to come, Senna defies the hypothesis with only seven victories, suggesting that strike rate comparisons require a minimum number of starts to allow more or less productive periods of winning to even out. One hundred starts could be

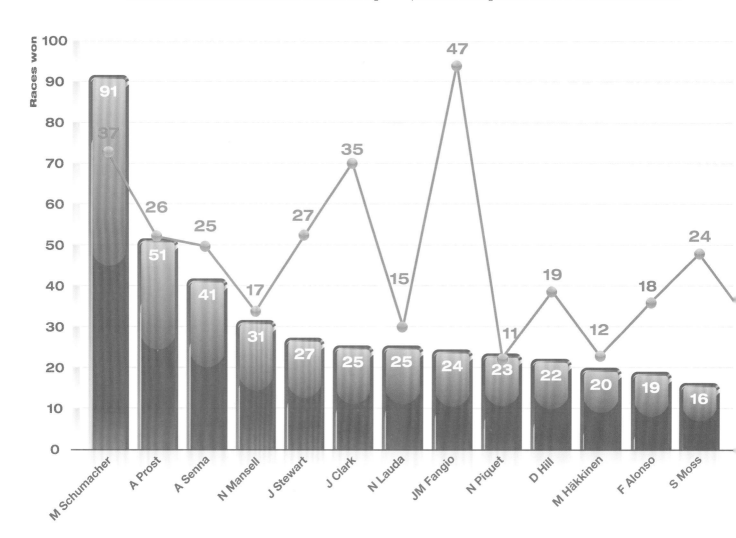

considered (equivalent to around six seasons of Grand Prix racing today), but this would eliminate such as Fangio (24 wins from 51 starts = 47 percent strike rate) and Jimmy Clark (25 wins from 72 starts = 35 percent strike rate). Fangio and Clark each raced over between seven and eight seasons – lengthy careers, albeit little more than half that of Schumacher. Their lower race-start numbers are also a function of the fact that, in the 1950s and 1960s, there were far fewer World Championship Grands Prix and, regrettably, at that time highly successful careers could be abruptly curtailed by death or serious injury.

Fangio's 47 percent strike rate is truly phenomenal. To place it in perspective, Michael Schumacher would have needed to add a further 26 successive Grand Prix victories to his vast tally in order to reach and match Fangio's record!

Other examples may be taken from the 1950s and 1960s that point towards strike rate being a sound comparative indicator. When the cars of Alfa Romeo in 1950 and Ferrari in 1952 swept the board, each team won six and seven Grands Prix respectively. If there had been 10 or more additional races in the season, as there are today, would their team drivers have been just as dominant as Ferrari's Schumacher and

Barrichello in 2002 and 2004? Yes – without question.

In 1963, when Jim Clark won seven of 10 races, would his 70 percent strike rate have translated into 12 victories over a 17-race season of today's duration? Yes – without question, and probably more!

So, strike rate is a simple yet effective way to compare winners across different eras. However, to a born winner, that first Grand Prix win has been likened to releasing a genie from the bottle. Once they know they can do it – as well as how to do it – they can repeat it again and again.

Some of the top 27 winners had lengthy early careers before they were able to release that genie, perhaps because they were not driving potentially winning machinery. Others had long career 'tails', bereft of winning, often associated with the development of a new car or team, as the following examples show:

MOST PRE-WIN STARTS		MOST POST-WIN STARTS	
Mika Häkkinen	96	Jacques Villeneuve	132
Nigel Mansell	72	Emerson Fittipaldi	78
Ronnie Peterson	40	Graham Hill	70

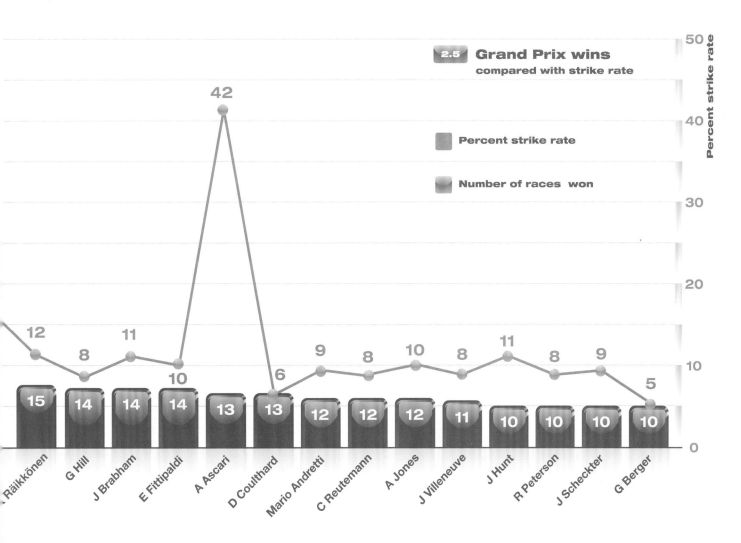

2.5 **Grand Prix wins**
compared with strike rate

Percent strike rate

Number of races won

These considerable variations between the commencement or cessation of winning during a driver's career make it worth exploring a revised definition of strike rate, one which calculates wins as a percentage of those races between the first and the last win, eliminating lengthy winless periods at the beginning or the end of a career. However, when the numbers are reworked accordingly (Graphic 2.6), does revised strike rate bring a totally new perspective to the interrelationship between our Grand Prix winners?

In short, no! It does not rewrite the pecking order of our top 27 race winners. Alberto Ascari takes over from Fangio at the top; Clark moves ahead of Schumacher to third; Moss moves up to number six. But the broad shape is not significantly disturbed – with one notable exception.

With the longest 'tail' in the business (Graphic 2.7), Jacques Villeneuve soars to sixth place, and in so doing, introduces a further qualification to the definition of the Grand Prix 'serial winner'. This is sustainability: the capacity

Alberto Ascari winning the 1953 Swiss Grand Prix at Bremgarten. This was the last of an extraordinary sequence of 13 victories from just 16 starts.

not only to reach the summit, but to stay at or near the top, season in, season out.

Villeneuve's enhanced position is based on two prolific winning years. So too Ascari's revised strike rate, derived from a two-year purple patch between the 1951 German Grand Prix and the 1953 Swiss Grand Prix. Ascari won all 13 of his victories from a mere 16 race starts, for a remarkable strike rate of 81 percent. This included nine successive wins, a record of domination and consistency which still stands to this very day. Both of these examples point to the need to add a further dimension to the term 'serial winner'.

Sifting through the facts suggests that, to become eligible, a driver must have achieved at least five 'winning' seasons in his Grand Prix career. Such a cut-off point would mean that, as well as Ascari and Villeneuve, such great names as James Hunt, Alan Jones, Mario Andretti and Ronnie Peterson are also eliminated, although all six drivers, for very different reasons, enjoyed magnificent yet comparatively short periods in the ascendancy.

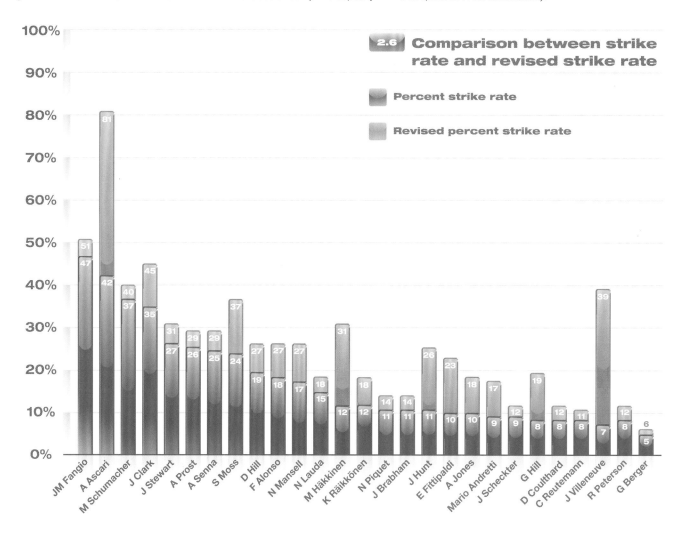

2.6 Comparison between strike rate and revised strike rate

Percent strike rate

Revised percent strike rate

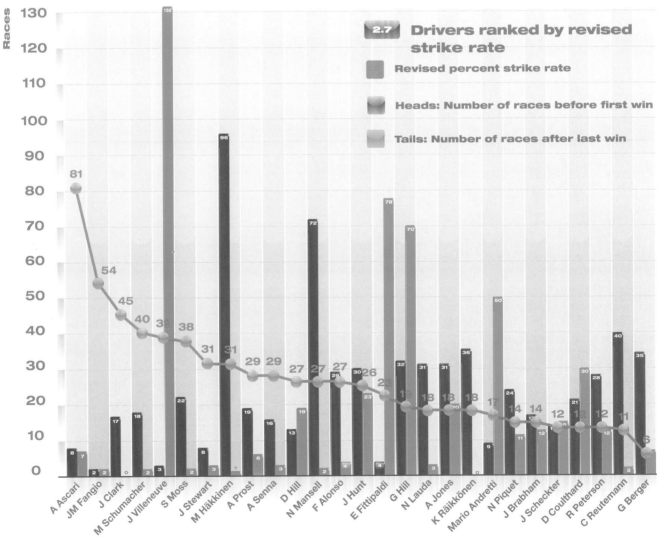

Races

130
120
110
100
90
80
70
60
50
40
30
20
10
0

| 2.7 | **Drivers ranked by revised strike rate** |

Revised percent strike rate

Heads: Number of races before first win

Tails: Number of races after last win

A Ascari · JM Fangio · J Clark · M Schumacher · J Villeneuve · S Moss · J Stewart · M Häkkinen · A Prost · A Senna · D Hill · N Mansell · F Alonso · J Hunt · E Fittipaldi · G Hill · N Lauda · A Jones · K Räikkönen · Mario Andretti · N Piquet · J Brabham · J Scheckter · D Coulthard · R Peterson · C Reutemann · G Berger

W hat mechanisms can be used to narrow the field further, and isolate the truly prolific winners in an equitable fashion? Put another way, when does a multiple Grand Prix winner become a 'serial winner'?

Examining the preceding analysis, it is not difficult to identify the most appropriate measures which differentiate a 'serial winner'. Three clear-cut criteria emerge which, for reference purposes, may be called the 20/20/5 rule.

Logic dictates that the first measure is a driver's absolute number of wins. Setting aside the top three really heavy-hitters (Schumacher, Prost and Senna), 20 wins offers a clear and significant threshold.

Second, any driver who has achieved a strike rate of 20 percent (one win for every five starts) surely qualifies. Such success levels require a high penetration of wins per season and/or a high frequency of wins over the seasons.

Which leads to the final criterion – sustainability, or the number of seasons a driver can keep on winning. Sifting through the evidence suggests that, to become eligible as a 'serial winner', a driver must have attained at least five 'winning' seasons in his Grand Prix career. So a minimum of five winning seasons becomes the third and final factor.

What happens when the 20/20/5 rule – at least 20 wins or 20 percent strike rate over five winning seasons

– is applied to the list of the top 27 winners? Fewer than half survive. Only 12 drivers (Graphic 2.8) still qualify as authentic 'serial winners'.

A time series (Graphic 2.9) of the specific winning years for these 12, with the number of wins made in each year also shown, indicates that, across 58 years there is barely a season when at least one of these was not victorious. These drivers account for more than half of all Grands Prix victories ever – a massive 55 percent, or 397 races, attributable to just 12 drivers.

By definition, dominance can rarely be a concurrent attribute, so it might be expected that the careers of these 12 'serial winners' tended not to overlap. To some extent, this is true, at least until the mid-1980s. At that time, something changed, which will be explored more deeply in later chapters. What can be said now is that, for a decade or so, four of the most prodigious winners of all time were in direct competition together.

Overall, however, the incidence of dominating drivers across each passing decade nicely illustrates that each era has normally produced its 'serial winners'. The supremacy of just two drivers since the turn of the century, Schumacher and Alonso, is not a wholly new phenomenon.

The most unexpected 'serial winner' is Damon Hill. He won regularly over the years against more highly regarded team-mates and rivals. Here Michael Schumacher offers a sporting hand after Hill beat him in their gripping duel at Suzuka in 1994.

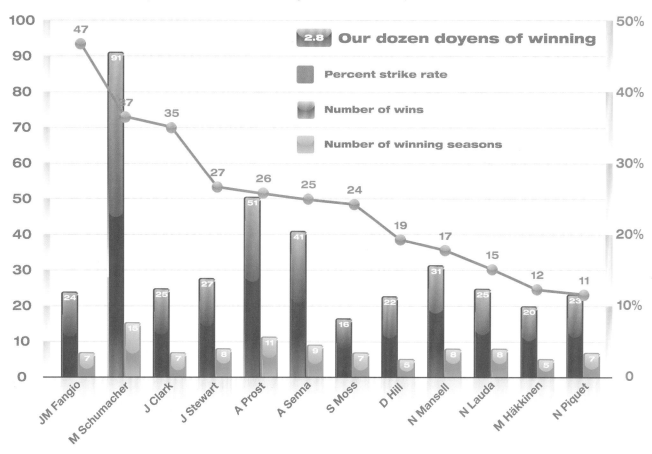

Driver	1950	1951	1952	1953	1954	1955	1956	1957	1958	1959	1960	1961	1962	1963	1964	1965	1966	1967	1968	1969	1970	1971	1972	1973	1974	1975	1976	1977	1978	1979	1980	1981	1982	1983	1984	1985	1986	1987	1988	1989	1990	1991	1992	1993	1994	1995	1996	1997	1998	1999	2000	2001	2002	2003	2004	2005	2006	2007
JM Fangio	3	3		1	6	4	3	4																																																		
S Moss						1	2	3	4	2	2	2																																														
J Clark													3	7	3	6	1	4	1																																							
J Stewart																1	1		3	6	1	6	4	5																																		
N Lauda																									2	5	5	3	2				2		5	1																						
N Piquet																															3	3	1	3	2	1	4	3			2	1																
A Prost																																3	2	4	7	5	4	3	7	4	5			7														
A Senna																																				2	2	2	8	6	6	7	3	5													
N Mansell																																				2	5	6		2	1	5	9		1												
M Schumacher																																											1	1	8	9	3	5	6	2	9	9	11	6	13	1	7	
D Hill																																												3	6	4	8		1									
M Häkkinen																																																1	8	5	4	2					

But which is 'the man'?

So with our 12 'serial winners' now firmly established by the facts, the next and inevitable question is: Which is the greatest winner of them all?

A simplistic answer would be Schumacher, with his incredible 91 victories.

Or should it be Fangio due to his remarkable 47 percent winning strike rate?

Some would be in no doubt that it should be Clark because of the dominant nature of his wins in a regrettably foreshortened career.

But what about Senna and Prost? They unquestionably had the greatest on-track rivalry, and had simultaneously to contend with the likes of Nigel Mansell and Piquet.

Moss? Has to be! Then there's Stewart. And Lauda... and, and, and!

Among our final dozen, there are some who, although great, will never be acknowledged as 'the man'. On that basis, it becomes clear that yet one more iteration is required to identify the final short-list. To achieve this, it is better to raise the bar for our existing measures, rather than introduce yet more criteria. One possibility is to raise the number of winning seasons qualification from five to seven, but this eliminates only two, namely Damon Hill and Mika Häkkinen. Raising the number of race wins to 20 eliminates Moss alone.

In 1993 Alain Prost returned from a sabbatical to challenge Ayrton Senna one more time. He won the World Championship, but not in a manner that usurped Senna as 'the man to beat'.

Which leaves the most telling qualifier of the three: percent strike rate. By upping the ante for strike rate to over 20 percent, we eliminate five, finally leaving – The Magnificent Seven.

Now, at last, we have a list of Grand Prix greats who not only possess extraordinary winning credentials but, during their particular periods at the summit of Grand Prix racing, were each acknowledged by common consent as 'the man to beat'. These seven giants of the sport span more than five decades, providing joined up brilliance with the exception of the seven years between 1974 and 1980. So who is the missing link?

Niki Lauda makes by far the most compelling case to fill the vacuum between Stewart's retirement and the emergence of Prost. In between Lauda's high points, however, too many lean years produce a strike rate well below par.

With the fourth highest all-time win tally, Mansell also pressures for a place in the final grouping but, again, as we have seen already, his record suffers from four barren early seasons at Lotus.

In the end, such considerations merely serve to emphasise the outstanding credentials of the seven. Their victory records can genuinely be described as 'magnificent', as the next chapter describes.

THE MAN TO BEAT	WHEN	KEY CHALLENGERS
FANGIO	1950–1957	Ascari, Moss
MOSS	1958–1961	Brabham, Brooks
CLARK	1962–1967	G Hill, Brabham, Surtees
STEWART	1968–1973	Ickx, Rindt, Fittipaldi, Peterson
Interregnum	*1974–1980*	*Lauda, Andretti, Hunt, Scheckter*
PROST	1981–1987	Lauda, Piquet, Senna, Mansell
SENNA	1988–1993	Prost, Piquet, Mansell
SCHUMACHER	1994–2004	D Hill, J Villeneuve, Häkkinen

The Magnificent Seven

Seven remarkable drivers averaged at least one win every fourth race they ever started, and were each acknowledged by their peers as 'the man to beat'.

'The men to beat':
Juan Manuel Fangio,
Stirling Moss, Jim
Clark, Jackie Stewart,
Alain Prost, Ayrton
Senna and Michael
Schumacher.

The king is dead, long live the king! As with a monarchy, in Formula One only one sovereign can reign at any one time as the acknowledged ruler, as the man to beat. Unlike a monarchy, the process of succession is complex in F1, and not always apparent immediately. Very often, it is only with hindsight that it becomes clear who has been anointed and assumed the throne. It also remains a comparatively rare occurrence.

Across the 58 years since the FIA World Championship of Drivers began, Michael Schumacher's successor will be only the eighth. Of these, in the dangerous game which is F1 racing, the reign of three ended tragically through death or injury. All three left so many unanswered questions, each beginning with the phrase, 'What if...'? Two others retired, or abdicated their throne to another. Perhaps their desire, essential to competitive motivation, was quenched or had dissipated. Perhaps they saw the writing on the wall or simply tired of being the acknowledged ruler in a dangerous sport. The remaining two, both of whom had exceptionally long Grand Prix careers, were usurped, deposed by another while still at the height of their powers. Neither went quietly. The first coup produced an enmity that developed into the most intense personal rivalry that Formula One has ever witnessed. The second was Michael Schumacher who, following his 2005 débacle, fought like a champion but lost in his final season.

Who Schumacher's successor will be is not yet certain. Fernando Alonso and Kimi Räikkönen stand first in line but neither has yet totally vanquished the other, and other drivers seem to have quite different visions of the future. As to Schumacher's predecessor, there is no question. In effect, Schumacher inherited the man to beat mantle on a tragic day at Imola in 1994. That black May Day was one of many which came to blight the Formula One World Championship, the inaugural race of which had also been held in the month of May, some 44 years earlier.

Due to the Second World War, motor racing development had been frozen in time for almost a decade. This accounted for the essentially pre-war technology of the cars and the age maturity of the drivers assembled for that first World Championship race at Silverstone in 1950.

Juan Manuel Fangio was the first in Formula One to establish among his peers a natural order as 'the man to beat'. This is the 1953 French Grand Prix at Reims, where Froilán González (20) is the man trying to beat Fangio (18) at the start.

It is often a source of surprise when it is pointed out that, as a 22-year-old, Stirling Moss was a participant in the World Championship of Drivers from as early as 1951. For this reason, his opinions about the pecking order in the formative 1950s should count for a great deal. He stated: "I have never driven against, nor subsequently identified, a driver who was better in a single-seater than the great Argentine, Juan Manuel Fangio, although Alberto Ascari and Giuseppe Farina and a few others ran him pretty close."

Perhaps that throwaway at the end – "and a few others" – is Moss's way of not ignoring his own claims to greatness, but we will come to that shortly. What Stirling's assertion does is to identify the three drivers who were the leading protagonists of 1950s Grand Prix racing, the greatest exponents of taming those large, front-engined machines with their narrow, treaded tyres, so evocative of the period.

The first Drivers' World Champion, Farina, was almost 44 years old when he won in 1950 and, quite reasonably, it could be considered that he was already past the zenith of his driving skills. Before the war, he had driven in Alfa Romeo's works team, at that time run by Enzo Ferrari, and these were the teams with which he was associated post-war. As well as his World Championship, he won five Grands Prix, the last in 1953 before his retirement two years later, but in truth he was eclipsed by Fangio at Alfa Romeo and by Ascari at Ferrari.

Ascari's star burned brightly for a comparatively short time, but long enough for many to regard him as the greatest driver of his age. To this day, he holds the record for the number of successive Grand Prix victories – nine. At the end of 1951 and for the following two seasons, he was almost unstoppable, achieving his tally of 13 Grand Prix victories from just 16 starts. In 1955, aged 36, he died in an unexplained accident at Monza while testing a Ferrari sports car.

On learning of Ascari's death, Fangio is reported to have said: "I have lost my greatest opponent." It is true to say that, at the time of the tragedy, both had won the World Championship twice, while Fangio had just nudged ahead of Ascari in terms of race victories, albeit one of them a shared drive. Fangio had missed the 1953 season due to injury, but it is a testament to their shared superiority – both veterans by today's standards – that, up until then, they had won 71 percent between them of all the races since the inception of the World Championship.

In fact, there were few races in which they had been pitted against each other when driving potentially race-winning machinery. They finished first and second only three times, Ascari beating Fangio on two of these occasions. Perhaps the more significant was at the Nürburgring in 1951, when Ferrari and Ascari were making a late-season charge to topple the might of Alfa Romeo

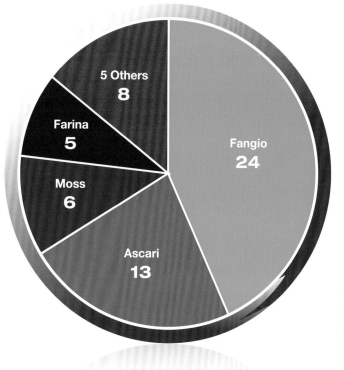

Race victories: [1950–57]

5 Others **8**

Farina **5**

Moss **6**

Ascari **13**

Fangio **24**

3.1 Juan Manuel Fangio

JM Fangio 24

A Ascari 13

S Moss 6

G Farina 5

5 Others 8

and Fangio. Indeed, they went into the final race of the championship that year separated by only two points.

The records show that, after Ascari's death, Fangio went on to win the championship on a further three occasions, amassing a tally of 24 victories from 51 starts, for a strike rate of 47 percent – which remains unsurpassed to this day. One of the qualities which made him the man to beat of his era was his sustained level of achievement over many years, winning races in every season in which he took part except the partial season of his retirement year, 1958.

Some say that Fangio simply had the knack of being in the right car at the right time. But is that luck? More usually, it shows the judgement required which makes an outstanding champion. He gained the respect of the new young chargers who joined the Grand Prix circuit after the war, the likes of Moss, Mike Hawthorn, Peter Collins and Tony Brooks. He was after all, almost twice their

age, but this deference was much more than the normal patronage of those times. On and off the track, Fangio wore the champion's mantle with panache, exceeding or matching the challenges laid down to him on the circuits, and conducting himself with grace and dignity away from them. This behaviour was not through any misplaced sense of importance – quite the reverse. His demeanour was natural, unforced, and if anything based on how he thought others expected a champion should behave.

Fangio's final Grand Prix victory is widely regarded as his greatest. At the formidable Nürburgring, he brought his 250F Maserati from behind to beat Hawthorn and Collins in their Lancia Ferraris at the 1957 German Grand Prix, effectively cementing his fifth World Championship at the age of 46. In 1995 'The Maestro', as Fangio became known, died at the grand age of 84 and to the end maintained that special aura which surrounds a champion and the man to beat.

Stirling Moss's assertion that Fangio was 'the man to beat' came from first-hand experience. This is the 1955 Dutch Grand Prix at Zandvoort: after 100 laps and almost three hours' racing in their Mercedes W196s, the pair finished just three-tenths of a second apart.

The exploits of Stirling Moss gave him legendary status in his home country, Britain, where he was known as 'Mr Motor Racing'. A London bus driver, irritated by the antics of a motorcyclist weaving in and out of the traffic, leaned out of his cab window at some traffic lights asking: "Who do you think you are? Stirling Moss?" As the rider looked up at him, grinning, the bus driver was flabbergasted to recognise that it was indeed Stirling, a household name in those times.

Moss was at the epicentre of a seismic shock-wave that pulsed through international motor racing in the late 1950s, and from which the Grand Prix world has never fully 'recovered'. British cars and British drivers began to win with increasing regularity, and have continued to do so ever since. Cause or effect, this resulted in British-based companies and organisations, run and populated by British work forces, being at the heart of the Formula One industry, an infrastructure broadly still in place to this day, 50 years on.

When Stirling took over Brooks's Vanwall and raced to victory at Silverstone in 1957, he became the first driver to win a Grand Prix in a British car. Achieving this feat at the British Grand Prix added to the delight of a highly patriotic driver as well as the appreciation of a grateful nation – a sporting nation, which had had to endure the humiliation of the BRM V16 saga some years earlier.

Moss had already been the first Briton to win his home Grand Prix when he controversially led home Fangio at Aintree in 1955. However, to Hawthorn went the accolade of the first race win for a Briton in the World Championship of Drivers when, at Reims in 1953, he beat Fangio fair and square, by a single second.

The rivalry with Hawthorn added immensely to the myth surrounding Moss. Here were two highly contrasting characters, the playboy versus the professional. Their 1958 championship battle gripped the British public: who would succeed, the athlete in the British Racing Green Vanwall, or the hedonist, the turncoat, in his scarlet Ferrari? Hawthorn won the championship with a single race victory to Moss's four. To this day, Stirling is widely known as the 'greatest driver never to win the championship'.

For the flamboyant Hawthorn, the ending was pure tragedy. Grieved by the death of his 'Mon Ami Mate', Pete Collins, at the Nürburgring in August, Mike, still not yet 30, decided to throw in the towel and not defend his title. Ironically, before his championship year was ended, he had lost his life in a high-speed road accident on the Guildford by-pass.

With Hawthorn and Collins no more, and Brooks throwing in his lot with Ferrari, once more Moss became the British talisman, this time up against the new dual

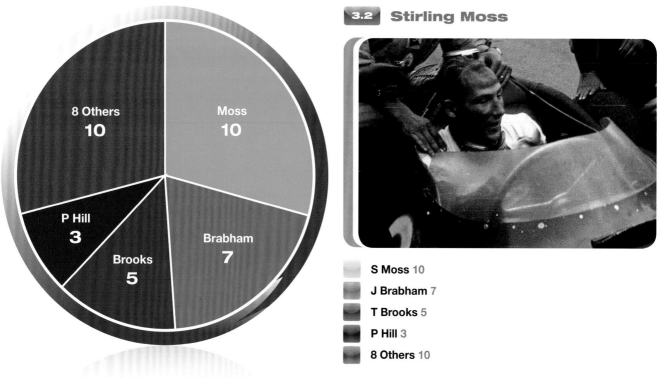

3.2 Stirling Moss

Race victories: (1958–61)

- S Moss 10
- J Brabham 7
- T Brooks 5
- P Hill 3
- 8 Others 10

Pie chart labels:
- 8 Others 10
- Moss 10
- P Hill 3
- Brooks 5
- Brabham 7

driving force from the Antipodes, Jack Brabham and Bruce McLaren, both racing for the Cooper Car Company.

Over the following three years, it was largely patriotism that caused Moss to drive for the Rob Walker's independent team, for which he sustained a regular success rate of wins. But the next and final milestone in this gifted driver's brilliant career came in 1961, up against the might of Ferrari. His wonderful wins against superior machinery at Monaco and on the Nürburgring won him deserved acclaim, proving that, at least on a 'driver's circuit', genius behind the wheel could overcome superior equipment. Rightly, Fangio's natural successor as the man to beat was later honoured with one of just three motor racing knighthoods.

Moss, seen at Monaco in Rob Walker's privately entered Lotus 18, was at the height of his power in 1961.

Moss's dreadful accident in 1962 at Goodwood and enforced retirement left the way clear for the next man to beat, and on this occasion he emerged quite quickly.

Prior to his 'tortoise and hare' championship battle with Graham Hill in 1962, Jimmy Clark had already spent two seasons with Lotus, the team for which he drove throughout his illustrious, if foreshortened, career. In his first season, the final year of the 2.5-litre Formula One, Clark scored points in his second ever race and reached the podium on his fifth Grand Prix outing: obvious signs of exceptional potential. Further podium finishes followed in the first year of the new 1.5-litre formula but, without a Cooper in 1960 or a Ferrari in 1961 – unless your name was Moss – the chances of winning were slight.

The mid-engine revolution spearheaded by Charles and John Cooper had moved Grand Prix car design on apace, but it was Team Lotus that took the concept into its next phase. Colin Chapman's brilliant monocoque Lotus 25, powered by the new Coventry-Climax V8 engine, brought new meaning to lightness, compactness, rigidity and nimbleness in chassis construction. Such was Clark's supremacy over this period, he could have matched Fangio's four successive titles with just a little more reliability in 1962, and again in 1964 with its updated successor, the Lotus 33. As it was, he won 20 of the 38 Grands Prix run

between 1962 and 1965, twice as many as his nearest rival, Graham Hill.

The 1966 season heralded the new 3-litre formula but, without fully competitive engines, it was a lean year for Chapman and Clark, although they did manage one fortuitous victory due, ironically, to reliability!

The following year held far more promise when Team Lotus had exclusive use of the brand new DFV V8 engine from the Cosworth Engineering company, funded by Ford. Chapman was again innovative, using this specially designed engine as a stressed chassis member on which he hung the rear suspension. With this car, the Lotus 49, Clark's reputation soared to even greater heights. The combination won on debut and on three other occasions that season, but it was yet another typical Team Lotus season of win or bust, and the more reliable Brabham-Repco of Denny Hulme took the World Championship, with two wins fewer than Clark. That season, Clark and his Lotus 49 led each of the nine Grands Prix they started and 100 more laps than the nearest competitor, the 1967 World Champion!

That Clark was the man to beat had long since been accepted by his peers, but that year – even more so than in 1963 and 1965 when he totally demolished the opposition – he seemed to be on a plane higher than any of his rivals. How could his pole position lap at the Nürburgring be nine

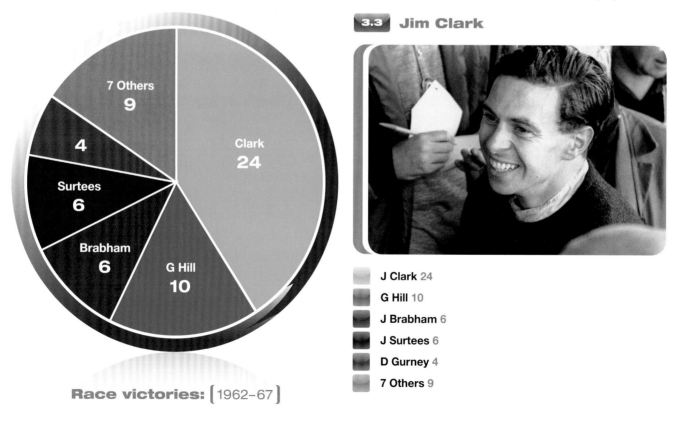

3.3 Jim Clark

Race victories: [1962–67]

J Clark 24
G Hill 10
J Brabham 6
J Surtees 6
D Gurney 4
7 Others 9

seconds faster than the next man? Having lost a lap at Monza due to a puncture, how did he make up the lap and reclaim the lead? It was cruel that he was robbed of victory with fuel starvation on the final lap.

When the news first broke, it was impossible to grasp that Clark was gone. He was such a superlative driver that a tragic ending just made no sense. In a racing car, he was masterly, yet out of it he came across as reserved, even nervy. He did not cut a self-assured figure at all. Witness the television advertisement he made for the British School

of Motoring: "Driving a Formula One Lotus needs special training, but teaching people to drive needs special training too." The voice with its soft highland burr, lacking any conviction, was hardly the TV presence one would associate with a World Champion and sporting hero. This was the Berwickshire farmer somewhat out of his depth in the world of advertising. But the very same man could step into his Formula One Lotus and become 'The Flying Scotsman', possibly the greatest racing driver the world had yet seen.

Typical Jim Clark. After just one lap of the 1965 British Grand Prix at Silverstone, 'The Flying Scotsman' has streaked into a dominant lead.

The names Jackie Stewart and Ken Tyrrell became as synonymous as Jim Clark and Colin Chapman. Stewart came to the attention of the motor racing fraternity driving Ken Tyrrell's Formula 3 Cooper-BMC, with which he thrashed allcomers, winning 15 from 18 races in 1963. The Grand Prix world had been given notice that here was a hot property ready to join their ranks, a new young driver with all the hallmarks of star quality. Chapman attempted to lure him into a seat next to Clark, but Stewart chose to learn his trade beside Graham Hill at BRM. Again, in his first season, all the classic signs of potential greatness were there, as he secured a point in his very first race and won from only his eighth start, at Monza. Between these two landmarks, he finished second to Clark three times. The motoring press made much of their Scottish ancestry with headlines such as 'Highland Fling' and 'Double Scotch'.

After posting a commendable 11 Grand Prix victories over four years, BRM made a poor transition to the 3-litre Formula One and the following two years were largely wasted for Stewart. The 3-litre BRM H16 engine took time to develop and, when it eventually materialised, it underperformed. With an old V8, Stewart did win at Monaco in 1966 and became the BRM team leader when Hill switched to Lotus in 1967, but the defining point in those two years was his crash at Spa in 1966 – a life-changing ordeal.

This traumatic event triggered Stewart's campaign for increased safety for which, even today, racing drivers should applaud him, although at the time his efforts were not always understood or appreciated.

Another 'life change' for Stewart was in his outward persona. In the early years with BRM, his appearance could be described as normal, even conservative – hardly the glitzy, showbiz style it was to become. By the time of Roman Polanski's movie, 'Weekend of a Champion', featuring Stewart at the 1971 Monaco Grand Prix, he and his wife, Helen, looked very much the style of fashion icons. Jackie was sporting long hair and sideboards, along with his John Lennon cap and Ray Burns. Thankfully, he decided against flares on his racing overalls!

Alongside his BRM commitments in 1967, Jackie continued to drive for Ken Tyrrell in Formula 2 in a highly successful partnership. Tyrrell used chassis supplied by the French aerospace and automotive company, Matra. This relationship was one of the essential ingredients which enabled Tyrrell and Stewart to enter Grand Prix racing together the following year. Another was Ford's decision to limit the exclusive arrangement with Lotus for the Cosworth DFV to one year, so in 1968 it was made more widely available.

Stewart's challenge for the title that year in the Tyrrell Matra-Ford was thwarted by a wrist injury sustained in Formula 2, but his three Grand Prix victories included

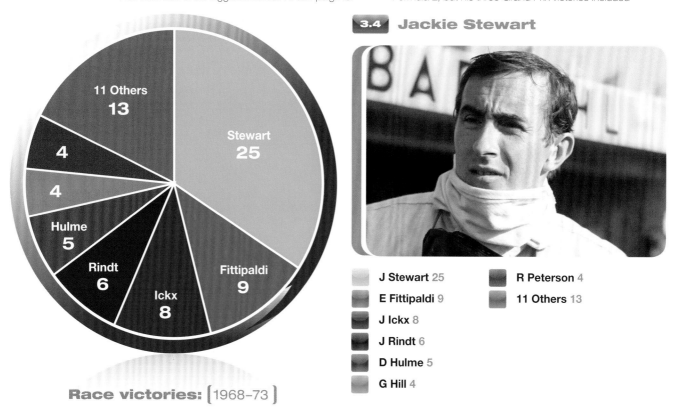

3.4 Jackie Stewart

Race victories: [1968–73]

- J Stewart 25
- E Fittipaldi 9
- J Ickx 8
- J Rindt 6
- D Hulme 5
- G Hill 4
- R Peterson 4
- 11 Others 13

a virtuoso performance at a rainy and misty Nürburgring, where he won by the extraordinary margin of four minutes!

Stewart's three championship years of 1969, 1971 and 1973 were each commanding triumphs during which he won 17 of his eventual total tally of 27 race victories. In the two intervening years, he was competitive but his campaigns were compromised by injury or poor health at a time when he needed to be at his best to resist the challenge of his two greatest track rivals: Jochen Rindt in 1970 and Emerson Fittipaldi in 1972, both armed with Colin Chapman's Lotus 72.

The nature of Stewart's friendship, and rivalry, with Rindt is well illustrated by a cameo from the 1969 British Grand Prix. In well matched machinery, these two supremely talented Grand Prix drivers thrilled the capacity crowd when they duelled for lap after lap. In qualifying, Stewart had crashed his Matra MS80, spinning across the track and crunching heavily into the vertical railway sleepers on the outside of Woodcote, the corner still in its full-blooded, pre-chicane form. The cause of the accident was a sudden tyre deflation, which in turn was due to a loose kerbstone at the apex of the corner. Stewart had clipped this kerbing in his attempt to rest provisional pole from Rindt's Lotus 49B. With qualifying over, a little group gathered at Woodcote to inspect the offending kerb, including a cigarette smoking Jochen and a long-haired JYS. Good-natured banter ensued between them with Jackie having much the upper

hand, the repartee including: "I'd steer clear of this corner tomorrow if I were you, Jochen." With no glib answer forthcoming, Rindt just took another pull on his fag, with the resigned smile of one who had lost this particular psychological skirmish.

The race the next day was also Stewart's but, three years later at Brands Hatch, in a similar duel for the lead, he was beaten by four seconds by his other arch-rival, Fittipaldi. Rindt and Fittipaldi were the only drivers to mount a sustained competitive challenge to Stewart during his six-year reign as the man to beat.

With 27 victories and three World Championship titles, Stewart's was a glittering career but, for one so engaged by matters of safety, it had an ill-fated ending.

The inferno that consumed poor Roger Williamson during the 1973 Dutch Grand Prix at Zandvoort was another factor which made Stewart resolve that this would indeed be his final season. During Stewart's nine-year Grand Prix career, Williamson was the eighth fatality at a Grand Prix meeting. Stewart was only too conscious that such as Jimmy Clark, Mike Spence, Bruce McLaren, Piers Courage and his close friend, Jochen Rindt, had all perished in these or other motor racing accidents. His final race, the US Grand Prix at Watkins Glen, was to have been his 100th Grand Prix start.

But it did not happen. The charming young Frenchman, François Cevert, his Tyrrell team-mate, was tragically killed during practice, and the Tyrrell team was withdrawn.

British Grand Prix, Silverstone, 1969. After crashing during qualifying, Jackie Stewart took over his team-mate's Matra MS80 for the race the next day. In a thrilling duel, he beat Jochen Rindt on his way to the first of his three World Championship titles.

Stewart's abrupt departure from the scene left something of an interregnum. The natural successor seemed to be Fittipaldi, now driving for McLaren. In fact, Emerson won his second championship that year, but by no means in dominant fashion. Indeed, ever since being somewhat overshadowed by Ronnie Peterson in the second half of the previous season, when they raced side-by-side at JPS Lotus, Fittipaldi was never able fully to assert himself as the man. In any case, in 1976 he took himself out of contention by joining his brother in an unsuccessful five-year foray with their own team.

In 1974, there were no fewer than seven drivers victorious in a close, 16-round World Championship battle. Peterson (Lotus) and Carlos Reutemann (Brabham) both matched Fittipaldi's three wins, but there was another driver who won only twice that year, but who led more races and more laps than any of them. He raced a Ferrari. His name: Niki Lauda.

Lauda's emergence as a future three-time World Champion and, if not the man to beat, the most successful winner of the period, was somewhat unexpected. He entered his first full season of Grand Prix racing in 1972 with the STP March team on a rent-a-drive basis. The car was hopeless and such a disastrous season might well have finished a lesser man. However, his tenacity and business acumen resulted in a seat at Marlboro BRM for 1973. Despite the limitations of his equipment over those first two

The start of the Austrian Grand Prix in 1977. This was a period when no single driver became 'the man': remarkably, the grid at the Osterreichring contained five existing World Champions and a future one – Alan Jones, who was the surprise winner of this race from 14th on the grid.

seasons, Lauda had shown enough glimpses of his innate talent to have come to the notice of the perceptive people at Maranello.

The Lauda period at Ferrari is described more fully in the next chapter. Suffice to state here that together they won the World Championship in 1975 and 1977, having lost by a mere point in 1976. That historic intervening season concluded in controversy within Ferrari because of Lauda's decision to withdraw from the streaming wet finale in Japan, thereby losing his title to James Hunt. This, effectively, created a rift within the team that never healed.

Those doubters in the Ferrari camp were made to pay when Lauda left the Scuderia before the completion of the 1977 season, just when further spoils of victory might well have been expected. Before he turned his back on Ferrari, Lauda had delivered another championship title and had made the talented Reutemann, who had been drafted into the team in case Lauda was not fully up to the task following his appalling Nürburgring accident, look quite ordinary.

Niki still had one more display of his single-minded personality to inflict upon Formula One. This was when he retired from motor racing following practice for the Canadian Grand Prix in 1979, claiming he was fed up with driving "round and round in circles". His switch to Bernie Ecclestone's Brabham Alfa Romeo team for 1978–79 had

3.5 An interregnum

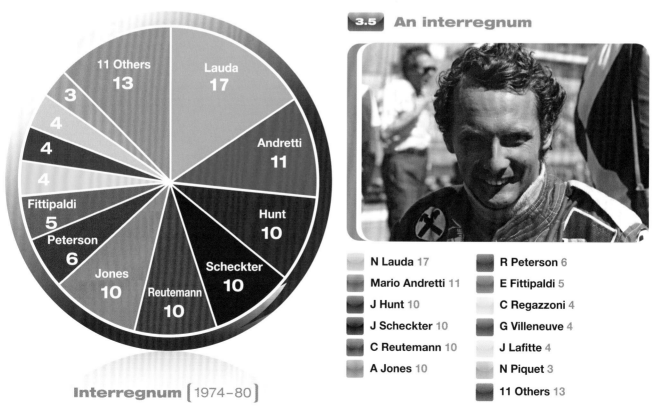

Interregnum (1974–80)

N Lauda 17		R Peterson 6	
Mario Andretti 11		E Fittipaldi 5	
J Hunt 10		C Regazzoni 4	
J Scheckter 10		G Villeneuve 4	
C Reutemann 10		J Lafitte 4	
A Jones 10		N Piquet 3	
		11 Others 13	

not really worked out, and any claim Lauda may have made as the man to beat finally dissolved over those last two seasons. Not that the likes of Peterson, Mario Andretti, Jody Scheckter or Gilles Villeneuve had supplied a fully convincing alternative.

Lauda's departure from the scene was not forever. In 1982, he returned for a further four-year stint with McLaren, winning eight more races (including the fourth race after his return), and lifting the 1984 World Championship. He won it by just half a point from the very man who, from 1981, had genuinely assumed the mantle as the man to beat – the diminutive Frenchman, Alain Prost.

By contrast with Lauda eight years before, Prost's entrance into Formula One took a more conventional route. He arrived with a burgeoning reputation established in the lower echelons of the sport, having won various championships culminating in the European and French Formula 3 titles of 1979. Marlboro McLaren snapped him up for the 1980 Formula One season to race alongside John Watson, and immediately Prost began to show the characteristics which were to define a remarkable career.

Above all else, Prost knew how to make a car work for him. It began with analysis and understanding. This he could translate into specific engineering-led solutions. Once the car was right, he maximised its benefits through a silky smooth driving style augmented by a tactical racing savvy second to none. Thus 'The Professor'.

On his retirement 13 years later, the fruits of his singular approach to racing were four World Championship titles and an impressive 51 victories. At the time, he was the most successful driver in history and even now his wins tally is only surpassed by Michael Schumacher's.

Before the end of 1980, McLaren was to go through a major restructure which brought Ron Dennis and John Barnard into the organisation. In the meantime, the team had lost its way and was falling back down the grid. Despite this, Prost scored points in his first two races and looked good against his more experienced team-mate, so much so that McLaren was keen to retain him for the following season. But Prost had been bitten by a sense of patriotism which compelled him to drive for Renault, his national team. By the same token, Renault wanted Prost, the best French prospect for honours since the championship had begun, 30 years before. Prost and Renault looked to be a match made in heaven, particularly as the turbocharged engine technology, pioneered by Renault, was finally coming into its own.

Their three years together brought success in the shape of nine Grand Prix wins, but not the ultimate triumph they craved and had expected to enjoy together. For the innovators of the 'turbo', the loss of the 1983 championship by just two points to Nelson Piquet's turbo Brabham-BMW was too much for the Regie, and heads had to roll. Prost became the scapegoat. But an indication of where the true culpability lay is that Renault disappeared into obscurity during the seasons that followed, while Prost began to win championships. Although Renault had considerable success as an engine supplier during the 1990s, they had to wait another 20 years, until

France's only World Champion, Alain Prost, was also powered by French engines near the start and at the end of his star-studded career. His first success was at the 1981 French Grand Prix in the Renault RE30 (above), his last – 50 victories later – was in the 1993 German Grand Prix in the Williams-Renault FW15C (below).

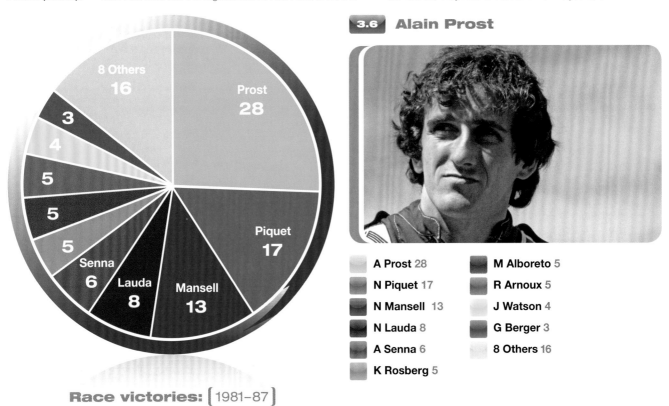

3.6 Alain Prost

A Prost 28   M Alboreto 5
N Piquet 17   R Arnoux 5
N Mansell 13   J Watson 4
N Lauda 8   G Berger 3
A Senna 6   8 Others 16
K Rosberg 5

Race victories: [1981–87]

Adelaide, 1993 – their final race, their rivalry over. Just this once Senna is magnaminous, secure in the knowledge that Prost is now retired and the Frenchman's seat at Williams is his for 1994.

2005, for Fernando Alonso to deliver its first title as a chassis-engine constructor.

Prost's first title, meanwhile, was just two years away. For 1984, he rejoined McLaren, now led by Dennis, with Barnard supplying the technical nous. Another principal player in the set-up was Mansour Ojjeh of Techniques d'Avant Garde (TAG), who provided the crucial sponsorship for a bespoke, and exclusive, turbocharged V6 engine supplied by Porsche. The financial muscle still came from Marlboro.

At McLaren, Prost raced besides none other than Niki Lauda, whom Dennis had lured out of retirement two years earlier. Using the McLaren-TAG turbo, Prost and Lauda made a formidable pairing and they utterly dominated the 1984 season, with Lauda securing his third World Championship title albeit with a half-point advantage over his team-mate. Prost conclusively triumphed the following season.

Over those two seasons and 32 races in which they were pitted against each other in the same team, Prost's success rate was double that of Lauda's, as he took the chequered flag on 12 occasions. In this McLaren-TAG period, there was little argument that Prost was the man to beat. This fact was endorsed further when, against the odds this time, he followed up with a second championship in 1986, becoming the first man to win back-to-back titles in over 25 years, since Jack Brabham in 1960.

The Formula One 'turbo era' – which broadly covered the six years from 1983, when they became de rigueur, to the end of 1988 when they were banned – was a highly competitive period. Car manufacturers, following Renault's example, saw turbo engine technology as a relatively painless means to enter Grand Prix racing, while also obtaining valuable R&D feedback. Ferrari, now owned by FIAT, was the first to emulate Renault, followed by BMW, Alfa Romeo, Ford…and Honda.

Unlike Renault, Honda had chosen the engine-supplier route. By the end of 1985, it was increasingly apparent that this was the engine in the ascendant. 'Powered by Honda' was the legend required on the engine cover of a winning car, and this fact was not missed by Ron Dennis. The TAG turbo struggled to keep pace with Honda R&D as regulations progressively placed limitations on power output, demanding higher combustion efficiency.

As well as the turbo era, the 1980s was also a period when Grand Prix racing was blessed with more than the usual one or two exceptionally talented drivers racing against each other. To maintain his unofficial title as the man, Prost had to see off the likes of Nelson Piquet and Nigel Mansell, as well as a young man many regarded as a driving phenomenon: Ayrton Senna.

At the close of 2005, Ron Dennis stole the Formula One headlines with another of his visionary coups: the announcement that Fernando Alonso and Vodafone would join McLaren from 2007. Back in 1987, it was little different: McLaren would pair Senna, the young pretender, with Prost, the acknowledged master, both

'Powered by Honda'. Could anyone compete against such a super-team? The answer, an emphatic "No", unfolded throughout the 1988 season as Marlboro McLaren Honda accumulated 15 race victories from a possible 16, including no fewer than eleven 1–2 finishes.

There were more than 1000 racing laps across the breadth of the season, and one McLaren driver or the other led all but 28! Such domination by one team may convey an impression of monotonous racing, but the reality was far from that. The racing was not always exciting, but it was invariably packed with high tension. This was pure motor racing, and between two of the greatest exponents of the art: no team orders, no stage-managed finishes, no quarter given. It was a 16-round heavyweight contest to become the undisputed champion, to be crowned the man.

Prost made a strong start, winning the opening round, and he was 3–1 ahead after round four. By mid-fight (er, mid-season), Senna had rallied and they were at parity again, and now he exerted the pressure by taking four consecutive rounds. At 4–7 down, Prost could easily have been out of it, but to his credit he came back to win three of the final four rounds. It was a very close points decision. The MC would have announced the verdict: "The winner… pause…and new World Champion, Ayrton Senna." By winning eight rounds to Prost's seven, Senna had done enough to shift the balance of power.

The end of Prost's reign coincided with the conclusion of the turbo era. Despite regulatory constraint, the power outputs from these engines spiralled upwards, such that they were banned after 1988. There was talk that, in race trim, they developed well over 1000bhp. For qualifying, as much as 1400bhp was rumoured.

Prost was the most prolific 'turbo winner' with 35 victories from 126 starts (28 percent strike rate). His smooth style enabled the conservation of tyres and fuel. That said, Prost's strike rate in five non-turbo seasons was 22 percent. As this included two barren years – his debut season and the 1991 Ferrari débacle – it provides irrefutable evidence that Prost was most definitely no one-trick pony!

But he did cut a controversial figure. They say once is excusable, twice is unfortunate, but three times is unacceptable. In Prost's case, he fell out with his teams at least three times for one reason or another, Renault in 1984, McLaren in 1988 and Ferrari in 1991. Was it always the fault of the other side? Even his departures from McLaren in 1980 and Williams in 1993 were not without hullabaloo. His ultimately unsuccessful five-year tenure as the principal of his own team (né Ligier) reflected poorly on Prost the man, but could take nothing away from Prost the driver.

Although Senna became the man from 1988, Prost still had a further two championships ahead of him. They raced head-to-head over nine seasons, during which Prost won 42 races to Senna's 41. As previously stated, Prost did not relinquish easily his status as the man to beat.

The name Ayrton Senna da Silva reached the headlines in a big way in 1983 as a consequence of his battle with Martin Brundle for the British Formula 3 Championship. Although Senna won the title, it was by no means a one-sided contest, and both drivers were clearly destined for Formula One. They duly made their debuts on the grid in Rio de Janeiro for the opening round of the 1984 World Championship.

Neither of these two young guns had managed to land a seat with a top team, which was highly surprising, in view of the impact one of them was to make on Formula One. Senna joined Toleman, a team entering only its fourth season and using a privately developed, four-cylinder Hart turbo engine. Inevitably its performance was modest but, despite the limitations of the equipment, all the signs were there: a handful of points finishes (the first in his second race) and three podiums, including the celebrated rain-shortened Monaco race, which he would have won had it been stopped one lap later.

Senna used Toleman purely to put himself on the Formula One map, knowing that to start winning races and challenging for a championship, he would need another team. He made a curious choice, which was unquestionably a mistake, although when he won his first Grand Prix in only his second race with Team Lotus – his virtuoso performance in the pouring rain in Portugal – it must have looked like an inspired decision.

Senna stayed with Lotus for the next three seasons. Under Colin Chapman, Lotus had been at or near the summit of Grand Prix racing for almost two decades. Over the 1960s and 1970s, seven Constructors' and five Drivers' championships had been achieved, all derived from brilliant, Chapman-inspired, leading-edge innovation. C.A.B. Chapman's untimely death at the end of 1982 was a hammer blow for Lotus, but even before that it seemed that his Midas touch may have deserted him. Since the heady days of 1978, when Mario Andretti and Ronnie Peterson had cleaned up with the JPS Lotus 79 'wing car', the team had achieved little in the way of hard results. Six years had passed between then and Senna's arrival, during which time Lotus had led a mere 20 laps in just two races, one of which had resulted in a somewhat fortuitous win.

Was Senna allured by the renown of Lotus, or simply perceived an underachieving team with massive potential that could be moulded around him?

Certainly all the ingredients were there: a Renault turbo motor in a Gérard Ducarouge-designed, advanced composites chassis and strong title sponsorship from Imperial Tobacco. All this, plus the Senna factor, promised so much but delivered relatively little, due in part to poor reliability but also to inadequate fuel efficiency,

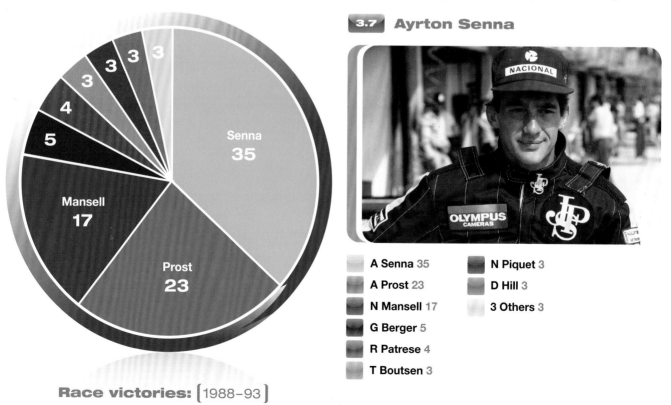

3.7 Ayrton Senna

Senna
35

Mansell
17

Prost
23

5

4

3

3

3

3

A Senna 35	N Piquet 3
A Prost 23	D Hill 3
N Mansell 17	3 Others 3
G Berger 5	
R Patrese 4	
T Boutsen 3	

Race victories: [1988–93]

an essential element in the turbo-powered racing of the period. Up against stiff competition in the shape of Prost in the McLaren-TAG and Piquet and Mansell in Williams-Hondas, Senna could win only four times in 1985–86, despite starting from pole position on a remarkable 15 occasions. In the first year, he finished only fourth in the World Championship, even though he led more racing laps than any other competitor. In 1986, Senna finished fourth again, although he was fully in contention for the title until his campaign fell apart in the final few races of the season. One of the iconic images of the 1980s is the photo-call of the four championship contenders at Estoril – Prost, Mansell, Piquet and Senna – perched on the pit wall, arms around each others' shoulders.

Circumstances conspired that Senna would give Lotus one more chance in 1987. Renault had withdrawn and Honda was keen for Senna to drive a car powered by its now dominant V6 turbo. Lotus was also developing active-ride suspension and, with plenty of cash from new sponsor R.J. Reynolds's Camel cigarette brand, once again the package looked highly promising. The switch to Honda also shed light on the poor fuel efficiency issue. Had it been the Renault motor, the Lotus chassis, or Senna's highly individual yet effective driving style, blip-blipping the throttle through slow corners? Honda engines duly dominated the 1987 season with 11 victories, but Senna only accounted

for two of them, registering the poorest fuel consumption of the three Honda drivers.

Whether it was car or driver, it was a mortifying conclusion to his career at Lotus and enough to cause Senna to reconsider his driving technique. Countering this view, it should be remembered that, the following year, defending World Champion Nelson Piquet was also unable to make a significant impression using the Lotus-Honda combination. And so it transpired that, the single 1985 win by Elio de Angelis apart, Ayrton Senna's six victories in three years were the last hurrah for the famous marque.

For 1988, Senna encroached upon Prost's territory in a very direct manner by joining the double World Champion at McLaren. Over the next six years, their careers became inextricably linked and their rivalry the stuff of legends. Although Senna brought Honda engines to McLaren, as well as to Prost, it is to the Frenchman's credit that he did not attempt to bar Senna's access to the team, as Senna had done with Derek Warwick at Lotus a few years earlier. Each driver, Senna and Prost, thought they had the measure of the other, one with his raw speed and hunger for success, the other with his greater experience, guile and race-craft...

Senna recognised that this was a make-or-break year. Although his reputation was high, Prost still remained

Ayrton Senna won his first Grand Prix in the atrocious conditions of Estoril, Portugal, in 1985. After crossing the line he flung back his seat belts and waved both arms wildly. Such jubliation became a rarity, his demeanour on the podium often impassive.

the man. Now they would slug it out, head-to-head, using exactly the same equipment.

Looking back from today, it is possible to state that in 1988 Prost stood no chance. But this is only in the knowledge of what the coming years held for these two great drivers, and their subsequent behaviour towards each other on and off the track. In motor racing, as in all sport, motivation counts for so much in winning… and losing. Prost, six years older and already with two World Championships, was up against a man on a mission, an irresistible force.

This was not just pent up frustration from the three wilderness years at Lotus, it was something rather more… well…scary!

Senna possessed true charisma, a presence that commanded attention. This aura contained a mystical, almost eerie quality, steeped in strong religious faith. Self-belief in his driving superiority was unshakable, his driving style and rhythm often mesmeric. He was the best, destined to win, but did this mind set contain an element of divine guidance? Was it providence which allowed him to take himself to the edge and sometimes beyond, whereby his 'win at all costs' philosophy involved ruthlessness, intimidation, even recklessness? Beating his opposition was not enough, he had to destroy them. "If he wants the championship that badly, he can have it." That was Prost's reaction after he was dangerously squeezed towards the pit wall by Senna during a 190mph overtaking manoeuvre at Estoril.

That was towards the end of 1988, and the first overt sign that their relationship was degenerating owing to the intensity of their rivalry. Its final collapse came in the second race of 1989, at Imola, where Prost accused Senna of reneging on a private pre-race agreement not to fight each other for the first corner. From there, the bad blood intensified, with suggestions that Senna was receiving preferential treatment from Honda. Later it became an all-out feud at Suzuka when they collided at the chicane, the race finish almost in sight. Prost reasonably refused to cooperate with Senna's attempt to bully his way past for the lead and closed the door, the consequence of which was a collision. Prost took the championship back from Senna, and the coveted No 1 to a new team – Ferrari.

Twelve months later, again at Suzuka, Senna saw his opportunity for revenge. He took out Prost's Ferrari at the first corner, a move which ushered the title back once more to Senna. In the midst of this, it should be noted that Prost was no saint, and neither was Jean-Marie Balestre, the president of FISA and also a Frenchman, who added a political and nationalistic dimension to the Senna/Prost affair. By the same token, despite his sometimes tearful intensity, Senna was not a monster and could show considerable humanity both on the circuit and away from it.

When, in 1988, Senna deposed Prost as the man to beat, he deservedly held that status until the tragedy at Tamburello six years later. That fateful final season apart, he drove for McLaren, 'Powered by Honda', until the Japanese company's withdrawal at the end of 1992,

and over that period won the World Championship again in 1990 and 1991.

Nigel Mansell dominated the 1992 World Championship in the supreme Williams FW14B Renault, but Senna's position as the man was never usurped. In many ways, Mansell came closer than Prost to wresting this tacit title from Senna. 'Il Leone', as Mansell became known during his two years at Ferrari, showed a similarly indomitable strength of character on the race track. Prost took the more pragmatic approach, bringing himself and his team into a position to win, which normally required less on-track heroics.

Some of the great Senna images came from those last two seasons with McLaren, when he won in lesser equipment. If evidence of car inferiority were needed, of his extraordinary Formula One career record of 65 pole positions, those two particular years contributed a paltry pair. The association of Williams with Renault had produced an Adrian Newey design which, by 1992, was in a class of its own, and Mansell used it to devastating effect. At Monaco, a venue Senna had made his own with no fewer than six victories, the Brazilian managed to keep the hard charging Mansell behind him as the laps counted down to the flag. Mansell, in the faster car, was catching up after a pitstop to replace a punctured tyre. He jinked, he weaved and feigned passes, doing everything he knew to force Senna into a mistake. It was to no avail, and Senna crossed the line 0.215sec to the good.

Much to Senna's chagrin, the following year Alain Prost managed to get his hands on a Williams-Renault, and another Prost championship looked a formality. Senna attempted, but failed, to jump ship from McLaren and muscle in beside Prost at Williams, even offering to drive for nothing! Prost duly won his fourth World Championship, scoring seven victories, although this was only two more than the remarkable Senna. These Senna wins included what many regard as his greatest, in the rain at Donington Park, England.

Some even say that his first lap, when he sliced through the field to lead after a poor start, was possibly the greatest lap ever driven in the history of Grand Prix racing. Only fourth on the grid behind the clearly superior Williams-Renaults of Prost and Damon Hill, and Michael Schumacher's Benetton-Ford, Senna fluffed his start and arrived at the first corner down in seventh place. Some 80 seconds later, Senna completed lap one: in the lead.

During the course of that brief 2.5 miles of streaming wet track, Senna overtook six other Grand Prix drivers – each with his own machismo ego, competitive spirit, and adrenalin-fired desire to win – including arch-rival Prost and young pretender Schumacher.

Frank Williams knew that, when he gave Senna his first Formula One test, way back in July 1983, he had allowed gold dust to run through his fingers. At last, over a decade later, in 1994 he would drive for Williams. The third round of the championship was at Imola. The accident on Saturday which killed Roland Ratzenberger was disastrous, but the loss of Ayrton Senna on live TV the following day was cataclysmic.

On 1 May 1994, the Grand Prix world changed forever.

On that fateful May Day at Imola, Michael Schumacher won round three of the 1994 Formula One World Championship. Rounds one and two were already in the bag. To some, it may have seemed he had already stolen Senna's crown as the man to beat. Not so: Senna was undoubtedly struggling with the initially quirky Williams FW16 Renault – witness the spin in his first race with the car in Brazil – but those in the know realised that it was only a matter of time before this same car, in Senna's hands, would surely become unstoppable. Three out of three pole positions were indicative of the promise of this potent combination. Schumacher's two wins and 18-point advantage was simply setting up a thrilling championship because Senna was now chasing for the title.

As events turned out, it was still an exciting championship, but the tragedy within the Williams team necessitated that a little-known understudy, Damon Hill, was required to substitute for the deceased star, Ayrton Senna.

Records show that Schumacher was the 1994 World Champion but...by a single point. The closeness of this result may be put down to the doggedness of Hill on the one hand, hanging on to Schumacher's coat tails, and, on the other, the whiff of scandal surrounding Michael's performances.

For 1994, the FIA had banned 'driver-aids', such as launch control and traction control. At that time, the use of such electronic technology was not easy to police so, by introducing the ban, the FIA was relying on a certain amount of integrity among the teams. Throughout the season, there were rumours and allegations surrounding the Italian funded and led Benetton team.

Was this the factor that made the penalties that the FIA metered out to Benetton during the 1994 season appear almost draconian? Without robust proof of electronic misdemeanours, were the FIA sending a message to Benetton, and their competitors, not to cross the line?

The aftermath of Imola was a range of safety measures, one of which was a control of ride-height, perceived as a possible contributory factor to the Senna accident. In such a hi-tech business as Formula One, the solution decided upon was ludicrously simple. By attaching a wooden plank, or 'skid plate', to the underside of each car, and allowing only minimal wear to the plate arising from contact with the track surface, a minimum ride height could be regulated.

After winning at Spa, Schumacher's Benetton was thrown out due to excessive wear to its skid plate. This was his second disqualification in four races, the first having occurred after Schumacher had overtaken Hill, who had pole position, during the parade lap (to the grid formation) at Silverstone. Worse still, the FIA later excluded Schumacher from two further races for improperly

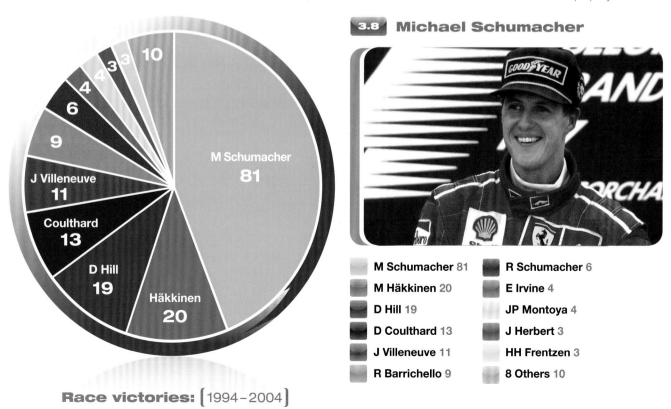

3.8 Michael Schumacher

Race victories: (1994–2004)

- M Schumacher 81
- M Häkkinen 20
- D Hill 19
- D Coulthard 13
- J Villeneuve 11
- R Barrichello 9
- R Schumacher 6
- E Irvine 4
- JP Montoya 4
- J Herbert 3
- HH Frentzen 3
- 8 Others 10

observing the black flag that he had been shown for the Silverstone transgression.

By scoring maximum points, Hill made the most of these four opportunities. In addition, his tenacity and application meant that, whenever Schumacher won, he was very often next on the road. If ever Schumacher faltered, he was there to pick up the pieces. Even more, Hill could also beat Schumacher in his own right, as he proved decisively in the streaming rain in the penultimate round at Suzuka, Japan.

These were the elements that conspired towards the outrage committed by Schumacher at the showdown race, the season finale in Adelaide. Leading the race, but under serious pressure from Hill, Schumacher cracked and struck the barrier. Rather than allow Hill to take the lead, and most probably the title, Schumacher lunged his crippled car back onto the racing line just as Hill arrived at the scene. A collision was inevitable and now both drivers had damaged cars and were eliminated…handing Schumacher the title.

Three years later, a similar yet more obviously deliberate coming-together with Jacques Villeneuve settled the 1997 Formula One World Championship, on this occasion not in Schumacher's favour. These two incidents left many to conclude that Schumacher's was a flawed genius, that he was a victim of human frailty, his massive

accomplishments in this most perilous of sports soured by this personal failing: he had to win, at any cost to others…or himself.

Car-to-car contact is not part of Formula One racing and never can be. On-track confrontations – when the stewards regard them as non-contentious or where no fault can be apportioned – are deemed to be 'racing incidents'. Most controversial are those that involve accidental car-to-car contact. But contact resulting from behaviour that is deliberate, premeditated or even threatened is completely unacceptable. Even in Schumacher's miserable 2005 season, the 'give way or we crash' mind set was apparent at Indianapolis, when he overtook Rubens Barrichello as he was exiting the pits.

Some are of the opinion that the Prost/Senna feud which caused those championship-deciding collisions at Suzuka in 1989 and 1990 was akin to Pandora's box. The significance of these two infamous acts, along with greatly increased levels of cockpit safety, would not have been lost on Schumacher, one of the most intelligent of drivers and possibly the most 'complete' ever seen. Schumacher diagnosed every facet of a race and his execution of each part was almost invariably perfect.

His physical stamina and superb concentration meant that he could gain vital track time during any or every phase of a race, from a meteoric opening lap to slicing

The 1994 World Championship showdown at Adelaide. Damon Hill applies the pressure, forcing Michael Schumacher into a costly error, but the German was prepared to take his first title by fair means or foul…

through traffic. At Ferrari, he and Ross Brawn contrived to make pitstop strategy an art form.

Schumacher's arrival on the Formula One scene was shrouded in scandal and controversy. In 1991, the ebullient Irishman Eddie Jordan decided to break into Grand Prix racing, achieving modest success almost from the start by finishing fourth in the Constructors' Championship in that first year. For the drivers of the pretty 7-Up Jordan 191, designed by Gary Anderson, Eddie had combined youth with experience. The young firebrand, Bertrand Gachot, was placed alongside a former firebrand, Andrea de Cesaris.

When, in mid-season, Gachot had a contretemps with a London taxi driver and found himself in prison, Eddie had to cast around for a suitable replacement. He came up with a 22-year-old German named Michael Schumacher. At the time, Schumacher was contracted to Mercedes-Benz, one of a number of young 'junior drivers', including Heinz-Harald Frentzen and Karl Wendlinger, who were racing Group C Sauber sports-racing cars for the Three-Pointed Star. This was the means by which Mercedes was grooming youthful

German driving talent for their proposed return to Grand Prix racing in 1993, almost 40 years since the last foray of the Silver Arrows.

Schumacher's phenomenal talent was manifest from the moment he was strapped into a Formula One car. In his first race, at Spa-Francorchamps, a renowned 'driver's circuit', he qualified the Jordan seventh behind such illustrious and established drivers as Senna, Prost, Mansell and Piquet, plus Riccardo Patrese and Gerhard Berger in superior machinery. Despite losing his clutch and retiring at the start of the race, Schumacher had done enough to be widely recognised as the new 'wunderkind', and as the first German with championship potential since Wolfgang von Trips 30 years before.

His German birthright, combined with this palpable talent, meant that for his second race at Monza, only two weeks later, Schumacher sat on the grid not in a Jordan, but in a Benetton. Many consider this as a watershed in Formula One – the moment when Grand Prix motor racing unequivocally became a business first and a sport second. Germany was (and is) the largest market in Europe. Bernie

Ecclestone's TV rights and Benetton's clothing business would benefit massively from a credible German contender for Grand Prix honours.

As minnows, Jordan did not really stand a chance of holding on to its new driver. Crossing the paddock at Monza, old hand Ron Dennis found himself in step with newcomer Eddie Jordan. "Welcome to the Piranha Club." That was Ron's rationally sympathetic observation to Eddie.

With Benetton, Schumacher scored championship points in his first three races and in his initial full season with the team registered his first Grand Prix victory – patterns of success that have come to be associated with future greatness. In 1993, there was another single victory before the tragedy of Imola, and the dubious showdown with Damon Hill for the 1994 title.

For 1995, Benetton acquired engines from Renault, the French V10 that powered the winners of all but one race that season. With the addition of this power plant, a truly formidable package was created at Benetton, and the team notched up 11 victories. Schumacher, now a

double World Champion, equalled Nigel Mansell's 1992 benchmark of nine wins in a season.

By joining Ferrari in 1996, Schumacher took his career into a totally new phase. The most charismatic team in Grand Prix racing was at rock bottom. It had failed to win a Drivers' Championship since 1979, had lost Enzo Ferrari, its founder and mentor, in 1988, and had been out of contention since 1990. Indeed, the five seasons preceding 1996 had realised a meagre two Grand Prix victories.

Gianni Agnelli, the chairman of FIAT, charged Luca di Montezemolo to restore the Scuderia to its former glories, and his first key appointment was that of Jean Todt as the team principal. These three decided to build the team around Schumacher, whom they lured with a large bag of gelt, although the German was in any case keenly motivated by the challenge of a shared cause, almost a crusade, to resurrect the Prancing Horse.

Other key Ferrari appointments were those of Ross Brawn and Rory Byrne, both of whom had made substantial contributions to Schumacher's two titles at Benetton, not only from a design and technical perspective but, in Brawn's case, also from a tactical racing aspect. With Schumacher the nucleus, it was a highly talented and formidable group. It largely remained together over 11 years, a lengthy period that may be considered in three phases: four years to reach the top (1996–99); five extraordinary years at the top (2000–04); and the final two years (2005–06) before Schumacher's retirement and Brawn's 'sabbatical' brought the dynasty to an end.

It is important to recollect the struggle and frustration that this group had to endure together before they won both championships in 2000 – Ferrari's first Drivers' title in 21 years. No wonder they wore scarlet wigs on the podium as they celebrated their championship victory. It had been a long time coming and was richly deserved.

The frustrations during those initial years were numerous. They included Schumacher's broken leg at Silverstone in 1999; stalling on the grid at the deciding round in 1998, and the deliberate collision with Villeneuve in 1997, also in the title-deciding race. Such incidents at crucial, championship-determining moments could mark Schumacher out as something of a liability, with critics always suspicious about his temperament under pressure. A more sympathetic opinion would be that he could take much of the credit for the fact that Ferrari was in championship contention in the first place.

Some of his results clearly flattered the competitiveness of his equipment. Hungary 1998 was a spectacular case in point, along with his immense finesse in the wet, Spain 1996 and Monaco 1997 being outstanding examples.

Once the championship dam had been breached, titles flowed for both Schumacher and Ferrari. They held them both for an unprecedented five-year stretch.

Was such domination the consequence of the undoubted strength of Ferrari, or the weakness of the competition? Probably both. Ferrari's traditional combatants, Williams and McLaren, had lost impetus and their chosen drivers were not of the calibre to counteract the deficit. Mika Häkkinen's motivation was in decline over

Schumacher's first win for Ferrari, in the streaming wet 1996 Spanish Grand Prix, is commonly regarded as one of his finest. Sixth after the first lap, he caught and passed leader Jacques Villeneuve on lap 12 – "he just left me standing," said Villeneuve afterwards.

Schumacher's
podium leap
became a
regular sight.
After all, the
Red Baron
notched up 72
victories for
Ferrari. Next in
line come Lauda
with 15 and
Ascari
with 13.

his final two seasons and his departure from the scene in 2002 removed Schumacher's principal challenger. The Finn was probably the only driver of whom Schumacher did not have the full measure, and his absence diluted yet further the weak competitive line-up, further emphasising the supremacy of Schumacher's middle period at Ferrari.

The potential of Sir Frank Williams's promising partnership with BMW was unfulfilled and going sour, while Ron Dennis was preoccupied with futuristic projects such as his team's amazing new 'Technology Centre' HQ and the McLaren Mercedes 'supercar'. Dennis had replaced Häkkinen with another Finn, Kimi Räikkönen, but he was still on his learning curve, not yet championship material. Williams relied on Schumacher's brother, Ralf, paired with Juan Pablo Montoya, both good but distinctly incomplete, and certainly incapable of prising Schumacher's grip from the Drivers' crown.

With the exception of Montoya, during his early seasons in the Williams-BMW, the mere sight of Schumacher's scarlet Ferrari seemed to coerce other drivers to acquiesce to the inevitable. It was a facet taken from Senna's uncompromising approach, which the German would have analysed and adopted. Whenever Senna reached lapped traffic, he pulled further away from those behind. With the prospect of being vilified for baulking or taking out the race leader, that bright yellow helmet in the mirrors of an also-ran was a warning as effective as a scorpion's tail: 'Get out the way, or else…'

It was a form of intimidation that Schumacher developed still further to claim track position from the front-runners immediately after starts. Known as the 'Schumacher chop', it was based on the premise that car-to-car contact would ensue unless the opponent gave way. Not pretty, ruthless rather than skilful, it was highly effective and won far more races than were lost by the occasional tangle in the early days, while the proposition was being established in the minds of his peer group.

No wonder Schumacher saw no end to his career. But nothing is forever, and the end of the Ferrari Family era was abrupt when it did come, in 2005. That season ended ignominiously for Schumacher. There he was, stuck in the kitty-litter having spun off – during a safety car period! Martin Brundle, now a TV commentator, summed it up beautifully: "You can always tell when a driver knows it's his own fault. He doesn't remove his helmet!" Schumacher's helmet stayed firmly on his head, sparing his blushes.

This blank result in the finale at Shanghai was Schumacher's seventh pointless race of the season, equalling his previous low, way back in 1993, when the phenomenon was yet to be realised. How are the mighty fallen! It is hard to conceive how a driver so utterly dominant just 12 months earlier could become an also-ran. Although the record books show that Schumacher won a race that season, it was the débacle known as the 2005 United States Grand Prix, in which he led home his team-mate, as usual, plus two Jordans and two Minardis: Bridgestone runners all, the Michelin contingent having withdrawn from the race… Effectively, in 2005, Schumacher failed for the first time in 13 years to win a representative Grand Prix!

All the indicators pointed towards a Ferrari decline rather than a Schumacher crisis. Michael outqualified his team mate, Rubens Barrichello, 13–6, and outscored him in terms of championship points in the region of 2:1. So, no change there. It all seemed to come down to the inability of Ferrari and Bridgestone to adapt to the new 'single tyre' regulations. But whatever the cause, a season among the ranks of the ordinary was bound to affect the psyche of this extraordinary Grand Prix winner.

As the 2006 season beckoned, one and only one thought could sustain him during the winter break. Come January, when he stepped into the new Ferrari V8, he would want to feel instinctively that he was behind the wheel of a machine worthy of his talents. With that knowledge, he could again summon up the fierce motivation that he required to put together yet another championship-winning season. He recognised that, by regaining the championship in 2006, he would make an inexorable claim to become readily (rather than grudgingly) acknowledged not just as the driver with the best winning statistics, but as the greatest driver in the annals of the sport.

Defending World Champion Fernando Alonso, the man who had ended Schumacher's five-year supremacy the previous season, had other ideas. This time against a fully competitive Ferrari – the single tyre regulations having been rescinded by the FIA after only one season – Alonso repeated his triumph and in so doing seemed to reaffirm that Schumacher's reign as the man to beat was over. The German himself appeared to concur by announcing that he would retire at the end of the season.

As a postscript, two incidents in Schumacher's final season encapsulate the very essence of the man and his career. In his 249th and final race, he suffered an early delay due to a tyre problem, and fell to the very back. He drove a mighty race, catching up a whole minute on the leaders and overtaking with ease Kimi Räikkönen, the man who would replace him at Ferrari the following season. It was classic Schumacher, relentlessly reeling off blistering, inch-perfect laps one after another. Although he finished only fourth, it was a great way to draw his career to a close. Even his harshest critics were hugely impressed with this virtuoso demonstration of pre-eminent driving.

Five months earlier, at what turned out to be his final Monaco Grand Prix, he had feigned an 'off' at Rascasse corner in order – it seemed – to baulk Alonso's final qualifying lap and so steal pole position. Again it was classic Schumacher, but exposing his darker side. This incident rekindled memories of the contempt felt for the dirty tricks he employed to further his own ends in other incidents. He was a World Champion selfishly prepared, on more than one occasion, to bring his sport into disrepute.

And, lest we forget, at the pre-season weigh-in at Interlagos in 1995, when the minimum racing weight depended on the combined values of car and fully equipped driver, reigning World Champion Michael Schumacher weighed 5.5kg (the best part of one stone) more than he did four days later…

It is for such reasons that he will not be missed as other Grand Prix champions have been missed.

Formula 1™
DI SA
IMOLA 20
Marlboro
Bridgestone
M. Schumacher
FOSTER'S

Had Fernando Alonso won his third consecutive World Championship in 2007, few would have defied the assertion that he had become unquestionably the new 'man to beat'. The fact that he didn't, coupled with the manner in which he failed, leaves the question wide open.

Until the 2007 season, Alonso's outstanding succession of triumphant accomplishments since joining Régie Renault in 2003 had convinced even the more sceptical of F1 sages that here was a driver capable of joining the all-time greats. Even at the time of writing, late in 2007, Alonso's very next Grand Prix victory will elevate him from multiple winner to 'serial winner' (see chapter 2), and put him alongside just a dozen other drivers who across 58 years of Grand Prix racing have either reached or exceeded that exceptional level of excellence.

Alonso's transfer to McLaren for 2007 looked to be exactly the move that would ensure his continued prominence. He was already the destroyer of arch-rival Kimi Räikkönen in 2005, while in 2006 he had become the slayer of that champion of champions, Michael Schumacher, to remain in perpetuity like the man who shot Liberty Valence. Even if the championship eluded him in 2007, a bagful of wins would enhance his strike rate to the point where the 'Magnificent Seven' would become the 'Great Eight'.

Alonso might say that if Ron Dennis had given him the precedence enjoyed by Schumacher at Ferrari, the pre-ordained script which they had written together towards the close of 2005 would have been followed to the letter. What Fernando chooses to ignore is that even though Schumacher was given number one driver status, his superior on-track performance never, or extremely rarely, muddled perception with reality.

In 2007, on track where it counted, Alonso failed to fully assert himself over rookie Lewis Hamilton. Whether this was because Fernando isn't quite good enough or that Lewis is simply brilliant remains to be seen, but the 'man to beat' cannot be beaten repeatedly by his team-mate with equal equipment and still expect to retain that special status among his peers, let alone the watching world.

What's more, by sharing the McLaren spoils with Hamilton, Alonso also let Kimi Räikkönen back in through the half-closed door to re-stake his claim as Schumacher's true successor. Little wonder Alonso's demeanour on and off track began to fragment. New boy Hamilton was dismembering his date with destiny.

Alonso's or Räikkönen's claim to true greatness is not yet over, but neither driver gives the impression that they see themselves as Grand Prix lifers, still around in ten years' time, still retaining that Midas touch of the born winner, still slugging it out with the latest bright young thing…and winning. The coming years will see Schumacher's 'man to beat' mantle pass on elsewhere, but for the present the jury remains out.

3.9 To be determined

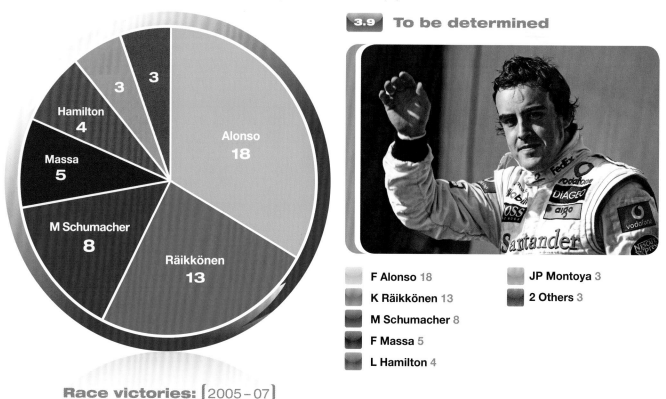

Race victories: (2005–07)

- F Alonso 18
- K Räikkönen 13
- M Schumacher 8
- F Massa 5
- L Hamilton 4
- JP Montoya 3
- 2 Others 3

One of these three (above) looks set to become Schumacher's successor as 'the man to beat'. Hamilton, Alonso and Räikkönen take the plaudits at Monza in 2007.

Alonso leads at Monza in 2007, but did not do enough during the season to stake his undisputed claim as 'the man to beat'.

The exceptional Grand Prix winners identified in the preceding chapters have been pared down successively. Twenty-nine World Champions became 12 serial winners, then ultimately the Magnificent Seven, each an incomparable driver considered in their time as 'the man to beat'.

But is this handful of true greats really incomparable? Surely it is possible to shrink the short-list and, relative to their extraordinary prowess, rank each one in some semblance of order? Does one of these seven magnificent winners clearly transcend the rest?

Some suggest it matters not: each driver attained their own right to greatness. Others say it cannot be done, because racing drivers cannot be compared across the decades. Maybe both these groups of opinion – the doubters – are right.

But equally, maybe they're wrong!

Perhaps they are sceptic because they have not really thought it through. Conceivably their strongly held beliefs are purely intuitive, the result of good old gut-feel as opposed to factual analysis. The journey on which *Analysing Formula 1* embarks is unreservedly fact-based. Whichever camp you tend to side with, it will be fascinating and fun discovering who is right!

Any attempt to challenge the doubters needs to begin with a quantitative and qualitative appreciation of World Championship Grand Prix racing over the half-century and more of its existence. How has the landscape changed? Are the fundamentals of the sport similar enough for a fair relationship to be drawn, or are there day-and-night differences which defy any form of comparability?

The following chapters set out to accomplish such an appreciation by studying the changing landscape of Grand Prix racing from three perspectives:

• Races and circuits
• Cars and teams
• Drivers and danger

This requires analysis of 774 Grand Prix races over a period of 58 years. Before contemplating a study of such depth and detail, it is important to establish a broad perspective of how Grand Prix racing has developed over time. These days, the rate of change is such that every race, let alone every season, seems to bring about some form of alteration to the fabric of the World Championship. Even so, over the scope of many decades, it is necessary to transcend the minutiae and identify specific watersheds of change. Couched more precisely: to identify the beginning, and the end, of each successive era.

Schumacher bridges the Grand Prix eras. At Silverstone in 2001, he commemorated the 50th anniversary of Ferrari's first Grand Prix victory by driving this Tipo 375, a sister car to the one with which Froilán González won the 1951 British Grand Prix.

1950-53: Phoney formulae

The Alfas of the three Fs – Fangio (6), Farina (2) and Fagioli (4) – lead away the 1950 French Grand Prix at Reims.

By definition, an era constitutes a period of time made distinctive by a significant development, feature, event, or personality. This description can be applied very successfully to Grand Prix racing. Some of the developments, features, events and personalities are incontrovertible in defining the end (or the beginning) of a Grand Prix era. They are so momentous that they have changed the landscape of Grand Prix for all time.

EVOLUTIONARY ERA		Years	Races
1950–53	Phoney formulae	4	28
1954–58	Fangio and fatalities	5	38
1959–62	Front to back	4	34
1963–67	Lotus blossoms	5	50
1968–73	Wings and things	6	74
1974–77	Ford versus Ferrari	4	62
1978–82	Suck (ground-effect)…	5	76
1983–88	… and blow (turbos)	6	95
1989–93	Gizmo Grand Prix	5	80
1994–99	Imola implications	6	98
2000–04	Ferrari family	5	85

After sifting through these and many other factors for the purpose of the exercise required, the 11 eras (see panel) have emerged, each of four, five or six years in duration, and concluding with the cessation of the Ferrari/Schumacher epoch in 2004. The difference in the number of years and the quantum difference in the number of races between each era are immaterial. It is clear from the chosen titles that neither time nor races are the defining factors. As becomes quickly apparent, and just as the dictionary definition cites, what delineates an era are developments (for example, aerodynamics), features (like TV coverage), events (such as the death of Ayrton Senna), and personalities (like Bernie Ecclestone).

The 12th era of World Championship Grand Prix racing is now in play, and only time and 20–20 hindsight will enable the accurate identification and description of this latest phase. For the moment, the spotlight must focus on the great happenings of history which delineate the passing from one era to the next, starting with 1950 when the World Championship began.

'Phoney formulae', the title chosen for this first era of Grand Prix racing, might strike a derogatory chord. That is not the intention, although it should be remembered that, during this formative period, Formula One effectively collapsed, being substituted by Formula Two for 1952–53. The initial Formula One regulations were based on the pre-war formula for Voiturette racing. When, for the 1952 season, Alfa Romeo withdrew and BRM failed to show, the FIA had little choice but to revert to F2

regulations in order to save the perpetuity of the still embryonic World Championship.

This first era could equally well have been called 'Sweet FA', serving as an acronym for the leading lights during these important first four Grand Prix seasons: drivers, Fangio and Ascari; teams, Ferrari and Alfa Romeo. Failing that, it might have been entitled 'The Italian Job', conveying the overwhelming influence of Italian cars and drivers in this opening era.

Of the 28 races held over these four years, every single one was won by a car of Italian stock. With one single exception, even the winner's tyres came from Pirelli. The same almost held true for the drivers, with three of the first four titles going to Italy. The exception was Argentina – and what an exception. Even after more than five decades of Grand Prix racing, to this day Juan Fangio is still considered as the greatest of all time. For the record, the other Argentine winner revelled in the nickname 'Pampas Bull'.

Froilán González was the epitome of the racing driver of these early post-war years. With the open cockpit and his open-faced helmet, a driver's individual style, even his facial expressions, were on full view to all. González was particularly good value, his bulky frame hunched in the cockpit, all arms and elbows as he see-sawed at the vast steering wheel, gripped tightly in gloved hands.

As illustrated by Graphic 4.1.2, Ferrari had already stamped its authority on the World Championship in this opening era. By the end of 1951, the Scuderia's mounting challenge had chased off Alfa Romeo. Whether or not the following year was to be a continuation of the extant Formula One, or the switch to Formula Two, a Ferrari festival was on the cards.

The first of Ferrari's successful cars was the 4.5-litre V12

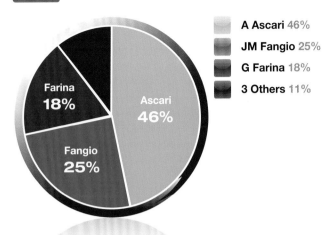

4.1.1 Drivers

- A Ascari 46%
- JM Fangio 25%
- G Farina 18%
- 3 Others 11%

Percent race victories: [1950–53]

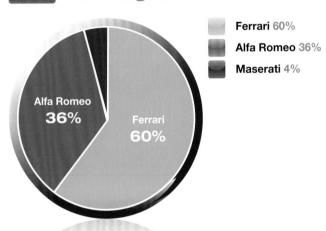

4.1.2 Cars/Engines

- Ferrari 60%
- Alfa Romeo 36%
- Maserati 4%

Percent race victories: [1950–53]

Tipo 375, the second the Ferrari 500. Each sported a de Dion rear axle and a four-speed gearbox en bloc with the differential, but the 500 was a new model intended for Formula Two and the first Ferrari not conceived around a V12 engine. Even with its 2-litre, four-cylinder engine, the 500 had a superior power-to-weight ratio than the 375, having been designed for lightness and agility.

Alberto Ascari's immense success with this car in particular made him appreciably the most successful driver of the era (Graphic 4.1.1). Such was the superiority of Ascari at the wheel of his Ferrari 500 that, even if Fangio had not been sidelined through injury for the whole of the 1953 season, it is unlikely that this statistic would have been greatly different.

In the decades to come, Ferrari 'rossa' would gratify the Italian tifosi on many occasions, but Giuseppe Farina and Alberto Ascari still remain the only Italians to be crowned World Champion. Drivers from Italy were never as dominant again as in this first era of the World Championship.

One feature of this second era was the emergence of British cars as race winners. Aintree 1957 saw the first British victory, for Vanwall, Stirling Moss having shared the drive with team-mate Tony Brooks.

New regulations from 1954 ushered in the first set of rules devised specifically for Formula One and the FIA World Championship. It attracted new blood in the shape of car manufacturers Mercedes-Benz and Lancia. After the stuttering start of the 'phoney formulae', which were based on inherited regulations, the 2.5-litre Formula One was highly successful and heralded a new racing era. Although the new regulations were to continue broadly unchanged over seven years, this second era was to last just five. It was characterised by (a) the rapid fall and decline of the front-engined Formula One racing car, (b) the dark side of motorsport depicted by death and danger, and (c) the extraordinary supremacy of Juan Manuel Fangio, who won the Drivers' Championship a further four times in this five-year period.

Fangio's exploits are well documented in earlier chapters. Suffice to say that he was by far the most prolific winner (Graphic 4.2.1), scoring towards twice the win rate of Stirling Moss, his only consistent challenger during this era.

Sadly, it was Fangio's Argentine protégé Onofré Marimon who became the first driver to die in pursuit of the championship. He crashed and died while practising his Maserati for the 1954 German Grand Prix at the Nürburgring. At that time, death was an ever-present spectre in motorsport. Many drivers lost their lives in the multifarious forms of the sport in which they also participated in parallel with their Grand Prix careers.

Things seemed to come to some sort of frenetic climax during the seasons of 1957–58, during which no

fewer than 12 Formula One drivers were killed, most of them when competing in other categories. Such as Ken Wharton, Eugenio Castellotti, Alfonso de Portago, Archie Scott-Brown and Peter Whitehead were lost to the sport over this grisly period.

But worse was yet to come.

Between 6 July and 19 October 1958, a period of little more than 100 days, three separate deaths occurred on the Grand Prix circuits during the actual races in France, Germany and Morocco. Luigi Musso (Ferrari), Peter Collins (Ferrari) and Stuart Lewis Evans (Vanwall) were the three sad losses which inevitably raised genuine questions over the future viability of Formula One.

Of the 12 fatalities over that 24-month period of 1957–58, no fewer than seven were at the wheel of Ferraris, a macabre testament to the significance of the marque in 1950s motorsport. As Graphic 4.2.2 indicates, however, Ferrari maintained success in Grand Prix racing, edging out Mercedes, Vanwall and Maserati as the most successful marque of the second era. Ferrari was victorious in every year bar one, but achieving this success required four

4.2.1 Drivers

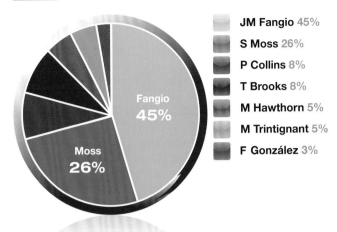

JM Fangio 45%
S Moss 26%
P Collins 8%
T Brooks 8%
M Hawthorn 5%
M Trintignant 5%
F González 3%

Percent race victories: [1954–58]

4.2.2 Cars/Engines

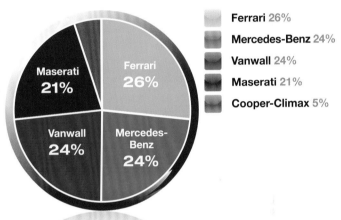

Ferrari 26%
Mercedes-Benz 24%
Vanwall 24%
Maserati 21%
Cooper-Climax 5%

Percent race victories: [1954–58]

separate models, the most successful of which did not even have its roots in Maranello. This was the Lancia-Ferrari D50 which won five Grands Prix in 1956.

Therefore the accolade as the most successful model of this period is shared by the Mercedes-Benz W196 (nine wins in 1954–55) and the Vanwall VW57 (also nine wins, in 1957–58). Close behind with eight wins came the Maserati 250F. These three wonderful machines superbly represented state-of-the-art 1950s racing car technology. It was a technology about to be consigned to history by the motor racing activities of a small company from Surbiton in Surrey, England.

Fangio's decision to retire in 1958 was in recognition of an inescapable truth: a sea change had occurred in Grand Prix racing. He is reported to have said: "Surrounded by rear-engined cars painted green, I realised it was the end of an era."

And so it was.

The beautiful Cooper-Climax T53 of 1960 was a major step forward over the 1959 T51, and Jack Brabham, seen here at Monaco, dominated that summer. The front-engined cars from BRM (2) and Ferrari (36) were beginning to look incongruous.

A mid-engine layout for Grand Prix cars, with the motor located behind the driver, was by no means new. The Benz company once raced a rear-engined car in 1923, and rear-engined Auto Unions fought for supremacy with Mercedes-Benz through the 1930s. But at that time the arrangement did not become *de rigueur*. The general conception in racing, as well as in road car production, was that the engine should arrive before the driver!

In the post-war Formula One World Championship, the first entry for a rear-engine car came as early as the second-ever championship round, the 1950 Monaco Grand Prix. American privateer Harry Schell qualified his 1.1-litre V-twin Cooper-JAP 20th and last, and was eliminated in a famous multiple accident before the completion of the first lap. It was hardly an auspicious beginning for what was soon to become – and remains to this day – the fundamental configuration of the Grand Prix racing car.

The Cooper Car Company did not enter Grand Prix racing until 1953, and then only with its orthodox Formula Two Cooper-Bristol. It was at the 1957 Monaco Grand Prix, seven long years since Harry Schell's visionary

Cooper entry, that the factory, in association with Rob Walker, fielded a 2-litre Climax-powered T43 with the engine behind the driver. Jack Brabham finished sixth, gaining a World Championship point despite pushing his car across the line, out of fuel, five laps in arrears of the winner.

And the rest, as they say, is history. It was to fall to Walker's privately entered Cooper T43 Climax, expertly piloted by Stirling Moss, to post the very first win for a rear-engine chassis, at Buenos Aires in January 1958. But it was Brabham, in the works Cooper-Climax, who went on to secure two successive World Championship titles in 1959 and 1960. Truly, this was a changing of the Grand Prix guard.

An intrinsic part of this change was the successful emergence of the role of the independent Grand Prix engine supplier – independent, that is, from the chassis constructor or racing team. Coventry-Climax was the first independent engine supplier to be used in a winning chassis, but this was by no means the first of that ilk. Names like Alta, Bristol and Lea Francis had powered the chassis of British racers such as HWM, Cooper

and Connaught, especially during the 1952–53 seasons of Formula Two Grand Prix racing. Over this four-year period, as portrayed by the engine Graphic 4.3.3, Coventry-Climax powered more than half (58 percent) of the winners, tucked neatly behind the driver in nimble, responsive chassis from Cooper and Lotus (Graphic 4.3.2).

As the drivers' Graphic 4.3.1 shows, Moss and Brabham were the leading drivers in this the third era of the FIA World Championship. Any reservation – and there was not much – that, since the departure of Fangio, Moss was the man to beat was completely shattered in the third year of this era. A new, 1.5-litre Formula One for 1961 gave Ferrari an advantage which Moss, and Moss alone, was able to confront.

The car chosen by Rob Walker for Moss to drive was a Lotus, the marque that reacted most quickly to refine Cooper's rear-engine initiative. As things transpired, the Cooper Car Company only had three more Grand Prix wins ahead of it, whereas Lotus was on the threshold of greatness. In the interim, Ferrari wrapped up the titles in 1961, and BRM succeeded the following year. Each success was wholly deserved, but they were simply improving on the Cooper breed, whereas Lotus was in the business of taking Grand Prix design into another new era when 1950s spaceframe chassis know-how was replaced by a completely new line of thinking, complemented by the brilliance of a new man to beat – Jimmy Clark.

4.3.1 **Drivers**

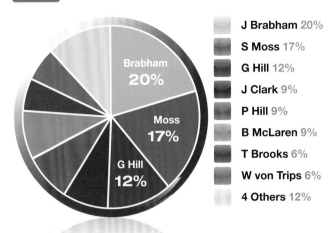

J Brabham 20%
S Moss 17%
G Hill 12%
J Clark 9%
P Hill 9%
B McLaren 9%
T Brooks 6%
W von Trips 6%
4 Others 12%

Percent race victories: [1959–62]

4.3.2 **Cars**

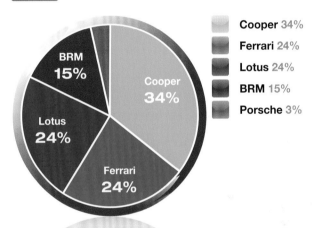

Cooper 34%
Ferrari 24%
Lotus 24%
BRM 15%
Porsche 3%

Percent race victories: [1959–62]

4.3.3 **Engines**

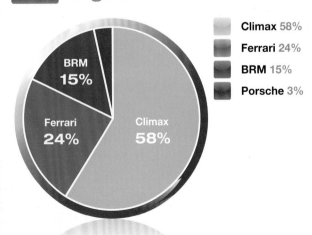

Climax 58%
Ferrari 24%
BRM 15%
Porsche 3%

Percent race victories: [1959–62]

A glance at Graphic 4.4.2 reveals that, despite the best endeavours of Ferrari, BRM and particularly Brabham, this era belonged to Lotus. The marque's enormous success was achieved by one of the great partnerships in Formula One folklore, that of Colin Chapman and Jim Clark. It was a fusion of greatness: a great and visionary racing car constructor in Chapman, and a great and sublime racing driver in Clark.

There is little purpose in trying to decide which of the two made the greatest contribution to their mutual success. Since Clark won every one of his 25 Grand Prix victories in a Chapman-inspired car, it is easy to suggest that everything sprung from Chapman's design genius, particularly as he went on to achieve so very much more after Clark's untimely death. However, comparative performances with some very talented team-mates at Team Lotus suggest that there were many occasions when Clark's genius flattered the equipment he was given. Even without Lotus, Clark would have found success. Clark and Chapman, Chapman and Clark, truly embodied the notion that two plus two can equal five.

Their first success together came in 1962, but the season fell well short of their full potential. Not so the following year, when they shattered all opposition with seven victories. Such

was the supremacy of which this remarkable combination was capable. Three wins in 1964 were followed by another dominant six wins in the final year of the 1.5-litre formula. Even in the fallow year of 1966, awaiting the new 3-litre engine from Cosworth, they scored a fortuitous victory together.

Once the Ford Cosworth DFV engine was delivered, yet more victories came, a total of four in 1967 which could have been more without teething troubles. Few doubted that 1968 would be another big one for Chapman, Clark and the Lotus 49 Ford.

Although at the end of 1967 the Lotus 49 had plenty of racing miles left to run, just as the 1958 Vanwall had previously, this car may be regarded as the end-point in an avenue of design philosophy before the arrival of the next big idea. Chapman had stunned the Formula One world when, at Zandvoort for the opening round of the 1962 World Championship, he replaced his latest creation, the svelte spaceframe Lotus 24, with something even better, the monocoque Lotus 25.

The rigidity of the chassis, combined with its light weight, had clear performance benefits, and everyone soon recognised that they too would have to follow this new design path. Except, that is, Jack Brabham and his designer

Fusion of greatness. Jim Clark and Colin Chapman confer at the 1963 Dutch Grand Prix. This race was the second in a four-race winning streak during which Clark was headed just once – and only for three laps!

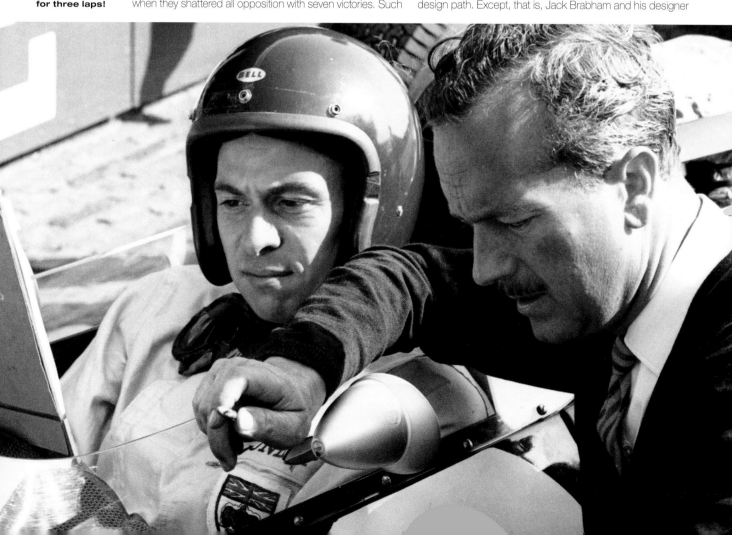

partner, Ron Tauranac, who for some time ahead continued very successfully to exploit the simplicity of spaceframe construction.

But it was Chapman who honed to perfection the concept begun by Cooper: the rear-engined, cigar-shaped racing car with front-mounted radiator. It started with the 'bath tub' monocoque construction of the Lotus 25 and culminated with the Lotus 49, with its engine designed as a fully stressed chassis member.

Chapman's deal with Walter Hayes of Ford in 1966 would revolutionise Formula One as much as his deal with the Imperial Tobacco Company (Gold Leaf, later John Player) two years later. The relationship between Lotus and Ford had become ever closer in the 1960s through both racing and road car projects. The highest-profile road car project was the Lotus Cortina, with which Jim Clark won the 1964 British Touring Car Championship, three-wheeling his little 1600cc car round the corners in true Clark style, seeing off the mighty Ford Galaxies and their 7 litres of American muscle. Why not a Chapman–Ford-Clark partnership in Formula One? Lotus required an engine for the new 3-litre Formula One of 1966 and so the Ford-Cosworth DFV was born. Keith Duckworth and Mike Costin and their Cosworth engine development and manufacturing company had created a strong reputation producing powerful racing engines built on Ford production blocks, which were used extensively by Lotus in other formulae.

So Ford would put up the money and the Blue Oval would grace the cam-covers. Cosworth would design and build it, while Lotus would have exclusive use for the first year before availability was extended to any other teams. That the car won on its debut, having also taken pole position and fastest lap, has become Grand Prix legend.

But Clark's untimely death meant that Chapman's vision of a super-team was never entirely fulfilled. The key components were the necessary financial resources from Players and Ford; an integrated chassis/engine design with the DFV; and two proven Grand Prix winners – Jim Clark and Graham Hill. Chapman and Hill did take both the Drivers' and Constructors' championships in that first year of Gold Leaf Team Lotus, but it was not the overwhelming success that the scenario might well have produced.

Alongside this, Chapman was feeding off what he had learned from his Indianapolis 500 campaigns, particularly through his relationship with Firestone. Comparative photographs of the Dunlop tyres on the Lotus 25 and the Firestone-shod Lotus 49 tell their own story of the intensive tyre development also associated with this era.

When, on New Year's Day 1968, Jim Clark, from pole position, won the opening round of the World Championship at a canter from his Lotus team-mate, Graham Hill, no one was in the least surprised. Their rivals prepared themselves for another Clark/Chapman/Lotus year of domination. Come the second round at Jarama in Spain the following May, a new era had commenced, characterised by three momentous events during those intervening four months. They had changed the landscape of Grand Prix forever: aerodynamic wings, sponsorship... and the death of Jim Clark.

4.4.1 Drivers

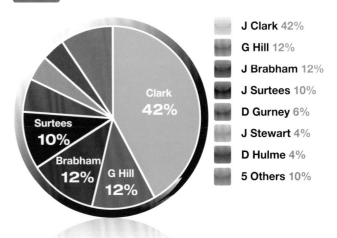

- J Clark 42%
- G Hill 12%
- J Brabham 12%
- J Surtees 10%
- D Gurney 6%
- J Stewart 4%
- D Hulme 4%
- 5 Others 10%

Percent race victories: [1963–67]

4.4.2 Cars

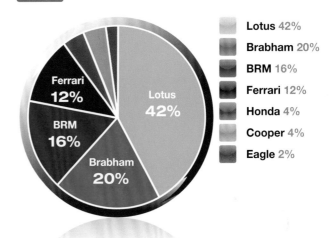

- Lotus 42%
- Brabham 20%
- BRM 16%
- Ferrari 12%
- Honda 4%
- Cooper 4%
- Eagle 2%

Percent race victories: [1963–67]

4.4.3 Engines

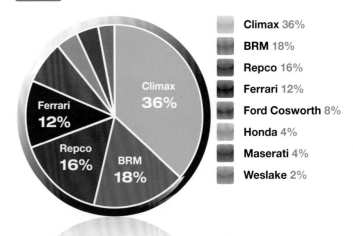

- Climax 36%
- BRM 18%
- Repco 16%
- Ferrari 12%
- Ford Cosworth 8%
- Honda 4%
- Maserati 4%
- Weslake 2%

Percent race victories: [1963–67]

1968-73: Wings and things

High-wing aerofoils lasted a little over a year before they were banned on safety grounds. Here Graham Hill (Lotus 49B) races to the 1968 title at Mexico City, followed by Jackie Stewart (Matra MS10).

Colin Chapman is widely credited with the introduction of sponsorship into Formula One. Those striking red, white and gold Gold Leaf Team Lotus cars had a major impact on the Formula One scene in early 1968. It was at this very time that aerodynamic wings were sprouting in all directions. The sight of the Lotus cars appearing to sail round the twists and undulations of Brands Hatch, their high rear wings in close formation, leading the opening laps of the British Grand Prix, did seem to be the start of something different, even extraordinary.

In truth, the financing of a Grand Prix team by a company without any direct involvement in motorsport – in other words, funding largely for advertising and promotional purposes – was not entirely new. Yeoman Credit, UDT Laystall and Bowmaker, all financial services companies, were the title names of privately entered Cooper and Lotus teams in the early 1960s. Up until then, sponsorship had been more on a quid pro quo basis. Companies for which motoring or motorsport was a primary business – supplying tyres, fuel and oil, sparkplugs, brakes, ignition systems, fuel injection, shock absorbers, wheels – would support a team by providing free supply or even technical assistance for the exclusive use of its products and the right to advertise their joint successes. For example: "FERODO FIRST. 1962 Italian Grand Prix: 1st BRM Graham Hill. Fit race-proved Ferodo anti-fade linings and disc brake pads."

What changed, and what Chapman exploited through Gold Leaf Team Lotus, was a loosening of the restrictions in Formula One regarding on-car advertising, which was already commonplace in the USA. With the relaxation in the number and the size of decals used to advertise suppliers or sponsors, money began to pour into the sport, particularly from the tobacco companies.

Formula One sponsorship for cigarette brands was a no-brainer. The fit was perfect: a global sport with all the right connotations – dynamic, exhilarating, colourful – and beamed round the world through its extensive television coverage. With cigarette advertising on TV banned in many key world markets, here was a way to continue to gain exposure and raise brand awareness via TV: paint a Formula One car like a cigarette packet, or plaster the brand name around the Grand Prix circuits – ideally both. Gold Leaf, JPS, Rothmans, Marlboro, Camel and Mild Seven were all brands successfully promoted by this means. The brand that took Formula One sponsorship to its natural conclusion was British American Racing (BAR),

4.5.1 Drivers

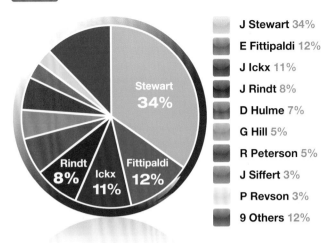

- J Stewart 34%
- E Fittipaldi 12%
- J Ickx 11%
- J Rindt 8%
- D Hulme 7%
- G Hill 5%
- R Peterson 5%
- J Siffert 3%
- P Revson 3%
- 9 Others 12%

Percent race victories: [1968–73]

4.5.2 Cars

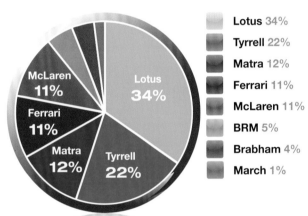

- Lotus 34%
- Tyrrell 22%
- Matra 12%
- Ferrari 11%
- McLaren 11%
- BRM 5%
- Brabham 4%
- March 1%

Percent race victories: [1968–73]

4.5.3 Engines

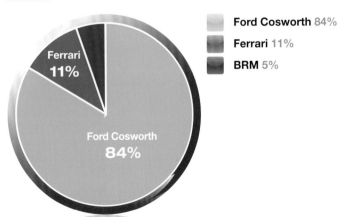

- Ford Cosworth 84%
- Ferrari 11%
- BRM 5%

Percent race victories: [1968–73]

a racing team specifically formed by British American Tobacco, the brand owners of Lucky Strike and 555.

It might be said that Dietrich Mateschitz's Red Bull organisation has even surpassed BAR, where the line between product marketing and racing becomes ever more blurred. That is not to say that the Red Bull and Toro Rosso teams are anything but serious about their racing. Numerous aspects of their evolving set-up indicate that they have grand designs on ultimate World Championship success against the pukka works teams.

Sponsorship completely changed the business model for Formula One teams and for circuits. It was potentially a classic win/win situation. The teams no longer had to scratch for financial security and investment in R&D. No longer was survival, let alone success, dependent upon the sales or servicing of cars (racing or otherwise), personal wealth, pay drivers, supplier companies and so on. Someone else would pick up the bills. In return, the sponsor obtained a cost-efficient platform for advertising and promotion, a tax-effective expenditure, and a great device for thanking loyal customers, schmoozing potential ones, showing appreciation to successful staff, building relationships with suppliers… the hospitality marquee could do it all! The only possible flies in the ointment were if the sponsor did not pay or the team did not win, but even winning was not compulsory for sponsors of the teams further down the grid.

For 1969, Chapman chose the exciting Austrian driver, Jochen Rindt, to partner Graham Hill at GLTL. In Montjuïc Park, Barcelona, both the works Lotus 49Bs crashed heavily when the long struts holding their high rear aerofoils collapsed. The two accidents happened at exactly the same point on the circuit and within a dozen laps of each other, confirming this to be a design fault exposed by the specific forces exerted by this magnificent but undulating track. Rindt was injured, not only colliding with the barrier but also Hill's wreck. It was a mercy that both drivers escaped with their lives.

At the very next race, the Monaco Grand Prix – which Hill won for a record fifth time – high-level, unsprung wings were banned for reasons of safety. Wings of specific dimensions now had to attach directly to the chassis, a ruling which sensibly curtailed a bizarre line of aerodynamic development before it could become lethal.

Within Chapman's fertile mind, regulations requiring wings integrated with bodywork led to his next radical concept. The Lotus 72 was launched on an unsuspecting world in early 1970. Three key characteristics made this concept fundamentally different. First, the conventional cigar-shaped chassis was replaced by an aerodynamic wedge-shape, with flat rather than rounded surfaces. This was achieved by, second, replacing a single, nose-mounted radiator with twin devices hung in sidepods on the monocoque either side of the cockpit. Third, airflow around the wedge bodywork was extensively cleaned up through inboard disc brakes and torsion-bar suspension. The result was ample downforce with reduced drag.

Requiring development, the Lotus 72 took time to come good. However, in Rindt's hands, it was a winner by the

fifth round of the championship and proceeded to take four victories in a row. Despite the Austrian's tragic death during practice at Monza, this was enough to give Rindt and Lotus the 1970 Drivers' and Constructors' titles.

The cause was greatly assisted by a young Brazilian, Emerson Fittipaldi, who stepped into the breach left by Rindt. Using the Lotus 72 to great effect, he won from only his fourth start, simultaneously claiming the unofficial title of youngest Grand Prix winner. In 1972, still at the wheel of a Lotus 72, he capped that achievement by becoming the youngest World Champion, the car now resplendent in the black and gold livery of the John Player Special brand.

The winner of 20 Grands Prix, the Lotus 72 was a remarkable and highly successful racing car. It was used by Team Lotus over six seasons, taking the start in 74 races and ending its career in 'F' specification. This is six short of the record for a single Grand Prix model and

The John Player Special (Lotus 72) epitomised this era with its unique sponsorship, advanced aerodynamics and DFV powerplant. Here Ronnie Peterson sweeps to victory in the 72E at the magnificent Osterreichring in 1973.

its derivatives, which belongs to the McLaren M23, a car created in the image of the Lotus 72 a couple of years after it. The M23 won World Championships for Fittipaldi (1974) and James Hunt (1976).

Although his remarkable achievements did not define this particular era, by far the most successful driver (Graphic 4.5.1) of this period drove for neither Lotus nor McLaren. Following Clark's death, Jackie Stewart quickly assumed the mantle of the man to beat. After three years with BRM, Stewart joined Ken Tyrrell and created another legendary entrant/driver partnership, their six seasons campaigning together realising three Drivers' and two Constructors' championships. These were the halcyon days for the Tyrrell Racing Organisation, which outscored even Lotus (by one!) during the period using Matra, March and ultimately a chassis of Tyrrell's own construction (Graphic 4.5.2).

The engine used for every one of the World Championship successes between 1968 and 1973 was the brilliant Ford Cosworth DFV V8. Its contribution to the ultimate success of Formula One was massive. If not for aerodynamics and sponsorship, this would be known as the 'kit-car' era, because the DFV powered four of every five winners throughout this period (Graphic 4.5.3), sweeping the board in both 1969 and 1973.

But the image that most perfectly encapsulates the essence of this era is its most successful car – the Lotus 72. It was a so-called 'kit-car', powered by the fabulous Ford DFV. It pushed the boundaries of sponsorship, having been actually entered not as a Lotus but as a 'John Player Special' between 1972 and 1975. And, after Formula One had retreated from the high-wing cul de sac, the Lotus 72 took the science of racing car aerodynamics to new heights.

On reflection, maybe the 1968–73 era should have been called 'Lotus Blossoms 2'!

1974–77: Ford versus Ferrari

The start of the 1976 South African Grand Prix, and DFV-powered 'kit cars' predominate. When one Ferrari, two Alfa-powered Brabhams and the Matra-engined Ligier all retired, Niki Lauda's Ferrari (1) led home 16 cars from 13 teams – all with DFV engines.

The story goes that, in the 1960s, when the Blue Oval's attempts to acquire Ferrari were rebuffed, the unrequited Ford Motor Company decided to teach Ferrari a lesson on its own stamping ground, the Le Mans 24 Hours. With six successive victories since 1960, Ferrari had made the annual event in north-west France its own.

Veni, vidi, vici: after a faltering start to its Le Mans campaign, Ford came, saw and conquered in style. The Ford GT40 won Le Mans in 1966–67–68–69. Pretty much simultaneously, Ferrari also found itself up against Ford in Formula One. By 1973, matched against the plethora of DFV-engined teams, Ferrari was in the wilderness and had failed to lead even a single lap during the Grand Prix season.

Certain key elements came to fruition to generate a Ferrari revival. Now under the direction of Luca di Montezemolo, a new chassis was designed by Mauro Forghieri that packaged Ferrari's flat-12 engine to take full advantage of its low centre of gravity. The following year,

a transversal gearbox added the benefits of low polar moment of inertia to the mix. Next, the new Fiorano test track became fully operational adjacent to the factory. Lastly, Niki Lauda was on board, his relentless capacity for testing and intelligent technical feedback being the perfect foil for Forghieri's brilliance.

Together they made a winning combination, but in 1974 only managed to translate a remarkable nine pole positions into two race victories. The Ferrari 312T of 1975 fulfilled the promise and deservedly took both the Drivers' and Constructors' titles, but again five wins from yet another nine poles suggested that still more was to come.

And so it proved. Lauda won five of the first nine rounds of the 1976 World Championship. Against the multifarious talents of the Ford-powered teams, which had enjoyed such recent dominance and included proven winners like Lotus, McLaren, Tyrrell and Brabham, it was a remarkable achievement (Graphic 4.6.2). Where was a Ford-powered white knight to take on the Prancing Horse?

In the closed season, two events had occurred that were to contribute to the extraordinary story of the 1976 World Championship. Lord Alexander Hesketh's swashbuckling team was forced to withdraw due to lack of sponsorship. This left its driver, the dashing James Hunt, without a seat for the upcoming season. At the eleventh hour, Emerson Fittipaldi departed McLaren to drive in his own team, leaving McLaren bereft of a lead driver.

A marriage seemed the proper and inevitable consequence of these two unrelated events, and the prospect of Hunt in the top-flight Marlboro Team McLaren was exciting. Surely here was a combination that could take the fight to Lauda and Ferrari?

By the time the World Championship had reached the 10th of its 16 rounds, at the awesome Nürburgring, the Hunt/McLaren/Ford promise had materialised at least in part with two wins. But by then Lauda had racked up five, and held a massive 35-point advantage in the championship. The Austrian's fiery accident on the first lap at the Nürburgring changed everything.

With Lauda fighting for his life, it seemed certain that he would not return to racing that season, if ever. Suddenly the way to the World Championship was open for Hunt, and he duly won in Germany and again in Holland, narrowing the points gap to 14.

4.6.1 Drivers

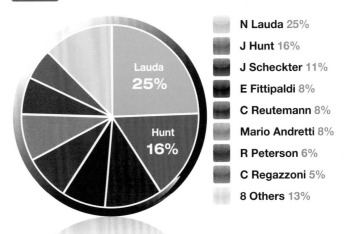

- N Lauda 25%
- J Hunt 16%
- J Scheckter 11%
- E Fittipaldi 8%
- C Reutemann 8%
- Mario Andretti 8%
- R Peterson 6%
- C Regazzoni 5%
- 8 Others 13%

Percent race victories: [1974–77]

4.6.2 Cars

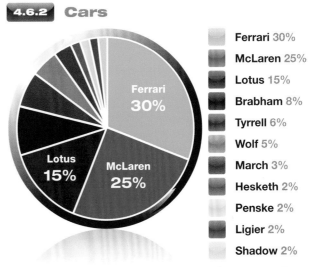

- Ferrari 30%
- McLaren 25%
- Lotus 15%
- Brabham 8%
- Tyrrell 6%
- Wolf 5%
- March 3%
- Hesketh 2%
- Penske 2%
- Ligier 2%
- Shadow 2%

Percent race victories: [1974–77]

4.6.3 Engines

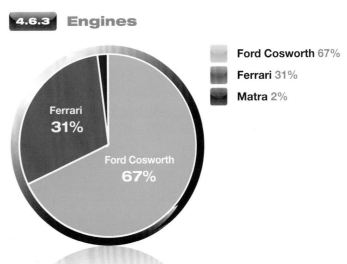

- Ford Cosworth 67%
- Ferrari 31%
- Matra 2%

Percent race victories: [1974–77]

In the meantime, Lauda somehow survived his traumatic accident. Not merely that – miraculously, he returned to the cockpit at Monza, a mere six weeks after his brush with death, having missed only two races. With his burns not fully healed and his head swathed in bandages, it is difficult to understand how he managed to finish the Italian Grand Prix at all. His accomplishment in finishing in fourth place demonstrated courage and determination beyond measure.

Following Lauda's return, Hunt won twice more, but a podium by Lauda at Watkins Glen meant that the protagonists came to the final round in Japan with Ferrari's man still holding a slender, three-point lead. Unless Hunt won, another strong finish by Lauda would be enough to secure the title, an outcome that had been against all the odds after his near-fatal experience.

What transpired is further testament to Lauda's strength of character. The weather at Fuji was appalling but, after many delays, the race was eventually run in atrociously wet conditions. Lauda retired to the pits after one lap with the perfectly rational explanation that the streaming wet track was unsuitable for racing, and the decision to start it had been irresponsible and dangerous. Inevitably his action was controversial.

Many recognised that he and Ferrari were only in with a chance of the World Championship as a result of Lauda's extraordinary tenacity. Others felt differently, particularly when Hunt went on to finish third and win the World Championship by one point.

What was it that made the 1976 championship so utterly compelling? Was it Hunt versus Lauda, McLaren versus Maranello, Ford versus Ferrari? Good versus Evil, even? Probably all these and more. It seemed to have every facet which transforms a good script into great theatre: the unexpected, disqualifications, reinstatements, intrigue, dirty tricks, last rites, courage, bravery, all culminating in a showdown at the Fuji finale. This 100 minutes of racing was in itself a microcosm of all the emotional turmoil that had gone before as, within the space of the last dozen laps, the World Championship was ripped from the grasp of one deserving player by the other equally deserving character, and back again, finally to be resolved by a single point!

This titanic struggle not only blew the minds of existing Formula One followers, it captured the imagination of numerous newcomers to the sport in the same way that Moss/Vanwall versus Hawthorn/Ferrari had almost two decades before. Most importantly, it galvanised the TV broadcasters who now had access to the satellite technology necessary to beam live coverage from around the world.

In the end, it would have happened anyway, but the 1976 championship was the catalyst that turned an extravagant minority sport into a global TV extravaganza. For that, beyond any other contributory factor, acknowledgement must extend to Ferrari and those behind its revival. Without Ferrari in one corner of the ring, this extraordinary prize fight would have lost much of its cachet. Against another Ford kit-car team, it might well

have been just another championship battle, as opposed to one of just a handful that have fashioned the legacy from which the magic of Grand Prix emanates. Ferrari brought with it more than just a great car and driver.

The Italian marque brought the legend, the images, the colour, the individuality – all the special ingredients that set the Scuderia apart. Hunt was the formidable white knight, the McLaren M23 his charger, together superbly championing the cause of a converse Grand Prix culture – the kit-car, the antithesis of everything which is Ferrari. Say 'Ford' and what words spring to mind? Henry, Model-T, mass-production. Now try Ferrari: Enzo, Berlinetta, pedigree.

That epic 1976 season was more than just a championship. It was the collision of two worlds epitomised by Ford and Ferrari. If Ferrari had not fought back during this era, Formula One could have taken a very different course, both as a sport and as the TV-fuelled business it has become.

Designed by Mauro Forghieri, the highly distinctive Ferrari 312T successfully fought the Ford-powered teams. Here at Anderstorp in Sweden, Niki Lauda completes a 1975 hat-trick of wins.

Often dubbed 'the greatest story ever told', the 1976 season had everything. James Hunt is seen splashing his way to third place – and the World Championship title – at Fuji in Japan.

1978-82: Suck (ground effect)...

The beautifully clean lines of the Lotus 79 looked magnificent in classic JPS livery. Mario Andretti and Ronnie Peterson play follow-my-leader at Jarama, one of four 1-2 finishes for the pair during 1978.

The 1976 World Championship showdown in Japan had been won by Mario Andretti in a Lotus – the marque's first victory in more than two years. The following season, although Lauda and Ferrari won and so closed out the preceding era, four wins for Lotus signalled that Colin Chapman was back, and once again it was with something new: ground-effect.

The application of ground-effect in motor racing may be traced to the activities of a Texan by the name of Jim Hall and his family of Chaparral sports-racing cars, which he evolved over a 15-year period from the mid-1960s. With partner Hap Sharp, Hall's principal avenues of innovative technological development focused on automatic transmissions and aerodynamics. In the hands of Phil Hill and Mike Spence, the Chaparral 2F won the 1967 BOAC

500 race at Brands Hatch sporting a high-wing aerofoil mounted on struts. This was a full 12 months before Jo Siffert won the British Grand Prix at the same circuit with a similar device attached to Rob Walker's privately entered Lotus 49B. The high-wing on the Chaparral was driver-adjustable, so that an oblique 'angle of attack' would be used to maximise downforce around the corners, but the wing could be feathered to minimise drag along the straights.

In 1970, Hall came up with the Chaparral 2J 'sucker' car, and ground-effect was born. Two large fans at the rear of the car, driven independently of the Chevrolet V8 engine by a small auxiliary motor, sucked the car towards the track surface. Where bodywork and track met, 'skirts' were used to prevent air ingress, so increasing the vacuum

effect. The 2J was very quick but unreliable, and was soon outlawed on safety grounds. Following drivers complained of being bombarded by stones and other track debris flung out from the rear.

To harness the enormous potential of ground-effect, the interpretation by Peter Wright at Team Lotus was deceptively simple: an inverted wing. An upturned aerofoil profile within venturi tunnels formed beneath the sidepods of the Lotus 78 generated 'suck' rather than 'lift'. The faster the speed of the car, the greater the dynamic flow of air channelled through the tunnels – and the more 'suck'. The technology proved highly promising in 1977, although it did not totally overwhelm the conventional approach to aerodynamics used by Ferrari, McLaren and the rest at that time. In any case, prospects were blunted by unreliability and accidents, so that the real 'magic' of ground-effect was not fully unlocked until the following season.

It was in 1978 that Mario Andretti and the Lotus 79 delivered the full potential of ground-effect at which the Lotus 78 of the preceding year had merely hinted. From 11 poles by Andretti and team-mate Ronnie Peterson,

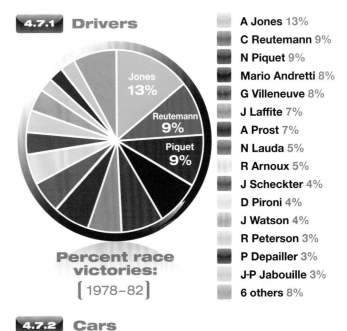

4.7.1 Drivers

Jones 13%
Reutemann 9%
Piquet 9%

Percent race victories:
[1978–82]

- A Jones 13%
- C Reutemann 9%
- N Piquet 9%
- Mario Andretti 8%
- G Villeneuve 8%
- J Laffite 7%
- A Prost 7%
- N Lauda 5%
- R Arnoux 5%
- J Scheckter 4%
- D Pironi 4%
- J Watson 4%
- R Peterson 3%
- P Depailler 3%
- J-P Jabouille 3%
- 6 others 8%

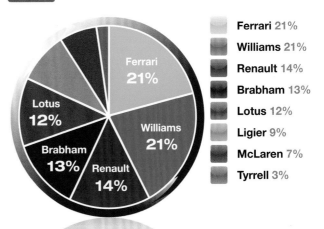

4.7.2 Cars

Ferrari 21%
Lotus 12%
Brabham 13%
Renault 14%
Williams 21%

- Ferrari 21%
- Williams 21%
- Renault 14%
- Brabham 13%
- Lotus 12%
- Ligier 9%
- McLaren 7%
- Tyrrell 3%

Percent race victories: [1978–82]

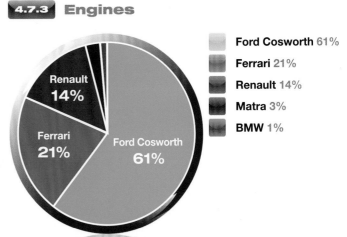

4.7.3 Engines

Renault 14%
Ferrari 21%
Ford Cosworth 61%

- Ford Cosworth 61%
- Ferrari 21%
- Renault 14%
- Matra 3%
- BMW 1%

Percent race victories: [1978–82]

Lotus swept to both championships with eight victories including four 1–2 finishes. The beautifully clean lines of the Lotus 79 twins looked magnificent in classic JPS livery, often playing follow-my-leader as they rounded fast corners as though on rails. But somehow triumph by Lotus often seemed to go hand-in-hand with tragedy. This time, Peterson lost his life after an accident shortly after the start at Monza, blighting the celebration of a World Championship success, as with Clark in 1968 and Rindt in 1970.

That season of 1978 was also the last major triumph for Colin Chapman as other teams, notably Williams, found greater performance gains through ground-effect than could the innovators of the principle. Peter Wright's next big idea was the twin-chassis Lotus 88, but it never raced, falling foul of the technical regulations. In late 1982, Chapman died suddenly at the early age of 54.

In 1978, another highly talented designer, Gordon Murray, had responded to ground-effect with his Brabham 'fan car', a concept akin to the Chaparral 2J, but it was promptly banned following its successful debut in Sweden in the hands of Niki Lauda. As the teams and their designers explored and exploited this new aerodynamic theorem, performance advantage seemed to shift from one team to the next. The first five rounds of 1979 included three victories for the French équipe headed by Guy Ligier, including a crushing 1–2 in Brazil. By Monaco, Ferrari had four victories in the bag and, from Silverstone onwards, Williams won five from six races. But Williams came good too late, and Jody Scheckter and Ferrari clinched the titles at Monza, where Gilles Villeneuve honourably kept faith in his agreed support role, finishing on his team leader's gearbox.

In two other ways, the 1979 season was highly significant. There was the first victory for a turbocharged car, Renault winning the French Grand Prix, two years after debut. The second was the appointment of the Frenchman Jean-Marie Balestre as the president of FISA, the sporting arm of the FIA. Balestre was committed to wresting commercial control of Formula One back from the Formula One Constructors Association, and a showdown between the two power bases was inevitable.

Led by Bernie Ecclestone, FOCA had been formed in 1973 to enable the constructors collectively to negotiate better terms with the race promoters and circuit owners. Progressively FOCA had become involved in more than

The Williams team first found success during the ground-effect era when Clay Regazzoni won the 1979 British Grand Prix, after team leader Alan Jones's car expired at half distance.

simply prize and starting money and, as it did so, it had increasingly trod on the toes of the governing body, the FIA. The single issue central to the upcoming dispute was Formula One racing's new golden egg: television rights.

In what became known as the 'FISA/FOCA War', one of Ecclestone's 'rebel' cohorts, opposing Balestre, was Max Mosley, the son of Nancy Mitford and Oswald Mosley, the 1930s British fascist leader. A barrister by profession, Mosley was one of the founding directors of the March Formula One team, and he and Bernie made a formidable pairing. And they still do today! They are two of the most celebrated examples of poachers turned gamekeepers because, 25 years later, they are still running Formula One, but now one is the owner of the commercial brand, the other the official organiser. Since 1991, Mosley has held the office of president of the FIA, having overall responsibility for the governance of world motorsport, and in particular its jewel in the crown, the FIA Formula One World Championship. Ecclestone is the CEO of the Formula One group of companies, which owns the TV rights and is authorised by the FIA to handle all commercial aspects of the championship, including fixtures.

But that is now. Back then, Balestre identified as his battleground ground-effect – or more precisely, the sliding 'skirts' which helped to seal the vacuum between the car and the track surface. For 1980, he moved to ban them, an action which quickly divided the Grand Prix teams between those aligned with FISA and the FIA – principally Ferrari, Renault and Alfa Romeo, the so-called 'grandees' – and those siding with FOCA, essentially the British based, DFV-powered kit-car teams. The design of the DFV was now approaching 15 years old, and scope for development was becoming limited. This placed those using the engine at a widening power disadvantage relative to the wealthier, manufacturer-owned teams (Graphic 4.7.3). Superior ground-effect chassis design was the main means by which the Ford-powered teams could remain competitive, particularly against the prodigious power now being developed by the Renault and Ferrari turbo engines.

Blown away down the straights, the Ford-powered cars could catch the Renaults and the Ferraris in the corners, and in this way competition remained finely balanced (Graphic 4.7.2). On the one side, the FOCA teams wanted turbocharging banned. On the other, Balestre contended that the phenomenal cornering power

Nelson Piquet's Brabham BT49C receives the thumbs-up from the Monaco scrutineers in 1981. Although the car's ground clearance exceeds the required 6cm, during a race the rubbing strips along the sidepods would be in contact with the track, thereby preserving the car's ground-effect advantage.

accessible through ground-effect must be restrained because, to ensure circuit safety, corners and run-off areas had to be constantly redesigned.

The 1980 Spanish Grand Prix was struck from the championship calendar when it was boycotted by the FISA aligned manufacturer teams, Ferrari, Renault and Alfa Romeo. Aerodynamic skirts were banned for 1981, and a consistent 6cm ground clearance required. FOCA announced a breakaway series and even held its own South African Grand Prix in January 1981.

The FISA/FOCA War rumbled on over three years but resulted in an arrangement under which the Formula One World Championship is run to this day. Known as the Concorde Agreement, it handed FOCA commercial control of Formula One, not independently of but on behalf of the FIA, which retained its control of all technical and sporting regulations through FISA. It seemed a classic win–win, but at times the dispute had turned extremely nasty. Even after the Concorde was signed in 1981, some tough calls were made which might easily have resulted in an equivalent of the CART/IRL disaster that has decimated single-seater racing in the USA.

Back racing with the 'grandees' following the Concorde, the FOCA teams soon circumnavigated the ground-clearance rule. Led by Brabham and Gordon Murray, they devised driver-adjustable hydro-pneumatic systems that could lower the suspension when the cars were out on the track, so that they could skim along the track surface and so retain the seal needed to profit from ground-effect. For scrutineering inspections, the hydraulics raised the suspension such that the car achieved regulation ground clearance... or more!

But what about the drivers caught between the two warring factions (Graphic 4.7.1)? The 1980 World Champion, Williams driver Alan Jones, was the most successful in a highly competitive era during which a record 21 different drivers took the chequered flag. Jones became disillusioned with the car designs now required to keep ground-effect working efficiently. In his view, rigid suspension plus high cornering G-forces made for a disagreeable, if not dangerous driving environment, and he announced his retirement at the end of 1981. Winning his final Grand Prix in style helped him to make his point, as did his decision to return to Grand Prix racing in 1985, albeit unsuccessfully.

The crunch came in 1982. At the second round of the World Championship, in Rio de Janeiro, Piquet's Brabham-Ford and Rosberg's Williams-Ford were disqualified from first and second places because their constructors were attempting to exploit what they saw as a loophole in the minimum weight regulations. Under these rules, fluids could be replenished before post-race scrutineering. The Brabham and the Williams were each fitted with a large tank of water that ran dry during the race, said the teams, because the water was being used to cool the brakes. In fact, these 'water-cooled brakes' were nothing more than a thinly disguised attempt to circumnavigate the rules in order to keep naturally aspirated cars competitive. Rightly, their appearance was brief.

Adding insult to injury, the disqualification of Piquet and Rosberg handed the race to one of the 'grandee' teams, Renault, with third-place finisher Alain Prost. The disqualifications reignited the disquiet and distrust between the factions, and the next piece of brinkmanship was a boycott of the San Marino Grand Prix by the FOCA teams. This led to a very sad sequence of events that may or may not have been some sort of tragic by-product of the FISA/FOCA wars. In the absence of the leading FOCA teams, and with the Renaults out with engine trouble, the two turbocharged Ferraris cantered to victory over the closing laps at Imola. Reneging on a pre-race agreement,

San Marino, 1982. A pair of 126C2 Ferrari V6 turbos, Didier Pironi leading Gilles Villeneuve. Events that day were a prelude to the tragedy that befell Villeneuve at the following race, at Zolder.

Didier Pironi stole the race from team leader Gilles Villeneuve on the final lap. A principled man, Villeneuve was genuinely shocked by his team-mate's deceitful action. At the following race, at Zolder in Belgium, Villeneuve perished during practice. Although the direct cause was attributable to the characteristics of the super-soft, 'one-lap' qualifying tyres of that time, one can only speculate as to the extent that Villeneuve's misjudgement was affected by his desire for revenge and his general state of mind after Imola.

The war was actually over before those 'water-cooled brakes' disqualifications. It was over in January 1982 when the Brabham team, led by FOCA president Bernie Ecclestone, entered a pair of Brabham BT50s for the 1982 South African Grand Prix. They were powered by turbocharged BMW engines! For 1983, a ban on 'skirts' and regulations stipulating a flat bottom between the front and rear axles effectively eliminated ground-effect.

So which side really won the FISA/FOCA War?

FISA? Ground-effect had been banned, whereas turbos had not. The FIA still ultimately controlled all aspects of Grand Prix racing and had reigned in a potentially renegade organisation.

Wrong. Bernie Ecclestone won the FISA/FOCA War because ultimately he came away with the television rights!

1983-88: ...and blow (turbos)

The turbo era is usually remembered with dewy-eyed affection thanks to Renault, who pioneered the turbo concept but failed to win a championship. Test and development driver Jean-Piere Jabouille is seen at speed in 1977 in the RS01 'yellow kettle'.

The new Formula One regulations for 1966 are often referred to as 'the return to power'. Engine capacity was doubled to 3 litres. Almost as an afterthought, the words, '... or 1.5 litres supercharged' were added. It was just a sop to manufacturers of the superseded 1500cc engines who, in theory, could supercharge their existing Formula One engines. Nobody really expected anyone to take up the proposition, and nobody did. Little was it realised at the time that this seemingly innocuous rider to the regulations would have colossal ramifications for the shape of Formula One and, 10 years on, radically alter its future.

Classically, the Regie Renault spotted a gap in the market and did the sums. Based on its Le Mans winning experience with sports-racing cars, the conclusion was that, subject to mastering the considerable heat management challenges, ultimately 1.5-litre turbocharged engines had greater Grand Prix winning potential than the ubiquitous 3-litre naturally aspirated motor. Renault first fielded a 1.5-litre turbo V6 car

in the 1977 British Grand Prix. The all-French team, car, driver and tyres – Michelin also making its Grand Prix debut – certainly created high novelty value, although no one took the project particularly seriously. The RS01 qualified on the penultimate row of the grid and lasted 16 laps before the turbocharger blew in a cloud of steam, giving the car its nickname – 'yellow kettle'.

Less than a decade later, new regulations for 1986 would mandate that only 1.5-litre turbocharged engines were eligible for Formula One!

The tipping point, when Grand Prix racing essentially became the domain of the turbocharged car, happened in 1983. In the preceding year the World Champion was powered by the Ford Cosworth DFV, which won nine from 15 representative races (Imola being boycotted by the leading DFV teams). But by the following year, the DFV could manage just three wins from 15 races, and the World Champion was turbo-powered. Turbos ruled, OK.

It is ironic that the first turbo-powered champion did not drive for the team that had pioneered the concept. Indeed, after missing out on the 1983 World Championships, the works Renault team went into decline and withdrew at the end of 1985. It would not be until 1992, as non-turbo engine supplier to Williams, that Renault would land a World Championship title, and not until 2005 that the titles would be Renault's in its own right.

As the turbo era was to a great extent about engines delivering extreme power, the graphic depicting engine wins (Graphic 4.8.3) deserves special attention. First with Williams and subsequently McLaren, Honda engines came to dominate the turbo epoch. In qualifying form, a turbo engine could deliver well over 1000bhp, and even 1400bhp was claimed. A great driver at the wheel of one of these beasts – popping and banging on the over-run, flames stabbing from the exhausts – was something to behold.

There was one shocking moment when the Formula One rulemakers realised that the turbocharged cars could not remain completely unrestrained. In qualifying on the pole for the 1985 British Grand Prix, Keke Rosberg manhandled his spitting and snarling Williams FW10 Honda round Silverstone at an average speed of 160.925mph! Considering that the Woodcote corner already incorporated a chicane, such a lap-speed was unimaginable.

The Formula One world was stunned and, when Grand Prix racing next visited Silverstone, further significant speed-restricting alterations had been introduced on the circuit.

Graphic (4.8.2) shows that the turbo period was McLaren's golden era, winning 41 times from 95 races, first using the superb, Porsche-designed TAG V6 engine (25 wins) and then, for the final turbo season in 1988, the Honda V6 to win 15 of the 16 races.

Over the six years of the turbo era, 26 of McLaren's 41 victories (63 percent) were attributable to Alain Prost, a driver widely recognised as the greatest exponent of the turbo-powered racing car. With superb racecraft, Prost's quick yet smooth driving style was perfect to optimise turbo tactics. By saving tyres and fuel in the first part of a race, Prost would finish strongly as others struggled to complete the distance on worn tyres or near-empty tanks. Wins just seemed to come to him.

Because he drove for Renault in the years before turbos became de rigueur, Prost made more turbo starts than any other driver – 126. Of these races, he won 28 percent, a turbo strike rate exceeding any other driver, but not so very different from his 22 percent strike rate in naturally aspirated cars, suggesting that Prost was more of an all-round winner than many might think. He and three others, Ayrton Senna, Nelson Piquet and Nigel Mansell, accounted for 75 percent of all victories during the six-year turbo era (Graphic 4.8.1), which came to an end in 1988, after which they were banned. With restrictions to turbocharger 'boost' pressure and/or fuel allowance as the only methods to constrain ever-spiralling engine power outputs, it was felt that this form of engine development had run its course for Formula One.

Only 11 seasons had passed since the debut of that 'yellow kettle' at Silverstone.

 **Drivers**

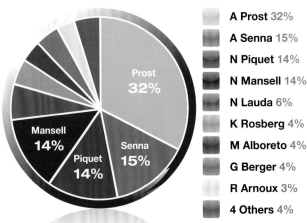

- **A Prost** 32%
- **A Senna** 15%
- **N Piquet** 14%
- **N Mansell** 14%
- **N Lauda** 6%
- **K Rosberg** 4%
- **M Alboreto** 4%
- **G Berger** 4%
- **R Arnoux** 3%
- **4 Others** 4%

Percent race victories: [1983–88]

4.8.2 Cars

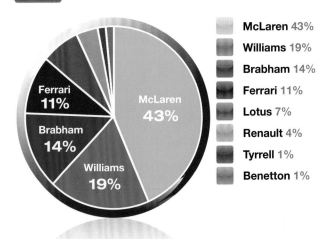

- **McLaren** 43%
- **Williams** 19%
- **Brabham** 14%
- **Ferrari** 11%
- **Lotus** 7%
- **Renault** 4%
- **Tyrrell** 1%
- **Benetton** 1%

Percent race victories: [1983–88]

4.8.3 Engines

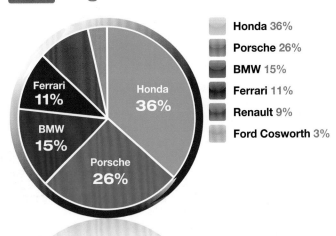

- **Honda** 36%
- **Porsche** 26%
- **BMW** 15%
- **Ferrari** 11%
- **Renault** 9%
- **Ford Cosworth** 3%

Percent race victories: [1983–88]

1989-93: Gizmo Grand Prix

In 1989 Ferrari drivers Mansell and Berger had the benefit of a 'gizmo' in the form of the paddle-shift gearbox. In Hungary Mansell sliced past Senna on his way to victory from 12th on the grid.

Just six seasons passed between the outlawing of 'suck' (ground-effect) and the banning of 'blow' (turbochargers). Where next would designers take Formula One, as each team strove to find the unfair advantage? The answer: gizmos!

The Williams FW14B Renault V10 of 1992 and the FW15C of 1993 are generally considered to be the most sophisticated cars ever raced. They were packed full of gizmos, a collective term for a range of electronic devices adopted by Formula One as computer chip technology really began to take-off in the late 1980s.

One of the principal applications of computer-controlled electronics was in the area of suspension technology. In view of the ever-increasing role played by aerodynamics, achieving stability of the wings and upper surfaces of the bodywork, as well as constant ground clearance between the car and the track surface, could pay dividends in aero performance. Electronically controlled 'active-ride' suspension could deliver a stable chassis platform in a way conventional springing could not.

Experimentation with active ride suspension can be traced back as far as Lotus in 1983. Indeed, both Lotus and Williams had won using such technology in 1987 but, at the time, the benefits seemed inconclusive. By 1992–93, its time had come, complementing the superior aerodynamic solutions brought to the Williams design team by Adrian Newey.

Active ride was not the only use of advanced electronics beneath the skin of those back-to-back World Championship winning cars from the Williams stable, although others were aimed more squarely at enhancing the driver's environment and experience, and as such were termed 'driver aids'. The first of these, the paddle-shift gearchange, had emerged in 1989 when Ferrari was under the technical leadership of John Barnard. A semi-automatic electro-hydraulic gearbox had numerous advantages over the conventional manual shift arrangement with foot-operated clutch. It was faster, less distracting of concentration, reduced physical effort over the race duration, and was less error-prone. A 'missed gear' had been the frequent reason for a trailing car to get a run on the car ahead.

Power steering and ABS braking systems were already prevalent on road cars, but could be just as helpful to the Formula One pilot on a Sunday afternoon as to the Sunday driver with granny in the back. And that was the nub over the development of driver aids:

4.9.1 Drivers

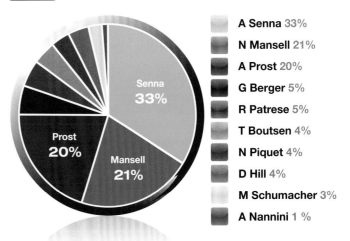

A Senna 33%
N Mansell 21%
A Prost 20%
G Berger 5%
R Patrese 5%
T Boutsen 4%
N Piquet 4%
D Hill 4%
M Schumacher 3%
A Nannini 1 %

Percent race victories: [1989–93]

4.9.2 Cars

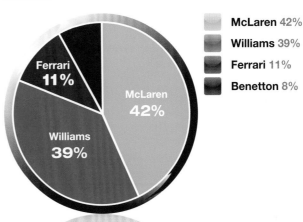

McLaren 42%
Williams 39%
Ferrari 11%
Benetton 8%

Percent race victories: [1989–93]

4.9.3 Engines

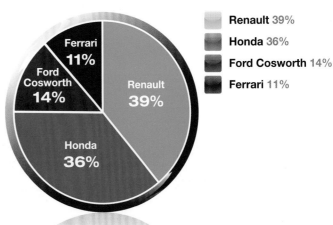

Renault 39%
Honda 36%
Ford Cosworth 14%
Ferrari 11%

Percent race victories: [1989–93]

By 1992 electronics were involved in the starting, accelerating, cornering, gearshifting and braking processes. Williams and Renault had taken the lead in these developments, which Mansell put to stunning effect with the FW14B, seen at Adelaide.

did they really have a place in Grand Prix racing, where driving skill and bravery are fundamental? Were not computerised driver aids simply dumbing down the skill ingredient? Taken to its logical conclusion, could a chimpanzee replace the driver? Indeed – why have a driver at all?

The gizmo which brought things to a head was 'traction control' and its close cousin, 'launch control'. Since its inception, one of the rudiments of Grand Prix racing has been the standing start. Getting the car off the start-line, ideally catapulting into the lead from the second or third row of the starting grid, was a driver skill to be cherished. So was throttle control, keeping a cornering car on that ragged edge between speed and spin. Computerised electronics could take care of all that. Just plant your foot on the loud pedal and the computer would work out the optimal throttle setting or cut the power to a spinning wheel. No more barp-barp-barp as Senna, now at his glorious summit (Graphic 4.9.1), fed in his own innate form of traction control.

Instead the spluttering stutter of an abused Formula One engine protesting at being switched on and off very fast electronically.

So by 1993 computerised driver aids, or 'fly-by-wire' as it is known in the aviation industry, were intervening between driver inputs, and car responses to those inputs, in the areas of starting, accelerating, cornering, gearshifting and braking. Steering was merely power-assisted, not fly-by-wire – yet.

Having fought and won an election against the incumbent, Jean-Marie Balestre, Max Mosley became the president of the FIA in 1991. Ultimately it was he who decided that driver aids were yet another performance cul-de-sac and were also 'dehumanising' the sport, and moved for a ban.

Prohibiting this particular line of development, which obviously had a big future, was a seminal moment for Grand Prix racing. Formula One has always positioned itself as the pinnacle of motorsport in terms of drivers and technology, attracting the best of the former and

pushing the boundaries of the latter. There were already precedents whereby the governing body had amended regulations to curtail developments considered to be not in keeping with the image or values of the sport. Most obviously, Wankel rotary, diesel, two-stroke and gas turbine engines were prohibited along with, in 1978, cars with more than four wheels.

Computer-based electronics was somehow in quite a different category. This was not a marginal or deviant development: microchip technologies were on course to change planet Earth, not just Formula One. What is more, a ban could prove exceedingly difficult to police!

Nevertheless, for the 1994 season, traction and launch control, ABS brakes and active ride suspension were all banned, along with pit-to-car telemetry whereby someone other than the driver could make adjustments to the car. The gizmo Grand Prix era was at an end.

Or was it?

One glance at the steering wheel of a contemporary Formula One car confirms that no regulations can stand

in the way of progress. Today's cars are simply packed with gizmos of one description or another. In the pits and on the grid, laptops are plugged into numerous ports distributed around the car, aerials and antennae sprout everywhere for telemetry and communications, a driver's personal race engineer advises him to "select setting 5" on the warm-up lap, backroom personnel study graphical readouts of every conceivable aspect of performance, and miniature television cameras observe car and driver from multiple angles.

There have been acceptable and unacceptable gizmos, but the latter category is not exclusively driver aids. Semi-automatic gearboxes were not outlawed in 1994 and have since been developed to the astonishing sophistication of today's 'seamless shift' technology. Even traction and launch control were reprieved from the 2001 Spanish Grand Prix because of the constant suspicion over cheating which pervaded the sport.

Launch control disappeared again in 2004, while traction control is slated to join it in 2008 when a standard ECU (Electronic Control Unit) for engine management was scheduled to be introduced. This is a move the FIA has been pushing to make in the belief that it is the only way in which mistrust over cheating can be totally eradicated.

Even so, the potential scope for gizmos in Grand Prix racing is such that major areas of possible future dispute and conflict remain. This is particularly so as the manufacturers would like to see greater use of 'intelligent' electronics which form such a significant part of today's 'clever' road cars. However, vehicles designed to wrap up the driver in ever more swathes of safety-first electronic bubble-wrap seem to be a line of development completely at odds with Grand Prix racing.

One glance at the steering wheel of a contemporary Grand Prix car, in this case a 2007 Ferrari, confirms that regulations cannot stand in the way of progress.

Over that dreadful weekend at Imola in 1994, with major accidents on both the Friday and Saturday, there was plenty to discuss, and Senna and Schumacher (facing page) look serious.

The events over that fateful two-week period in 1994 placed Formula One in crisis (see panel). The press, politicians, even the Pope were demanding answers about Formula One safety. Ayrton Senna's death was the first fatality in a Grand Prix race in 12 years. Over that time, there had been numerous major accidents in Formula One, even career-ending ones, along with fatalities in various other avenues of motorsport. However, the death of someone of the stature of Senna, killed on live Sunday afternoon TV, generated unprecedented worldwide publicity, much of it negative. Now Karl Wendlinger lay in a coma (for 19 days) with no certainty for his prognosis. The pressure on the governing body was immense.

They had not only to act but to be seen to be acting, which is exactly what FIA president Max Mosley decided upon. With immediate effect, and continuing on throughout the season, he introduced a series of measures. These targeted reduced car performance coupled with increased stability, the identification and minimisation of very high-risk corners, and improved pit-lane safety.

The measure probably best remembered is the skid block, or plank. Fixed to the underside of the chassis down its centreline, it is a simple but effective device to force the teams to maintain ground clearance, and remains to this day. By reducing downforce by up to 30 percent, and placing new restrictions on engine power output, the FIA curtailed cornering speeds, while eliminating 15 corners from 27 identified by computer analysis as 'very high risk'.

But probably the most important measure of all was the formation of the Advisory Expert Group to apply new technology to safety. The concept that the FIA itself should involve itself in research and development into safety was a revolutionary approach from which the sport has benefited immeasurably ever since. At last, nearly 30 years since

Sir Jackie Stewart's attempts to bring it proper recognition, safety would be integral to Grand Prix racing, technically, operationally and organisationally.

For a long time, fire was possibly the greatest single menace for the Grand Prix driver. There is some irony in the fact that, in 1994, its intrinsic risk was considered low enough that refuelling pitstops, having been outlawed during the turbo era, were once again permitted in order to spice up the TV show. Who will forget Jos Verstappen's Benetton erupting into a huge fireball during a routine refuelling stop at Hockenheim? Thankfully it was doused just as instantly as it had begun. A mere three months after Imola, if it had got out of control, the consequences for Grand Prix racing could have been severe.

Chaired by Professor Sid Watkins – who already headed up the FIA Medical Commission and had 15 years of hands-on Formula One medical experience – the Advisory Expert Group was given the responsibility for the safety of the cockpit (and any other aspect of the car), the integrity of crash barriers and a search for new materials, the configuration of the circuits and the size and length of run-off areas, and the protection of personnel within the pit-lane and in the public areas.

As the first point of these terms of reference indicated, car design was inevitably the primary area of consideration. The final point recognised that, although they take the greatest risks, safety does not confine itself to the drivers alone, but to the spectators, the pit crews, the marshals and other officials. The remaining two points confirmed that, in the constant struggle for improved safety in motorsport, the circuits remain a major focus of attention. To control the consequences of potentially violent accidents, the objective at the track is to arrest speed and dissipate the latent energy prior to impact, or on impact, within forces tolerable for the driver's survival.

14 days in 1994: A catalogue of disaster

29 April	Imola	Practice	Rubens Barrichello	Major accident. Left circuit, struck barrier.	Injured. Did not start race
30 April	Imola	Practice	Roland Ratzenberger	Major accident. Left circuit, struck barrier.	Killed
1 May	Imola	Race	J J Lehto & Pedro Lamy	Startline accident. Collision with stalled car.	Nine spectators injured by flying wheels
1 May	Imola	Race	Ayrton Senna	Major accident. Left circuit, struck wall lap 6.	Killed
1 May	Imola	Race	Michele Alboreto	Pits accident, lap 69	2 mechanics injured by flying wheel
12 May	Monte Carlo	Practice	Karl Wendlinger	Major accident. Left circuit, stuck barrier at chicane.	Severe head injuries. Made full recovery.

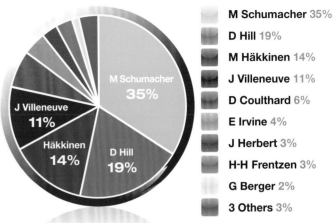

- M Schumacher 35%
- D Hill 19%
- M Häkkinen 14%
- J Villeneuve 11%
- D Coulthard 6%
- E Irvine 4%
- J Herbert 3%
- H-H Frentzen 3%
- G Berger 2%
- 3 Others 3%

Percent race victories: [1994–99]

4.10.2 Cars

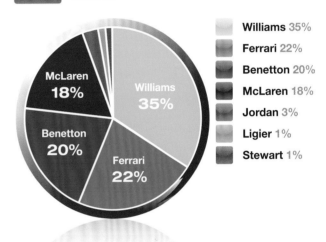

- Williams 35%
- Ferrari 22%
- Benetton 20%
- McLaren 18%
- Jordan 3%
- Ligier 1%
- Stewart 1%

Percent race victories: [1994–99]

4.10.3 Engines

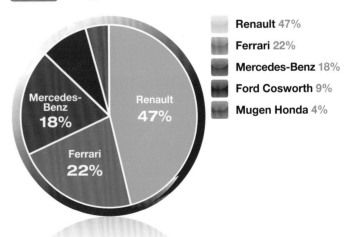

- Renault 47%
- Ferrari 22%
- Mercedes-Benz 18%
- Ford Cosworth 9%
- Mugen Honda 4%

Percent race victories: [1994–99]

A simplistic illustration of circuit safety is the evolution of perimeter protection from straw bales via steel barriers and catchfencing to the tyre walls of today, wrapped in conveyor-belting. Along with enlarged run-off areas containing appropriate materials, such measures have been hugely effective and would most certainly have led to a more favourable outcome of events on 1 May 1994 at Tamburello.

In addition, systems and procedures have also played an enormous part in achieving much-improved on-track safety. For instance, the start of every race is invariably steeped in danger. A loss or gain in position during those frenetic opening 10 seconds can be crucial to the outcome of the race for every driver on the grid. Adrenalin is pumping, cars with drivers of decidedly differing experience levels are packed together, gathering speed rapidly, jockeying for position before funnelling into the first corner. Thankfully, despite all its potential hazards, the standing start, one of the great spectacles of Grand Prix racing throughout the ages, has endured thanks to the sound stewardship of Bernie Ecclestone and his team.

The carefully choreographed starting procedure witnessed at every Grand Prix is in very sharp contrast to the idiosyncrasies of the past. Then, even grid formats could differ race to race. A 4–3–4 formation was commonplace up to 1967, and 3–2–3 was in use until Germany 1973, after which grids became 2–2–2. Rather than the invaluable experience of a permanent official starter for all races – Charlie Whiting – each race start was the province of the local organisers, sometimes even inviting a celebrity to conduct the starting 'ceremony'!

If there is a single fraught image which justifies and endorses the highly structured starting procedure of today it comes from the 1981 Belgian Grand Prix at Zolder. Riccardo Patrese stalled his Arrows on the second row of the grid just before the off. The starter did not observe Patrese's brave but foolhardy mechanic return to the stricken car to try to restart the engine. The race was flagged away and, ironically, it was Patrese's team-mate, Siegfried Stohr, starting from row seven, who had the misfortune to slam into the back of the stalled car just where the mechanic was

Main image: deployment of the 'Safety Car' remains controversial. It helps adherence to TV schedules, but are the tyres and brakes of the F1 cars that follow necessarily in a raceworthy state come the restart? This is Fuji 2007, where Lewis Hamilton received criticism for his conduct behind the 'Safety Car'.

Inset: Professor Sid Watkins has done much for the cause of F1 safety. A confidant of Senna, he counselled Ayrton not to race on that fateful day at Imola in 1994.

working. The anguish of poor Stohr as he came to grips with the realisation that he had unwittingly 'killed' a team mechanic was an image almost too painful to behold. Miraculously, the accident looked far worse than it was. The mechanic, Dave Luckett, suffered a broken leg when a fatality seemed inevitable.

Somehow it is the cars of 1998 that visually epitomise the wave of safety-related improvements which gathered pace in the seasons following the Imola tragedy and the creation of the FIA Advisory Expert Group on safety. A 10 percent reduction in maximum overall width to 1.8 metres gave these 'narrow' cars an unfamiliar appearance along with their treaded tyres, slicks now banned to reduce cornering speeds. What visually seemed to be a radical change did not significantly alter the balance-of-power on track. Mika Häkkinen won the final round of 1997 in his 'wide' McLaren MP4/12, and the opening round of 1998 in his 'narrow' MP4/13. The balance of power seemed far more to do with the allegiance of a handful of designers who were achieving 'guru' status.

Adrian Newey is given much credit for the spate of World Championship successes enjoyed by Williams between 1992 and 1997. Was it simply coincidence that, when he moved from Grove to Woking, McLaren won back-to-back championships in 1998–99 (Graphic 4.10.2). Most informed observers thought not and are now waiting to learn whether Newey's transfer to Red Bull Racing could bring that team to the winner's circle.

Another gifted designer, Rory Byrne, is given similar recognition for the championship successes by Benetton in 1994–95 and those by Ferrari in the first years of the new millenium. Pat Symonds or Ross Brawn might take issue with that statement, just as Patrick Head would be entitled to at Williams. However, what can be said is that a handful of brilliant people have been heavily involved in a sequence of success over more than a decade and have received deserved acclaim.

But this era will be forever associated with the consequences of the death of Ayrton Senna at Imola in 1994 – the first race-day death for 12 years. It is a tribute to those who shouldered the responsibility to effect new standards in safety that, since that watershed and thanks to a great deal of hard work, an even longer span of time has now passed without a fatality at a Grand Prix event. It does now seem impossible to imagine such a tragic event occurring – and yet the same feeling prevailed prior to Imola 1994.

Grand Prix racing remains highly dangerous. This was brought home with stark clarity during the first round of the 2007 Formula One World Championship in Melbourne. A self-confessed botched passing manoeuvre by David Coulthard caused his car to fly over Alex Wurz's car – inches from his head. Accidents will happen in any sport but, in inherently dangerous sports involving speed, contact or extreme conditions – boxing, mountaineering, skiing, motorsport – the consequences can be fatal.

2000-04: Ferrari family

Ferrari celebrations (below) in 2000, the first of five consecutive double championships (Drivers' and Constructors'). One factor in this sustained success was the retirement of Mika Häkkinen (right), seen winning his penultimate race, the 1981 US Grand Prix.

Starved of significant success for far too long, the sleeping Formula One giant at Maranello began to stir. Luca di Montezemolo was summoned by FIAT to restore Italian pride and passion in the nation's beloved Ferrari and the rest, as they say, is history: Todt, Schumacher, Brawn and Byrne, each knowing that individually they were less, together they were more, and united they were invincible. Five remarkable men with total commitment to a common cause, who would rouse hundreds more at Maranello to join them, to share the same goal, experience the same dream.

This was no longer Scuderia Ferrari. This was Family Ferrari.

Families thrive on harmony, not discord. Even the strongest family culture can be shattered by infighting and rivalries. Lessons had been learned from the experiences of Senna versus Prost at McLaren and Piquet versus Mansell at Williams. Intra-team competition can be positive up to a point, but once past that point – with rival factions

in opposition across the pit-garage floor – can become destructive. Ferrari would build their family around one inspirational driver whose on-track performance, plus his awesome commitment to his racing, would galvanise the family to yet greater attainment, certain in the knowledge that, given the tools, he would always finish the job.

There was no miracle. It did not happen overnight. It took resolute hard work with numerous near-misses to capture that first elusive Drivers' Championship. But the floodgates opened in 2000 and, like a scarlet tsunami, Michael Schumacher and Family Ferrari became unstoppable, crushing everything in their path to win both Drivers' and Constructors' titles for a record five successive seasons, during which Schumacher's personal strike rate was 56 percent (Graphic 4.11.1).

Schumacher raced for Ferrari for 11 years and, throughout that time, the key players who made up Family Ferrari stood shoulder-to-shoulder with him. The stability this consistency brought to the team was another key element of the Family Ferrari philosophy, a strategy which realised untold rewards and records over their time together. Family Ferrari won together; Family Ferrari lost together. It was not just bravado. They really meant it and really felt it.

The flipside of this dominant episode was that it made the racing predictable and dull, so much so that, Germany and Italy apart, TV audiences were negatively affected, causing the FIA to look for ways to spice up the show. The problem was compounded by a number of other factors. Aerodynamic turbulence, short braking distances (due to carbonfibre brakes) and other characteristics of the contemporary Grand Prix car had conspired to restrict both close racing and overtaking, making races processional. Schumacher and Brawn together made the Grand Prix race into a formulaic exercise. With on-track overtaking opportunities limited, pitstop strategy and related fuel and tyre tactics became the essential route to victory, and Schumacher and Brawn made it look like child's play. Brawn could call the strategy or adapt the tactics brilliantly and Schumacher, being such a complete driver, could interpret them flawlessly due to the range and depth of his skills. Two-stop, three-stop, even on one occasion four-stop fuel and tyre strategies could be employed by Brawn in the knowledge that, once on a clear track, his driver could produce a succession of laps at qualifying pace. This would move him into a race-winning position by overtaking the opposition during the pitstops, his 'in' and 'out' laps another powerful Schumacher trait.

The victory over Mika Häkkinen's faster McLaren at Imola in 2000 was typical. Brawn fuelled him longer at the first stop, which created a four-lap window on a light fuel-load at the end of Schumacher's second stint. Despite fresh tyres, the heavily refuelled McLaren lost around 1.5 seconds a lap to the German's scintillating and risky laps on worn tyres, enough to take P1 from the Finn as he exited the pits. Game over!

Ferrari policy was another aspect which contributed to the Schumacher/Ferrari supremacy and the regrettable association it engenders with monotonous motor racing. The Scuderia demanded strict team orders. Schumacher's

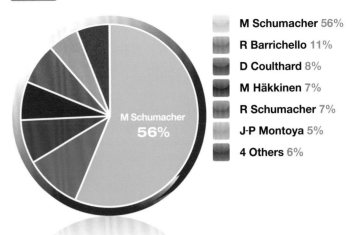

4.11.1 Drivers

- M Schumacher 56%
- R Barrichello 11%
- D Coulthard 8%
- M Häkkinen 7%
- R Schumacher 7%
- J-P Montoya 5%
- 4 Others 6%

M Schumacher 56%

Percent race victories: (2000–04)

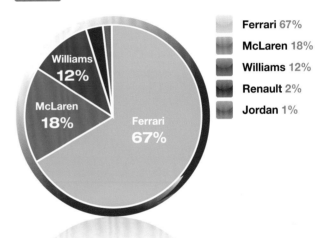

4.11.2 Cars

- Ferrari 67%
- McLaren 18%
- Williams 12%
- Renault 2%
- Jordan 1%

Williams 12%
McLaren 18%
Ferrari 67%

Percent race victories: (2000–04)

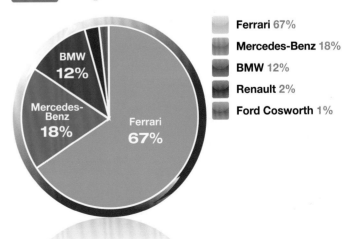

4.11.3 Engines

- Ferrari 67%
- Mercedes-Benz 18%
- BMW 12%
- Renault 2%
- Ford Cosworth 1%

BMW 12%
Mercedes-Benz 18%
Ferrari 67%

Percent race victories: (2000–04)

team-mates were required by contract not to race their team leader when his championship points situation might be compromised. Eddie Irvine (four wins between 1996–99), Rubens Barrichello (nine wins between 2000–05) and Felipe Massa (two wins in 2006) duly obliged. They knew that in a top team, even as the number two driver, they had the chance to collect some victories if or when Schumacher was sidelined, or when he deigned to gift them a victory for services rendered!

This subservience to Schumacher reflects poorly on the ambitions and hunger of these particular individuals (Massa excepted) but, in some ways, mirrors the general malaise of the competition Schumacher was up against during this period (Graphic 4.11.1). Principally they were David Coulthard, Ralf Schumacher and Juan Pablo Montoya, none of whom looked like true champions in the making.

With each succeeding season, winning became the rule for Ferrari and Schumacher, rather than the exception: a record-equalling nine in 2000; another nine in 2001. When it rose to 11 in 2002, the FIA acted. The late announcement of a regulation change put Ferrari on the back foot for the 2003 season and when, in August, Schumacher was lapped by the winner in both Germany and Hungary, it really did look as though the Ferrari stranglehold had been broken.

Not so. With their backs to the wall, this was when the true potential of this remarkable team of people probably reached its zenith. The victory at Monza, the very next race, was simply superb. Michael's overly sincere eulogy at the post-race press conference may have been a little hard to take, but his sentiments were spot on: it was one of his greatest victories, an amazing team effort, especially following on from the humiliation in Budapest. The pole position, the scrubbed front tyres, the 'skinny' aero set-up, the fuel levels, the pitstops – all beautifully conceived and executed. And the drive was truly sublime, from seeing off Montoya on the first lap to breaking his challenge in the traffic. This was a fast, immaculate, error-free drive despite the potentially skittish set-up.

Ferrari went on to win the two remaining races of 2003 and retained the twin titles for the fourth year running. Over the season, despite flashes of true brilliance, the young pretenders and their teams had failed to convince. It was always so that, in a close-fought heavyweight boxing contest, to be declared the victor you needed to be seen to take the crown away from the defending champion. Despite the contrivance of a revised scoring system which had duly helped to spice up the championship battle, the opposition failed to depose the reigning champions.

In 2004, normal if somewhat tedious service was

The Ferrari F2004, seen here at the Brazilian Grand Prix, was the ultimate expression of Ferrari family dominance. In the 2004 season it won 15 of 18 races, with a 94 percent finishing record.

resumed. Schumacher raised his own wins-in-a-season record to an astonishing 13, and Ferrari failed to win just three of the 18 World Championship rounds. This produced the astonishing statistic that two of every three races were won by Ferrari over this five-year era (Graphic 4.11.2).

So to 2005, when the FIA regulations were varied yet again, this time eliminating tyre changes altogether. The same set had to be used for practice, qualifying and the entire race, a scenario with which Ferrari and its tyre supplier, Bridgestone, seemed unable to cope successfully. A single, rather fortuitous victory was the sum total for the season. In another 12 months Schumacher had retired and an era had ended.

It was an era characterised by two things. First, the Ferrari Family approach to racing raised the bar massively in terms of the corporate resolve and resources, financial and otherwise, needed to win Grand Prix races in the new millennium. Second, this forced the governing body, the FIA, to add a second and a third imperative to ensure the success of Formula One. The first imperative had long been safety, which was now joined by the quality of the show and the question of costs. Measures to spice up the show largely centred on ways to mix up the grid – 10-place grid penalties

and single-lap qualifying – while constraints on costs mainly focused on the long-life engine concept under *parc fermé* rules.

One area that still needs to be properly addressed has much to do with both costs and the show – aerodynamics. There is universal acceptance that today's highly sophisticated, expensively researched aerodynamic designs reduce close racing and overtaking in Formula One. This is due to the aero performance of the trailing car being compromised by the 'dirty' or disturbed slipstream from the leading car. So aero spoils the show but, coincidently, massively increases the cost. Leading teams now have to absorb the massive costs of building and operating not one, but two wind tunnels as they seek to make aero improvements virtually on a race-by-race basis. As Renault's team principal, Flavio Briatore, remarked, with impeccable logic: "Why do we spend so much on something that spoils the racing?"

As the ecology debate intensifies, and Formula One being what it is, it is already a very big ask to persuade others that the sport possesses any 'green' credentials. This is a lot more difficult when calculations are made of the energy absorption by 20 or more wind tunnels, running 24/7 – and making overtaking ever more difficult!

This is a conundrum that leads us into the current era.

Michael Schumacher was the catalyst. Without him, Ferrari family would not have been possible. Or would it? Jean Todt (left) and Luca di Montezemolo, seen flanking Michael, will have gained enormous personal satisfaction from Kimi Räikkönen's 2007 triumph.

2005 onwards: An era still in play

When the current era is judged with hindsight, it will quite possibly be entitled 'Manufacturers, money...and Mosley'.

With the elimination of an important revenue stream from the sport due to the long-signalled constraint on tobacco sponsorship effective from 2007, the economics of operating a Formula One team may now have reached the point where the teams without manufacturer support find it difficult to survive, let alone compete. Fortuitously, in more than half a century of Grand Prix racing, manufacturer interest and involvement in Formula One is currently greater than in any previous era, although this could be considered both a strength and a weakness.

History can prove that manufacturer participation in Grand Prix racing has always been fickle. An abrupt withdrawal from Formula One of a few manufacturers could bring the sport to its knees unless pure-bred racing teams can operate viably and compete successfully while retaining their independence.

But it seems the FIA did not necessarily see it that way. It has been reported that Max Mosley, in conversation with Frank Williams, stated that his business model was "history". From now on, according to Mosley, it was "manufacturers and B-teams".

The term 'B-teams' refers to the return of customer teams, which are not bona fide constructors, effectively buying their chassis from their A-team counterparts. Already two teams are utilising the designs of their senior teams' cars, having arranged – deviously, at least one rival would say – to avoid the traditional barrier to such a practice by accessing the intellectual property rights to those designs. Many feel that this development will place the genuinely independent teams in an invidious position, bearing all the costs of a constructor (600-900 staff) but

few advantages over a B-team operation running on a third of that number.

At the time of writing, a genuine independent team, Force India (né Spyker, Midland and Jordan), was protesting the legitimacy under current Concorde Agreement rules of Super Aguri (Honda's B-team) and Toro Rosso (Red Bull's B-team). Although the outcome of this action remains unknown, this and threatened legal action by Williams has forced an overt customer team, Prodrive, to abandon their plans for 2008.

A new sense of unity between the FIA and the manufacturers, after five years in dispute, has brought about the prospect of significant change in Formula One. This goes back to the formation, in 2002, of the Grand Prix Manufacturers Association (GPMA), initially involving the BMW, Mercedes-Benz, Ferrari, Jaguar and Renault automotive brands. The manufacturers threatened to create a 'breakaway' World Championship series on the expiry of the Concorde Agreement at the end of 2007. Their issues included the inadequate share of the money from TV rights and other commercial ventures undertaken by the Formula One group, and the imposition of regulations designed to limit their spend on engine R&D. Their commercial grievances are apparently addressed in the new Concorde Agreement, originally due to come into effect from the 2008 season, whereas the FIA seem to have won the engine-development-cost argument by announcing a ten-year freeze.

Meanwhile proposals for an entirely new Formula One, embracing the most radical changes since the World Championship began in 1950, were under discussion. The proposed regulations incorporate elements designed to increase overtaking opportunities, various schemes to achieve cost reductions, and incentives for manufacturers to gain further benefit from the sport by opening up opportunities for the rapid development of new energy-saving technologies for their passenger cars. This also meets the FIA's fourth imperative for Formula One's successful future – the need to portray genuine 'green' credentials.

If B-teams and high-tech electronics, such as stability control, are accepted as the way ahead by the FIA, then the manufacturers' grip on Formula One has become considerable. Nothing can get away from the fact that with the departure of the only independent engine manufacturer, Cosworth, Formula One engine supply is now in the hands of just six companies: Ferrari (three teams), Renault (two), Honda (two), Toyota (two), plus Mercedes-Benz and BMW.

As an aside, it is ironic that Ferrari, whose founder treated anything other than self-sufficiency in engine provision with disdain, should have become the leading supplier to today's equivalent of what he himself called the 'garagistes'!

The deeper question concerning the manufacturers must be whether involvement alone is enough. If it is the stated or even the tacit understanding in the boardrooms of FIAT, Renault, Mercedes-Benz, BMW, Honda and Toyota that success is the key imperative, at least five

4.12.1 Drivers

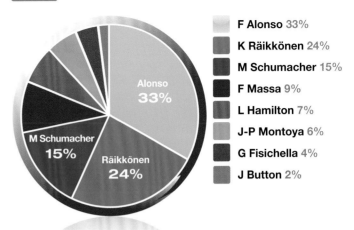

- F Alonso 33%
- K Räikkönen 24%
- M Schumacher 15%
- F Massa 9%
- L Hamilton 7%
- J-P Montoya 6%
- G Fisichella 4%
- J Button 2%

Percent race victories: [2005 – 07]

4.12.2 Cars

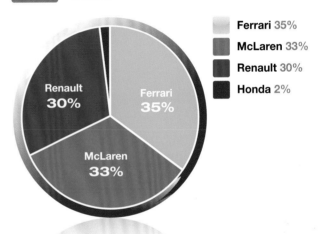

- Ferrari 35%
- McLaren 33%
- Renault 30%
- Honda 2%

Percent race victories: [2005 – 07]

4.12.3 Engines

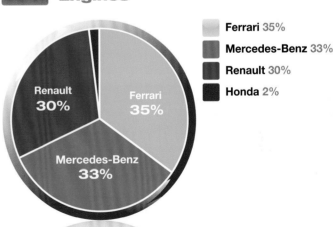

- Ferrari 35%
- Mercedes-Benz 33%
- Renault 30%
- Honda 2%

Percent race victories: [2005 – 07]

boards will be disappointed each and every season. When world market conditions get tough, or there is a change of philosophy at the top of a company, withdrawal becomes the most likely course for the repeatedly unsuccessful manufacturer-owned Formula One team.

Ford pulled out after five years of trying and failing with Jaguar, and it is hard to argue that this was not the right decision when 49 World Championship points was the return on an investment of millions to participate in 85 Grands Prix. To preserve the long-term participation of the manufacturer in motorsport, wins and ultimately championships must surely figure. Enter a Toyota dealership and take a look at the wall poster for yourself. Toyota has a straightforward ambition in Formula One: to win both World Championships. One aim – nothing less.

But even success guarantees nothing. More than once, manufacturers have withdrawn from Formula One at the height of their success. In 1998, Renault actually used their extended string of wins and championships as the rationale: there was nothing more to be gained.

Is there a philosophy which can justify Formula One but accept that success is not a given? Maybe the closest expression of such thinking is a quotation from Horihito Honda: "Success can only be achieved with pioneer spirit and the repeated use of three tools: failure, introspection and courage." These words recognise that simply facing up to the challenge presented by Formula One is the real return on investment. Those who, through introspection

and courage, can overcome failure, even repeated failure, are the real winners. The heat of Formula One offers every motor manufacturer an incomparably intensive laboratory for the research of technologies and the development of their people. It's a philosophy that may have attracted Ross Brawn towards Honda.

As this was written, a new Concorde Agreement was on the cards; a radical new formula on the horizon; the manufacturers apparently fully on board; new title sponsors such as Vodafone, AT&T and ING filling the hole vacated by tobacco; a new breed of enthusiastic, entrepreneurial patrons with very deep pockets has materialised (Red Bull/Toro Rosso, Force India); starting grids are expected to return to the full quota of 12 teams and 24 cars, if not in 2008, then soon; and Bernie Ecclestone announces new venues at regular intervals.

Just as long as a butterfly doesn't flutter its wings in some distant part of the globe, the immediate future for Formula One appears rosy indeed.

To conclude this chapter, take a look at one final Graphic (4.13). Very simply, for each evolutionary era, it compares the number of winning drivers, winning cars and winning engines extracted from the preceding graphics. Significant differences are immediately apparent, suggesting that, over time, the landscape of Grand Prix racing has changed appreciably. The following three chapters explain exactly what lies behind these variations, and why.

The commercial power of Formula 1 has never been greater, as the modern breed of purpose-built circuits illustrates. This is Shanghai, hosting the first Chinese Grand Prix in 2005.

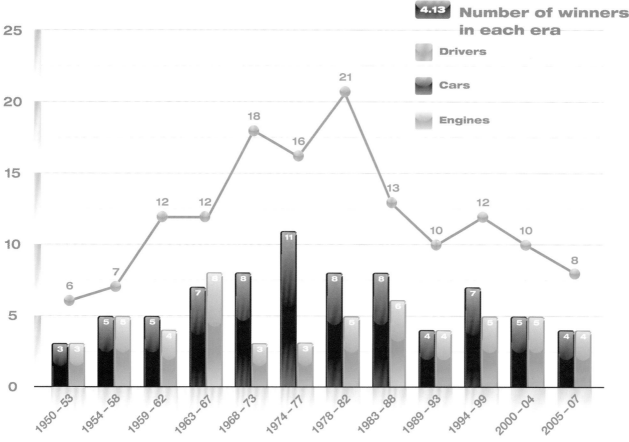

4.13 Number of winners in each era

Drivers

Cars

Engines

中国石化 SINOPEC
中国石化
SINOPEC
Panasonic Panasonic Panaso
中国石化

Grand Prix racing has long been regarded as the pinnacle of all motorsport. 'Grand Prix' is the traditional title for a major race on a national scale, attracting entries from the best international teams, with the top cars and drivers all vying to win the 'Great Prize'. As 2006 marked the centenary of Grand Prix racing, it is of no surprise that the sport enjoys a long and romantic history. In particular, the interbellum period between the two World Wars, in terms of cars, drivers and circuits, offers a great many evocative names: Sunbeam, Bugatti, Alfa Romeo, Auto Union… Nuvolari, Chiron, Varzi, Rosemeyer… Monza, Nürburgring, Spa, Donington.

Although various championships were devised between the wars, Grand Prix racing really operated as individual national events in countries across Europe, all springing from the very first major event to have the phrase 'Grand Prix' in its title – the 'Grand Prix de l'Automobile Club de France' at Le Mans in 1906. A few years later, the Great War, followed by the Great Depression, meant that it was not until the mid-1930s that Grand Prix racing reached what is often recalled as a 'golden age'. From mid-1934, racing in Europe was dominated by German teams with astonishing racing cars, after the Third Reich had chosen Grand Prix racing to strut its engineering prowess. The final pre-war race was held in Belgrade, Yugoslavia, on 3 September 1939 – a few hours after Neville Chamberlain's reluctant declaration of war on Germany. The great Tazio Nuvolari's Auto Union was the winner, over Manfred von Brauchitsch's Mercedes-Benz.

It was eight long years before Grand Prix racing could resume, in neutral Switzerland, at Bremgarten on 3 June 1947. The Swiss Grand Prix was run in compliance with a new set of rules known as 'Formula A'. It was soon renamed 'Formula One', and the link remains to this day. All post-war Grand Prix racing has been for Formula One cars except in the two seasons 1952–53, when Formula Two regulations applied.

An evocative scene – Eau Rouge, 1965. Eventual winner Jim Clark is barely just visible within a BRM 'sandwich'. Clark won a record four times on the classic 'long' Spa-Francorchamps circuit.

The date was 13 May 1950 and Silverstone, in England, was the venue for the opening race in the new World Championship that had been established by the recently formed Fédération Internationale de l'Automobile. The event was regarded as yet another sign of returning normality following the World War 2 years. There was a huge, enthusiastic crowd, and King George VI and Queen Elizabeth were there to greet the 21 drivers.

In that first year of the FIA World Championship, as many as 22 races were organised for F1 cars, many of which contained 'Grand Prix' in their title. For this reason, the six Grands Prix that counted towards the new championship were distinguished by the term 'Grand Epreuve'. The term fell into disuse during the 1970s as Grand Prix races and F1 races became entirely synonymous.

Non-championship F1 races were highly popular in the 1950s and 1960s (Graphic 5.1). There were comparatively few 'Grands Epreuves' by later standards, and minimal TV coverage, so they were viewed favourably by all concerned. At the heart of their success was the aura surrounding F1 cars and drivers which could always pull in a decent crowd. The circuit owners and the race promoters could bring in revenue and pay attractive 'prize' or 'appearance' money to the teams. In their turn, the teams had the opportunity to accept income while testing their latest equipment in the lead-up to the new championship season, Spring being the time of year when many of these races took place.

With the obvious exception of 1952–53, non-championship F1 races were abundant through much of the 1950s (no fewer than 24 were held in 1954) and were almost exclusively a European phenomenon. They enjoyed a resurgence in 1961 (21 races) due to the change in the F1 regulations and the existence of the parallel, but short-lived, 'Intercontinental Formula' that extended the use of outmoded 2.5-litre Grand Prix equipment. Within the long-term decline for such events, another, lesser peak occurred in the early 1970s that can be traced to the arrival of race sponsorship and to the promotional skills of John Webb, the outstanding English promoter at Brands Hatch.

In 1972, Webb's circuit hosted four races involving F1 cars, including the British Grand Prix. In March, July, August and October respectively, Webb put on the STP 'Daily Mail' Race of Champions, the John Player British (and European) Grand Prix, the Rothmans 50,000, and the John Player Challenge Trophy.

At that time, the appetite of the British motor racing public for Formula One was clearly insatiable. Indeed, towards their demise, non-championship events had become a rather British activity with races long-established on the F1 calendar at Brands Hatch,

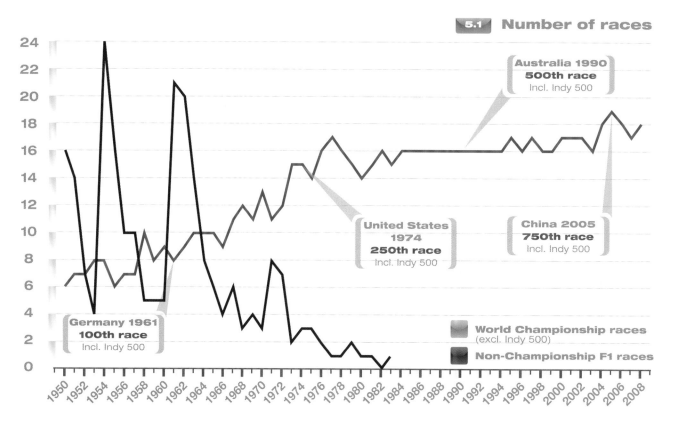

5.1 **Number of races**

Australia 1990
500th race
Incl. Indy 500

United States
1974
250th race
Incl. Indy 500

China 2005
750th race
Incl. Indy 500

Germany 1961
100th race
Incl. Indy 500

World Championship races
(excl. Indy 500)

Non-Championship F1 races

Silverstone and Oulton Park. Periodically other countries, or rather other countries new to Grand Prix racing, featured on the non-championship race roster for a year. This was because the FIA, before granting a new nation 'Grand Epreuve' status, required a rehearsal race the year prior. But steadily, as the number of World Championship races grew, so other F1 events petered out, and the last was held in 1983 – at Brands Hatch, of course. Non-championship F1 races had become an anachronism within the context of the progressively cohesive and commercially savvy Formula One Constructors Association (FOCA) under the leadership of Bernie Ecclestone.

FOCA was formed not very long after Ecclestone had purchased Jack Brabham's team in 1971. He had the vision to see that, as a united group, the F1 constructors could negotiate far better terms with the race promoters, and also have a much stronger voice with the governing body of motorsport about the way the sport should be run.

In short, Ecclestone has progressively run the commercial and operational aspects of the Formula One World Championship since the 1970s. Naturally, his focus has been the TV rights, the golden goose of Grand Prix racing. It is to meet TV schedules and to guarantee 'the show' that each three-day Grand Prix weekend is run to precision timetables. Ecclestone's organisational influence is apparent in the way the Grand Prix show has grown and evolved over the last 30 years to become the global colossus it is today.

Unlike the Olympic Games and the football World Cup – for which the world's nations congregate at a chosen venue every four years – Formula One is akin to a travelling circus. Every couple of weeks, an extravagant cavalcade arrives in each country and erects the most elaborate 'village' of mobile technology and hospitality centres in all of sport.

Each Grand Prix venue visited contributes to the overall championship through the point-scoring system. Originally points were awarded to the first five finishers, on the basis 8-6-4-3-2, with an extra point awarded to the driver setting the fastest lap. Today's version is 10-8-6-5-4-3-2-1, with the fastest lap disregarded. It is not very dissimilar in terms of the championship points. But there is a huge difference in the number of races counting towards the championship: there were six in 1950 (excluding the Indy 500), of which only the best four scores were counted. Compare this with at least three times that number these days (Graphic 5.1), with the scores from all races counting.

In the 1950s, a steady increase in the number of championship rounds was interrupted by the repercussions of the 1955 Le Mans 24 Hours disaster. More than 80 spectators were killed when a Mercedes-Benz crashed into the crowd. As a result, four Grands Prix were cancelled immediately, Mercedes-Benz withdrew from Grand Prix racing for almost 40 years, and Switzerland banned all motorsport on its soil.

During the 1960s, 10 World Championship races each year became the norm. This number rose steadily through the following decade, with a peak in 1977, to settle at 16 or thereabouts, where it has stayed until more recently. Currently there is the prospect of a 20-race calendar, so it is worth recording that, 1952–53 apart, there have been only three years when fewer than 15 F1 races were promoted (1959–60–66). In a number of seasons, the precedent has already been set for 20 or more events.

The paddock, Istanbul Park, Turkey. Mr Ecclestone insists on precision in everything.

Going global

One of the key drivers for (and key limiters of) the number of races in the World Championship has been the uptake for Grands Prix in countries outside Europe. Genuine 'World' status was always the FIA's aim for its championship so, from the outset in 1950, the governing body decided to include the Indianapolis 500 race in the United States. Before the war, Indianapolis cars had been built to comply with Grand Prix regulations – indeed, the 500-mile race had been won by a Grand Prix Maserati only 10 years earlier – but now the American regulations were quite different. This anachronism lasted for the first 11 years of the World Championship, but can be discounted for the purposes of this book (except where stated) because, from a driver or car perspective, the crossover was minimal. In 1959, in any case, the USA had its own Grand Prix, at Sebring.

This was not the first to be staged outside Europe. That honour went to Argentina, perhaps not surprisingly in view of the massive contribution to the sport made by the great Argentine champion, Juan Manuel Fangio. A Grand Prix in Buenos Aires was added to the championship as early as

1953. Remarkably, the second non-European venue, the year before Sebring, was Morocco in 1958, that historic race in Casablanca when Stirling Moss grasped the championship with both hands… only to have it slip through his fingers!

To date, 26 nations across six continents have staged World Championship Grands Prix but, because of its limited following in the USA, some have challenged Formula One's status as a truly worldwide sporting competition. The passion of F1 followers in Canada to the north and Latin America to the south suggests that it is the USA that is the exception – an impression substantiated, perhaps, by the 'World Series' tag that it attaches to its national baseball competition!

Despite the cagey relationship between the USA and Europe in motorsport (as well as most other things), there were few who did not welcome and anticipate with excitement the 'return' of Grand Prix racing to Indianapolis in 2000. At last, after many wilderness years, Grand Prix racing had perhaps found a permanent residence in the USA. It had been a long homecoming, via Sebring,

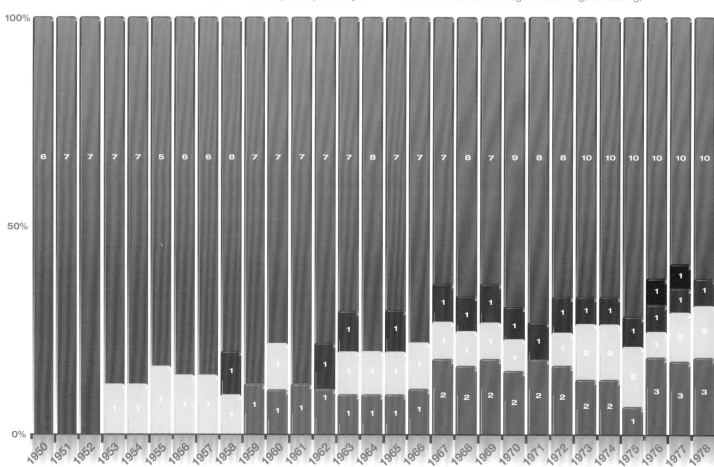

Riverside and Watkins Glen – a worthy foster parent for 20 years. Then there were the 'street' circuits in Long Beach, Detroit, Dallas, Phoenix and, lest we forget, an hotel car park in Las Vegas!

Indeed, the USA has held Grands Prix at more venues – nine – than any other nation, although some were not recognised as the official American round of the championship. Next in line, surprisingly, is the French Grand Prix, which has never found a permanent home in seven attempts.

For nine years between 1976 and 1984, at least two Grands Prix were held in the USA (three in 1982), but the bubble burst and there was no race in almost a decade leading up to Indy 2000. At the time of writing, 'The Brickyard' had been dropped from the 2008 F1 schedule, but there was still hope that it would return in the future as a permanent fixture run in tandem with the popular Canadian race at the Circuit Gilles Villeneuve in Montréal.

The naming of the Montréal circuit after the late Gilles Villeneuve illustrates how the spread and popularity of F1 racing across the world is stimulated by the presence, particularly the successful presence, of a driver from the host nation. In Latin America, the link between the Argentine Grand Prix and Fangio has already been mentioned, and it also holds true for Mexico and Brazil. Mexico City was added to the calendar in the early 1960s as the youthful and exciting Rodriguez brothers

came to the fore. Brazil joined up in 1972, the year its very first F1 hero, Emerson Fittipaldi, achieved his first World Championship.

Whereas Argentina and Mexico have been somewhat sporadic calendar entries (the Mexican race was dropped on safety grounds after poor crowd control during the 1970 race), Brazil has not missed a season to this day. This is unsurprising, because Fittipaldi was followed by Nelson Piquet, Carlos Pace, Ayrton Senna, Rubens Barrichello and Felipe Massa, just to name those Brazilian F1 drivers who became champions or race winners.

The region comprising the Middle East and Africa featured early on, with that one-off race in Casablanca. Until Bahrain was added in 2004, however, it was represented by South Africa alone. The South African Grand Prix managed to evade the anti-apartheid politics of the 1970s and defy the bans implemented by other sporting authorities, thereby owning a fairly regular place in the calendar over three decades. Regrettably, this race has been absent now for nearly 15 years.

Europe apart, the way that some countries, and global regions, have failed to maintain a slot on the annual F1 schedule can only be described as erratic. Some year-to-year variation of venues is naturally welcomed, but there also needs to be a framework of flagship Grands Prix in the calendar to endorse the World Championship status of the whole series.

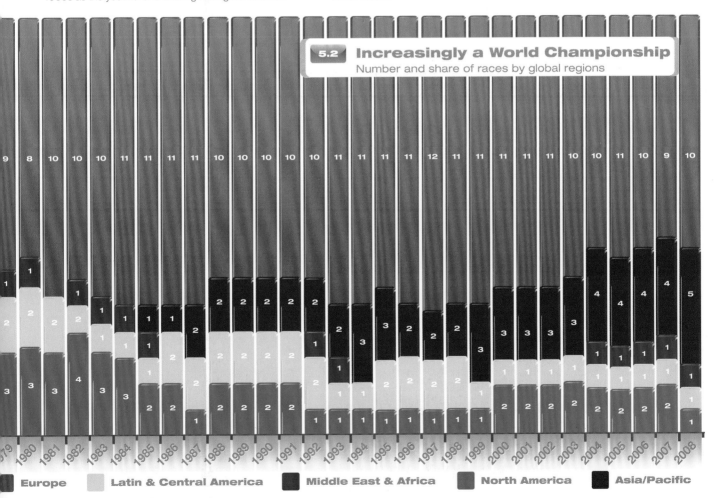

5.2 Increasingly a World Championship
Number and share of races by global regions

Europe   Latin & Central America   Middle East & Africa   North America   Asia/Pacific

Over the last 20 years, the region that has shown an unremitting commitment year by year has been Asia/Pacific. Ever since the first Australian Grand Prix in 1985 – joined by Japan in 1987, Malaysia in 1999 and most recently by China in 2004 – not one race has been missed. No wonder Bernie Ecclestone is looking east for additional venues and simultaneously promoting the concept of night racing as a way to maintain his substantial live TV audience in Europe.

Since Malaysia, four other new circuits have joined the circus (Indy, Bahrain, Shanghai and Istanbul), leaving the share Europe takes of all Grand Prix races at close to half (Graphic 5.2). This leads to another organisational conundrum, because these non-European 'flyaway' races place the greatest strain on the F1 teams and their entourages. The whole circus must be separated from its HQ hub in Europe, and airlifted to distant lands. Thoughtful scheduling of the 'flyaways' can minimise the logistics headache, and everyone becomes inured to a certain way of life, but all connected with the travelling show agree that long-haul travel is the major downside, contributing to physical and mental stress… and divorce!

These days the season lasts eight months, opening in early March with a handful of flyaway races. The European season, which begins in April and ends in September, is punctuated in June with the two North American flyaway races. There is usually a three-week break in August which allows everyone to catch their breath and families to take annual holidays. The season concludes in October with the remaining flyaway races.

For the race promoters, there has always been a certain kudos attached to staging either the opening or closing Grand Prix of the season. The opening race always attracts special attention as the pent-up anticipation of the closed season is finally unleashed. The country hosting the last race is ever hopeful of a grand finale with the championship still to be decided – and that has happened on 22 occasions in 58 years.

Australia features strongly for both opening and closing races. Melbourne has hosted the first round of the season 10 times, second only to Buenos Aires (15), while Adelaide has been the closing venue more than any other, on 11 occasions. In view of this, it is surprising that it has only been the deciding round twice, whereas Suzuka has enjoyed this experience four times from just six opportunities.

There was a time when the South African Grand Prix dictated the extremities of the Grand Prix season. In the middle of the European winter, there may be few better places in which to find oneself than Cape Province, where the East London circuit organised the first South African Grand Prix on 29 December 1962. The race brought to a conclusion an exciting, season-long championship struggle between Jim Clark and Graham Hill, which finally went in favour of Hill. After a similar December date in 1963, East London missed a year, to be rescheduled as the kick-off event for the 1965 championship trail. The earliest possible opportunity was chosen: New Year's Day!

This was the pattern for 1967 and 1968, the race now staged at Kyalami near Johannesburg, after which a March date was deemed more in keeping with the remainder of the season. Nevertheless, 1968 will be remembered for two reasons: first, it was the longest season on record, finishing in Mexico City on 3 November, having begun at Kyalami on 1 January. And second, by the time the European season got started at Jarama on 12 May, the driver who won that opening race on New Year's Day would sadly no longer be a participant. His name? Jim Clark.

The most bizarre location ever for a Grand Prix must be the hotel car park in Las Vegas (right) that hosted the US Grand Prix in 1981 and '82, the latter year being pictured.

Facing page. From the ridiculous to the sublime. The circuit for the night race at Singapore could be Grand Prix racing's most exotic location so far.

Raffles Hotel

Suntec City

Swissotel The Stamford

MILLENIA WALK

City Hall

PAN PACIFIC HOTEL

Supreme Court

WAR MEMORIAL PARK

T7

T9

STAMFORD ROAD

T8

NICOLL HIGHWAY

Arts House

MARINA MANDARIN HOTEL

T6

RAFFLES BOULEVARD

RITZ-CARLTON MILLENIA HOTEL

T5

Pit Building

ST ANDREWS ROAD

PADANG

T15

RAFFLES AVENUE

MARINA SQUARE

MANDARIN ORIENTAL HOTEL

T20

T21

Singapore Flyer

ESPLANADE PARK

T10

T11

T16

T17

T18

The Esplanade

SEATING GALLERY

T19

T22

T24

T12

T13

ESPLANADE DRIVE

FLOATING PLATFORM

T23

MARINA CHANNEL

Victoria Concert Hall

ANDERSON BRIDGE

SINGAPORE RIVER

T14

MARINA BAY

REPUBLIC BOULEVARD

T1

T2

T3

T4

The long and the short of it

Within the changing landscape of Grand Prix racing, one of the most striking transformations has been in race duration. The very first Grand Prix in 1906 was run over a mere 12 laps of a road course near Le Mans. However, the lap measured 64 miles, so the race distance totalled almost 770 miles! The race took more than 12 hours to complete at an average speed of a little over 60mph – an impressive figure for 1906, particularly considering the protracted duration of the race, fuel stops and so forth.

With this historical backdrop, it is perhaps understandable that, come the start of the new FIA World Championship in 1950, the regulations stipulated a minimum race distance of 300km (186.41 miles) or three hours. Endurance remained an important part of the game. Indeed, it should be remembered that the title given to Grand Prix races counting towards the World Championship, 'Grand Epreuve', translates to 'great test'. In those times, the Grand Epreuve vision was men of steel controlling powerful monsters on spindly tyres at dangerously high speeds for sustained periods of time.

Perhaps it should be of no surprise to discover that France, also the home of the Le Mans 24 Hours endurance race, has also staged a World Championship Grand Prix over the furthest distance. The 77 laps of the 1951 French Grand Prix at Reims-Gueux covered close to 374 miles. Fangio, having taken over the Alfa Romeo of his team-mate Luigi Fagioli, crossed the line after 3hr 22min 11sec, and the winning car averaged more than 110mph. This was still almost 24 minutes faster than his finishing time for the 1954 German Grand Prix on the slower Nürburgring. On that occasion 'The Maestro' drove his Mercedes-Benz W196 for 3hr 45min 45.8sec around the Nordschleife circuit, averaging less than 83mph.

Since then, alterations in the F1 regulations regarding the duration of races were numerous until 1989, when 305km (189.52 miles) or a maximum two hours became the standard used to this day. The changes that caused the most dramatic effect on race duration (Graphic 5.3), whether distance or time, occurred in 1958 and 1971, intriguingly a timeframe preceding Ecclestone's concerns over TV transmission schedules. Graphic 5.4 clearly illustrates the way that Grand Prix racing has evolved from the 1950s concept of a three-hour endurance race into effectively a 90-minute sprint. It has gone from fewer longer races to more shorter ones, but the championship is fought over many more miles than in the early days. The 19-race 2005 season exceeded 3500 miles for the first time, well over double the 1521 miles over which the inaugural championship was decided (Graphic 5.5).

Of course, the race distances represent only a fraction of the mileage put in by the teams as they reel off lap after lap in testing, the aims of which are to enhance car performance and reliability and to advance tyre development. During the 2005–06 closed season, Honda 'won' the unofficial winter testing prize by completing more mileage than any other team: 35,000 miles! Little wonder dedicated test drivers and test teams are required, numbering 40 or more people.

With a view to constraining costs, testing was subsequently limited to 36 days and track testing banned through August as Formula One takes its annual vacation. The introduction of a 'control' tyre and the new concept for race weekends, during which Friday is given over to testing, were also intended to bring sanity back to the activity of F1 testing.

With lap speeds so high these days, there is little likelihood of the two-hour time limit being imposed unless it is a wet race. The round-the-houses format at Monaco has for long been at the one extreme of circuit characteristics: shortest lap distance, lowest average lap speed, longest race duration. This holds true today even in the somewhat sanitised format of the Grands Prix, where lap time and race duration have broadly become standardised.

Hermann Tilke, the FIA's preferred F1 track designer, has been responsible for many of the more recent

2007	LAP (MILES)	F LAP (MPH)	F LAP (TIME)	RACE (TIME)
Sepang	3.444	128.249	1m 36.701 secs	1h 32m 14.930s
Sakhir	3.363	128.725	1m 34.067 secs	1h 33m 27.515s
Istanbul	3.317	136.815	1m 27.295 secs	1h 26m 42.161s
Shanghai	3.387	125.121	1m 37.454 secs	1h 37m 58.395s
Hockenheim (06)	2.842	133.999	1m 16.357 secs	1h 27m 51.693s
Hockenheim (01)	4.241	149.960	1m 41.808 secs	1h 18m 17.873s

additions to the calendar, and the fundamental dynamics of his circuits make interesting comparison (see panel).

The Hockenheimring has been included because Tilke was also responsible for the extensive modification to the track layout that was completed in time for the 2002 German Grand Prix. Traditionalists were sorry that this corrective surgery removed the quintessence that made Hockenheim special. No longer the flat-out blast through the forest section down to the Östkurve, the mighty blare of noise trapped in the branches of the trees. Lost was that intensity of listening out in the early laps for the wail, ever closer, as the pack charged and jostled its way back on the return loop, to burst into the stadium section to the roar of a huge crowd.

Gone, too, was the intimate association of Hockenheim with Jim Clark, who lost his life there on a tragic April day in 1968. The piece of track from which he skidded and crashed, probably after a tyre failure, has been ploughed up and the humble monument, built close to the spot where he died, has been resited. There is now a shorter, slower track with a lap-time almost half a minute shorter but a race time almost 10 minutes longer. A longer race with 20 more laps, plus a new hairpin designed to promote overtaking, which it does very effectively, all contribute towards a better show for trackside spectators and TV viewers alike. In an age when 'the show' is all-important, some may regard the loss of a circuit's character and heritage as a small price to pay.

At more than 14 miles in length, the Nordschleife at the Nürburgring is generally regarded as the longest lap distance in the modern Grand Prix era. Actually, at 15.894 miles (25.579km), the Pescara circuit in Italy, used just the once in 1957, edges out the Nordschleife, but by little more than a mile (Graphic 5.6). The other famous circuit of abnormal length was the picturesque Spa-Francorchamps in the Ardenne mountains, host to the Belgian Grand Prix. At 8.774 miles, it offered little more than half the lap distance of Pescara or the Nordschleife, but it was the first circuit to be axed from the Grand Prix calendar for reasons of safety. Circuits with long lap distances could not guarantee an acceptable level of safety at their remoter extremities. Assistance took too long to arrive at an accident scene. Spa after 1970 and the Nürburgring after 1976 were both sidelined, the latter following the fiery accident to reigning World Champion Niki Lauda, which so nearly cost the great Austrian his life.

In the annals of Grand Prix racing, the Nordschleife has legendary status. Because of its unique challenges, many consider it to have been the ultimate test of a Grand Prix driver. An undulating road circuit, much of it tree-lined, it had numerous blind brows and corners and finding any sort of driving rhythm was difficult, adding to the enormous powers of concentration required. Unless a driver was racing closely with others, he could feel strangely isolated out there in the countryside, with its sparse sprinkling of spectators. Also playing on his mind was the fact that, for a 14-mile circuit, it was simply impractical for safety standards to reach the accepted norm around its entire length. In the event of an 'off', how

5.3 Distance of World Championship races

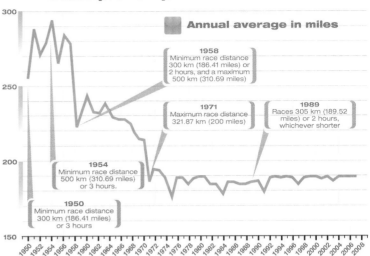

5.4 Duration of World Championship races

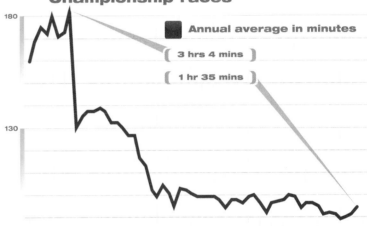

5.5 Racing miles of World Championship series

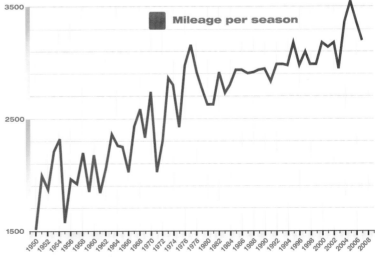

In winning the German Grand Prix at the Nürburgring in 1954, Fangio raced his Mercedes-Benz W196 for the better part of four hours – the longest ever World Championship Formula 1 race.

long until help reaches him – even finds him? And there was the awareness of the death toll... Seven Grand Prix drivers attempted to master the Nordschleife and died in the attempt: Onofré Marimon, Erwin Bauer (non-F1 race), Peter Collins, Carel Godin de Beaufort, John Taylor, Georges Berger (non-F1 race) and Gerhard Mitter.

Driving fast in the unique environment which was the old Nordschleife, fast enough to win and to beat others also seeking glory, required supreme self assurance and enormous courage, especially when inclement weather – another frequent feature in the Eifel hills – was added to the scenario. It is little wonder that the term 'Ringmeister' was coined to acknowledge the special status of those who had conquered the treacherous track and its cerebral devils. As the table shows, only 15 drivers won the 22 World Championship races held on the Nordschleife. Five of them were very special, victorious more than just the once, and two of that number were unquestioned Grand Prix kings of the Nürburgring.

At the time when Fangio won for the third time, and so magnificently, at the Nürburgring in 1957, only one driver had perished during the German Grand Prix. At the time when Jackie Stewart had equalled Fangio's feat, in 1973, the death toll had risen to five, more than any other Grand

Prix event before or since. Demonstrating such personal on-track courage, Stewart possessed every credential to become the self-styled champion of driver safety.

WINS	DRIVER	YEAR
	GRAND PRIX RINGMEISTERS	
	Winning drivers on the Nordschleife	
3	JM Fangio	1954, 1956, 1957
3	J Stewart	1968, 1971, 1973
2	A Ascari	1951, 1952
2	J Surtees	1963, 1964
2	J Ickx	1969, 1972
1	G Farina	1953
1	T Brooks	1958
1	S Moss	1961
1	G Hill	1962
1	J Clark	1965
1	J Brabham	1966
1	D Hulme	1967
1	C Regazzoni	1974
1	C Reutemann	1975
1	J Hunt	1976

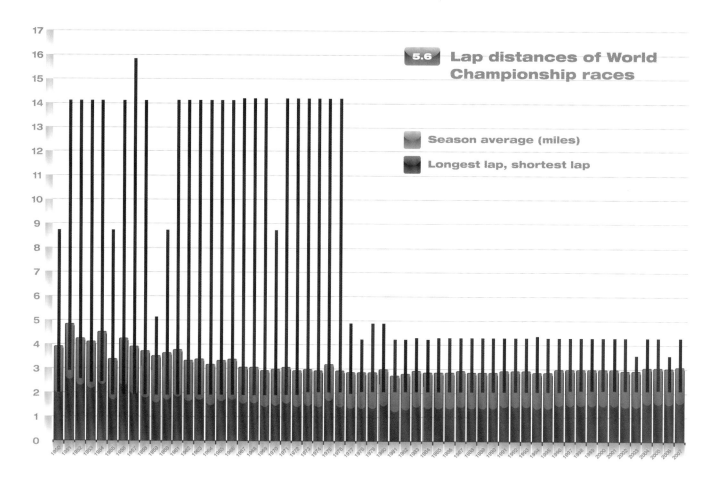

5.6 **Lap distances of World Championship races**

■ Season average (miles)

■ Longest lap, shortest lap

The ongoing challenge of safety is strikingly depicted by the annual average speeds over the 58-year period of the World Championship (Graphic 5.7). It is staggering to realise that the average speed around all 19 circuits used during 2005, the final year of the V10s, was almost 126mph! That is a 40 percent increase over the slowest equivalent statistic, the 90mph that was apparent half a century earlier (1957). Although an imperfect comparison, it is strongly indicative of relative performance levels. The top speed of a 1950s F1 car was not so very much less than one of today, so it is easy enough to appreciate that very much more of that 40 percent performance gain has been found around the corners than along the straights.

As a result of superior acceleration, traction and lower drag, coupled with phenomenal braking, the straight-line performance of the contemporary Formula One car is truly spectacular, but even that pales against the cornering powers available today.

Cornering has been totally radicalised by aerodynamic downforce and tyre technology, and it is during the negotiation of corners under high G-forces that the unforeseen is most likely to end in dire consequences. A study of the graphic reveals a sharp rise in average speeds towards the end of the 1950s as the better balance and lower frontal area of rear-engine cars shows up, ending with a distinct spike in the graph at 1960, the final year of the 2.5-litre formula. After that, the effect of the significant reduction in power due to the switch to 1.5 litres is detectable. With the return to 3-litre power in 1966, and the arrival shortly afterwards of aerodynamic wings and wide tyres, an incredible new performance spike is achieved by 1972. At that time, the general response to this challenge was to slow cars by introducing chicanes at strategic points on a circuit.

As the unrelenting upward trend of the graphic portrays, such measures provided only temporary respite. Various speed peaks and troughs ensue, most of which may be traced to specific events. One example is the peak associated with the performance breakthrough of ground-effect aerodynamics in the late 1970s until the concept was banned for 1982. Another is the trough linked to the range of safety-orientated measures taken in the wake of the death of Ayrton Senna in 1994.

Monza provides an ideal case history to observe the changing landscape of Grand Prix circuits over the decades (Graphic 5.8). It has featured in every one of the

5.8 CASE HISTORY: **58 years at autodromo nationale di Monza**
Pole lap in mph

Parabolica replaces Curva de Vedano

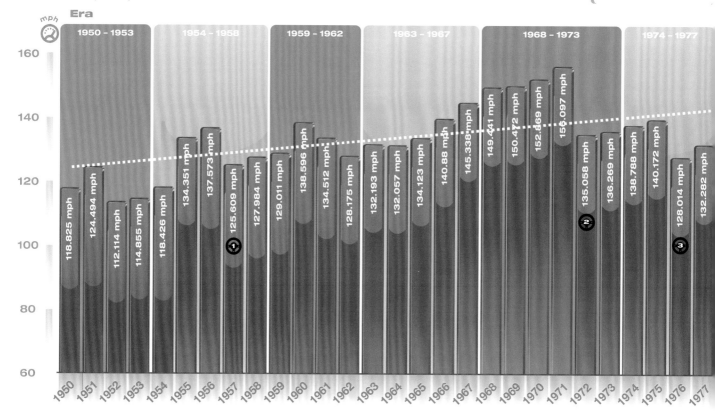

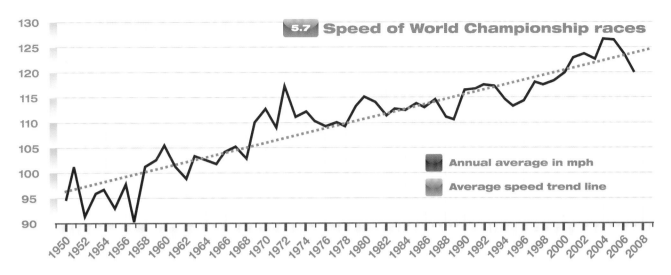

Annual average in mph

Average speed trend line

58 World Championships bar one, a record unmatched by any other circuit. Monza is also special because Ferrari naturally regards it as its home circuit, a place where traditionally a special effort is made to gain superiority over the rest of the field. The tifosi rarely fail to respond to Ferrari fever, which pervades a track steeped in history, having been built in the wooded grounds of the Monza Royal Park in 1922.

Monza's reputation as a high-speed circuit is well founded. The 1971 race, won at an average speed exceeding 150mph, still ranks as the fourth fastest Grand Prix of all time. Chicanes built for the race the following

took 20mph off the average lap speed and added more than 10 seconds to a lap-time. The graphic shows this as well as the subsequent series of attempts to counter the prevailing trend of faster and faster lap speeds.

But it took a further 33 years before the inevitable happened, and the Italian Grand Prix at Monza was at last won at a faster average speed than in 1971. It should be appreciated that, to achieve this despite the numerous alterations to the circuit layout, the Lesmo and Parabolica corners were taken by the 2004 winner, Juan Pablo Montoya, at speeds unimaginable to the 1971 winner, Peter Gethin.

 Chicanes added after start (Variante del Ratifilio) & at Variante Ascari

 Variante del Ratifilio modified & Variante della Roggia chicane added

 Second Lesmo tightened & Curva Grande reprofiled

 Ratifilio & Roggia chicanes modified

Ratifilio & Roggia chicanes redesigned

The Monza banking, adding >2.5 miles to the Grand Prix circuit, was used in 1955/56 & 1960/61. No race was held in 1980

Giuseppe Farina will forever be remembered as the winner of the first ever World Championship Grand Prix, held at Silverstone in 1950.

t seems inconceivable that Monza would ever be dropped from the Grand Prix calendar, but complaints by local residents about noise intrusion almost achieved the impossible in 2006. Neighbours taking legal action against something that has been in situ since 1922 is surely only possible in the politically correct age in which we now live. However, no circuit is free from the possibility of exclusion. As more new nations come on stream, some of the races in the European heartland of Grand Prix racing may have to go to the wall.

In the 21st century, Formula One has become a spectator sport drawing hundreds of thousands to the circuits, and a TV sport attracting millions who watch each of up to 20 races as the story of the World Championship unfolds year by year. Through the window of television, each racing circuit has become the means by which countries and cities promote themselves to the worlds of tourism and business, and brand owners expose their products and services to a worldwide consumer marketplace. Little wonder there is a waiting list of countries eager to join the Formula One Grand Prix bandwagon.

If a European circuit cull does become necessary, it is hoped that the powers that be will have an eye on the rich heritage of Grand Prix racing. This is undoubtedly maintained through racing teams or marques (particularly Ferrari), but unquestionably also through certain circuits. The number of races run in Europe has been 10 or 11 for more than 30 years, once reaching 12, in 1997. If heritage is to be a significant criterion for retention, then six Grands Prix (Graphic 5.9) and five circuits (Graphic 5.10) make irresistible cases.

Of the five circuits, the Neue Nürburgring is perhaps least evocative of its illustrious predecessor. Yet somehow the Burg Nürburg landmark provides an ever-present reminder of the majesty of the Nordschleife, which dates back to 1927.

Five of the races – Britain, Monaco, Belgium, France and Italy – and four of the circuits – Silverstone (first used in 1948), Monaco (1929), Spa (1924) and Monza (1922) – were on the calendar right at the start back in 1950. Indeed one of these, Silverstone, hosted the very first World Championship race.

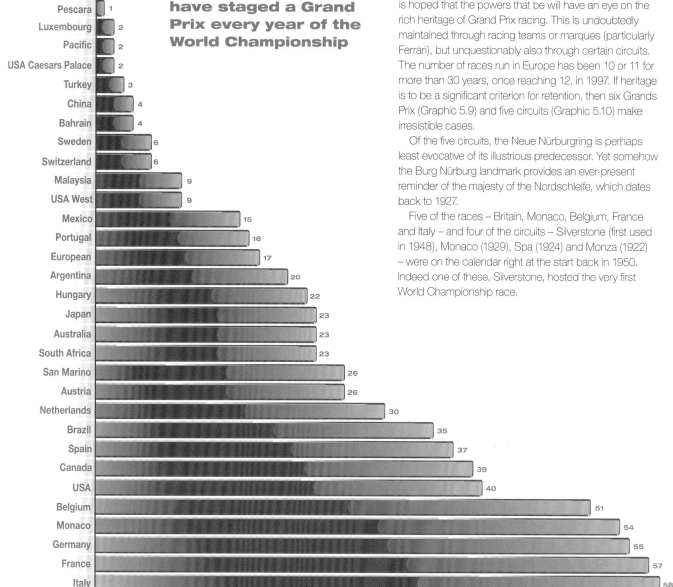

5.9 Just two countries have staged a Grand Prix every year of the World Championship

Country	Races
Morocco	1
Pescara	1
Luxembourg	2
Pacific	2
USA Caesars Palace	2
Turkey	3
China	4
Bahrain	4
Sweden	6
Switzerland	6
Malaysia	9
USA West	9
Mexico	15
Portugal	16
European	17
Argentina	20
Hungary	22
Japan	23
Australia	23
South Africa	23
San Marino	26
Austria	26
Netherlands	30
Brazil	35
Spain	37
Canada	39
USA	40
Belgium	51
Monaco	54
Germany	55
France	57
Italy	58
Britain	58

5.10 5 circuits keep the faith with Grand Prix racing's rich heritage

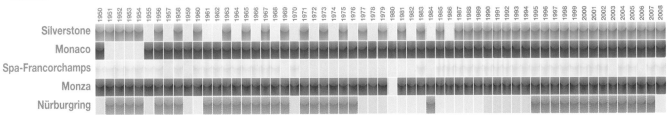

	1950	1951	1952	1953	1954	1955	1956	1957	1958	1959	1960	1961	1962	1963	1964	1965	1966	1967	1968	1969	1970	1971	1972	1973	1974	1975	1976	1977	1978	1979	1980	1981	1982	1983	1984	1985	1986	1987	1988	1989	1990	1991	1992	1993	1994	1995	1996	1997	1998	1999	2000	2001	2002	2003	2004	2005	2006	2007	2008
Silverstone
Monaco
Spa-Francorchamps
Monza
Nürburgring

The fusion of human skill with technological excellence is fundamental to the mix that makes Grand Prix racing so fascinating, colourful and exciting. While the drivers take the glory, the team owners wield the power and, as with the great football teams, certain Grand Prix cars and teams attract their own special following.

It is easy enough to comprehend what motivates the drivers of Grand Prix cars: talent, competitiveness, success, fulfilment... the list could fill the page and the language could become increasingly poetic. But truly to appreciate Grand Prix racing, there has to be an equal understanding of what inspires that select group who provide the machinery for each race – the entrants.

'The fusion of human skill with technological excellence.' Sir Jack Brabham, that great driver/constructor, characterises this definition of Formula 1 better than anyone. Here, at Reims in 1966, he is shortly to become the first driver to win a Grand Prix in his own car, the Brabham BT19-Repco.

G raphic 6.1 displays the number of entrants of Grand Prix cars over the decades. Although these are subdivided into four categories, there are essentially only two motivations for each to participate, and they could not be more diverse. One is largely sporting: the desire to go motor racing. The other, totally mercenary: the desire for financial gain. Over time, the four categories of entrant have narrowed to only two, and their motivations have become increasingly blurred.

A dip into early Grand Prix history provides an immediate clue as to why manufacturers participate. The first Grand Prix in 1906 was won by a Renault, and Renault's motivation then was the same as 100 years later: selling motor cars. What better platform could there be than motorsport for a car manufacturer to build awareness and create desire and demand? In the formative years of the sport before the Second World War, there were many other marques that, along with Renault, have remained household names in motoring, such as FIAT, Mercedes-Benz, Peugeot, Alfa Romeo and Maserati, as well as many that became no more than evocative names in the record books – Duesenberg, Delage, Delahaye, Auto Union, Bugatti (a brand name recently revived).

But Grand Prix racing was by no means the sole province of the factory teams. There were others who wanted to play a part in what was, and is, widely considered to be the ultimate expression of motorsport, entering cars privately for themselves or hired drivers. These privateers, often wealthy heirs (playboys) or gentlemen racers (business owners), purchased their cars from the constructors and competed against them. The factory team cars and their drivers usually held sway over the 'privateers', but not always, as some privateers operated their teams to extremely high standards. The supreme example is whisky heir Rob Walker's R.R.C. Walker Racing Team which, to this day, remains the only privateer Grand Prix winner.

There was a fine line between 'privateer' and 'customer' teams. Neither category was a constructor, their reason for participation being more to do with sporting ambition than any other stimulus. The distinction, such as it was, had more to do with the scale and professionalism of the teams. True privateers were largely a phenomenon of the 1950s and 1960s, a less sophisticated period for the sport. After 1970, it was not easy to identify a Grand Prix entrant of true privateer status. Ten years later,

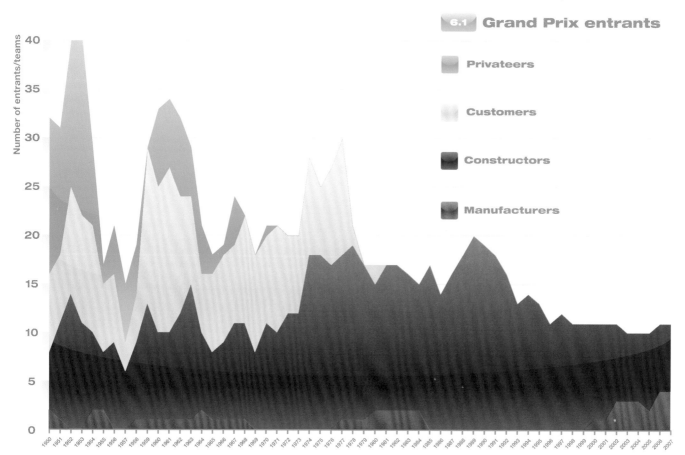

6.1 Grand Prix entrants

- Privateers
- Customers
- Constructors
- Manufacturers

the last customer car (for now) took to the grid. Rupert Keegan raced a Williams FW07B entered by RAM/ Penthouse Rizla Racing to finish ninth at Watkins Glen, two laps behind the winner. This was another Williams FW07B driven by Alan Jones, followed by his works team-mate, Carlos Reutemann.

'Works' was a term often assigned to the fourth and final category of entrant and, over its five decades, the category most important to the ongoing success of the Formula One World Championship. These teams constructed their own Grand Prix chassis but were not road car manufacturers although, more often than not, they had business interests in the motor trade – garages in the case of Cooper and HWM, engine bearings in the case of Vanwall (Vandervell). Motor racing was a logical sporting or promotional outlet where they could perhaps find advantage by producing their own machines, although very often using engines supplied by others. These days, the definition of the constructor/entrant is becoming blurred as the concept of 'B' teams gathers impetus.

The constructor/entrants are motor racing entrepreneurs – entrants who have made their racing team into successful businesses in their own right. McLaren and Williams are the outstanding examples of the genre. In the 1970s, these two joined with other, similarly minded entrants to form the Formula One Constructors Association, under the leadership of Bernie Ecclestone, the owner at that time of the Brabham racing team. Ferrari was never a member of FOCA, coming, as it did, from a unique position, being neither a mass car manufacturer nor merely a racing team.

In many ways, the origins of Ferrari were shaped by the history of the Mille Miglia and Targa Florio, the open-road endurance races that were so popular in Italy before and after the Second World War. Not only did Ferrari sell replicas of its works sports-racing machines, but the great Italian designer-coachbuilders – Bertone, Ghia, Zagato, Vignale and Pinin Farina – created exotic road cars that wowed visitors to the great 1950s motor shows in Turin, Paris, London and New York. The glitzy, glamorous positioning that Ferrari enjoyed was never truly occupied by Alfa Romeo or Mercedes-Benz, and only briefly by Maserati in the 1950s.

Today, that niche in the worldwide car market is known as the 'supercar' segment: very exclusive, high-performance machines, statements for the rich and famous… and Americans… and celebrities! In order to create that vital ingredient of exclusivity, Enzo Ferrari combined high desirability with high price. The price premium was the easy part, but first desirability had to be earned on the Grand Prix tracks of the world… and so the legend was born. And Ferrari have been faithful to Grand Prix racing for almost 60 years, making 1702 starts from more than 750 races (see 6.2), appreciably more than McLaren, which is next in the pecking order. To accrue its 630-race tally, McLaren began 16 years after the 'Commendatore' first entered his scarlet Grand Prix machines, in the second ever round of the World Championship at Monaco in 1950.

6.2	**Grands Prix started**	
197	BRM	
215	Sauber	
227	Renault	
227	March	
250	Jordan	
317	Benetton	
340	Minardi	
382	Arrows	
394	Brabham	
409	Ligier/Prost	
430	Tyrrell	
491	Lotus	
542	Williams	
630	McLaren	
757	Ferrari	

Monza 1967. The incomparable Enzo Ferrari in discussion with Mauro Forghieri. The car is Chris Amon's 312 V12, which was Ferrari's singleton entry that year.

Just like love and marriage, Formula One champion drivers go together with Formula One champion cars. Don't they?

In Formula One you can have one without the other, because there are two separate championships: the World Championship of Drivers and the World Championship of Constructors. In the 50 years since the inception of the latter, there have been as many as nine occasions when the car used by the World Champion of Drivers has not also been the winner of the Constructors' trophy. Rather against expectations, it seems that champion drivers and champion constructors are usually, but by no means always, two sides of the same coin.

As discussed earlier, the definition of an F1 constructor is an F1 racing team that owns the intellectual property rights to its chassis and builds it, even if it outsources to suppliers some of the components, such as the tyres, the brakes, the clutch, the gearbox and, most significantly,

the engine. The importance of the engine supplier is recognised in that Constructors' Championship points may only be scored for a specific chassis-engine pairing. Strictly speaking, for example, Williams-Ford, Williams-Renault and Williams-Honda should have all been regarded as separate entities. Thus following after Ferrari with 15 Constructors' titles are Lotus-Ford and Williams-Renault with five apiece, McLaren-Honda with four, and Cooper-Climax, Lotus-Climax, Brabham-Repco, Williams-Ford, McLaren-TAG, Williams-Honda and Renault with two.

It has become more usual for the Constructors' championships to be expressed in one or other of the two ways shown by the pie charts (Graphic 6.3). The first is for 'marques' – the collective term used for chassis constructors, whether they are factory (manufacturer) teams or works (constructor) teams. The second is for the engine suppliers to those teams.

The 1969 season brought the first of three World Championships for that durable partnership of Jackie Stewart and Ken Tyrrell.

The marques pie chart contains such names as Williams, McLaren and Lotus – dyed-in-the-wool racing organisations, privately owned companies whose whole *raison d'être* is motor racing. The engines pie-chart (6.3) comprises quite different names, Ford, Renault and Honda – dyed-in-the-wool motor car manufacturers, publicly owned corporations whose whole *raison d'être* is selling road cars. The manufacturers' role and involvement in Formula One and their relationship with the racing teams is a fascinating one, more so today than at any time previously. There is a great deal that unites them, but also much that makes them uneasy bedfellows.

The only name appearing on both pies is that of Ferrari. This fact alone is indicative of its special status. Ferrari is the only team to have participated in every one of the 58 years of the Formula One World Championship. Excluding the Indy 500, the Scuderia has failed to enter only two races and, throughout that lengthy period, has always sourced its own engine (the team's 1956/57 Lancia-based V8s excepted).

Ferrari and three other outstanding teams have made a massive contribution to the success of the F1 World Championship. From their differing roots and contradictory perspectives, these four – Ferrari, Lotus, McLaren and Williams – shared that crucial common goal: winning. Winning Grands Prix, winning World Championships, they have been competing head to head over many decades. Between them, they account for a staggering 78 percent (39) of the Constructors' championships since its inception 50 years ago, and 67 percent (39) of the Drivers' titles across its 58 years! These teams, and their drivers who have formed the essential and integral part of that success, are truly two sides of the same coin.

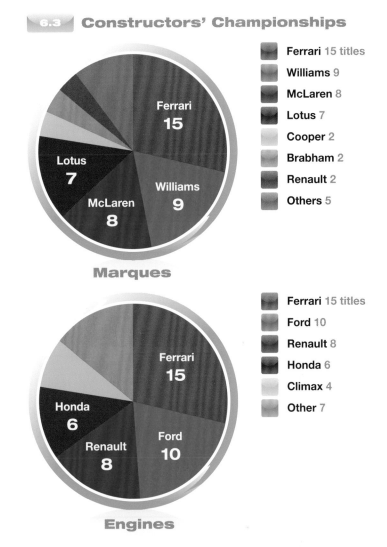

Ferrari 15 titles
Williams 9
McLaren 8
Lotus 7
Cooper 2
Brabham 2
Renault 2
Others 5

Marques

Ferrari 15 titles
Ford 10
Renault 8
Honda 6
Climax 4
Other 7

Engines

Sir Frank Williams is not known for a paternal attitude towards his drivers. Probably the closest he came to a special relationship was with Alan Jones, with whom he is pictured in 1981.

The rise and demise of winning marques

As the heading conveys, nothing is forever. Numerous evocative names from the annals of Grand Prix motor racing have been consigned to the museum. The tabulation below (6.4) lists every winning marque in the 58 years of Grand Prix racing, indicating the seasons in which they participated and the years in which they won (race victories depicted by the number). Purely for reference, blue is used to depict a season when a marque participated solely as an engine supplier. The table makes it easy to trace the early Italian supremacy, the incursion from British teams, the comings and goings of the manufacturers – the lasting emergence of some, and the brief flashes of brilliance of others.

One such was Vanwall, the team that made the breakthrough to establish the tradition for winning British cars and teams. Tony Vandervell's motivation for entering Grand Prix racing was as much patriotism as anything else. Frustrated by the lamentable BRM saga, he decided that the only way to bring Grand Prix success to Britain was to have a go himself. The success of the Vanwall project in 1957–58 was the forerunner of a glorious period for British motorsport, which included success even for the derided BRM concern, bringing succour to another great patriot, Raymond Mays, the founder of the British Racing Motors project.

Before founding his own Grand Prix race team, Colin Chapman of Lotus fame was involved in the BRM and Vanwall ventures in a consultative capacity. His story gives yet another twist to the motivations that lie behind the Grand Prix entrant. As with Cooper, it was the manufacturing and selling of racing cars for the lesser formulae which took him inevitably into Grand Prix racing, but from there Chapman became a road car manufacturer in his own right. Yet this does not place Lotus Cars in the same category as, for example, Renault as a 'manufacturer'.

The distinction between them is immense. One is a volume car producing conglomerate for mass market consumption, the other a small specialist performance car maker for the connoisseur. For Lotus, success on the race track and success in the showrooms was far more adjacent than for a Renault or a Honda. Even upmarket Renaults are far more to do with getting from A to B in a cosseted fashion than true aspiration of ownership. It is for this reason that Lotus aligns much more closely with the Ferrari business model than that of Renault. Ferrari, even

6.4 The rise and demise of winning marques

Marque	1950	1951	1952	1953	1954	1955	1956	1957	1958	1959	1960	1961	1962	1963	1964	1965	1966	1967	1968	1969	1970	1971	1972	1973	1974	1975	1976	1977	1978	1979
Alfa Romeo	6	4																												
Ferrari		3	7	7	2	1	5		2	2	1	5		1	3		2		1		4	2	1		3	6	6	4	5	6
Maserati			1	2		2	4																							
Cooper									2	5	6	1				1	1													
BRM										1			4	2	2	1					1	2	1							
Mercedes-Benz					4	5																								
Vanwall								3	6																					
Lotus											2	3	3	7	3	6	1	4	5	2	6		5	7	3		1	5	8	
Porsche													1																	
Brabham															2		4	4		2	1				3	2			2	
Honda																1		1												
Eagle																		1												
McLaren																			3	1			1	3	4	3	6	3		
Matra																			3	6										
March																					1					1	1			
Tyrrell																						7	4	5	2	1	1	1		1
Williams																														5
Shadow																												1		
Hesketh																										1				
Penske																											1			
Ligier																												1		3
Wolf																												3		
Renault																														1
Benetton																														
Jordan																														
Stewart																														

more so than Lotus Cars in its prime, was in the business of selling aspirational merchandise, highly expensive dream machines.

The incomparable Enzo Ferrari, the most charismatic of all the team principals, was actually dismissive of Lotus, Cooper and the other predominantly British racing teams which, in the late 1950s, had developed the practice of externally sourcing their engines, rather than building their own. With a curled lip, he referred to them as the 'garagistes', implying that they were back-street boys but with motoring connotations!

Well before the name Ferrari became a legend, the man himself had run Alfa Romeo's motor racing department from 1929–39. On being congratulated by Alfa Romeo's managing director on Ferrari's first Grand Prix victory, at Silverstone in 1951, Enzo's telegram reply stated: "Rest assured that I still have the adolescent tenderness of a first love and deep affection of a mother for our Alfa." With his car manufacturer background at Alfa, possibly Ferrari's mind-set could not progress from the idea that selling cars financed racing… and racing success sold more passenger cars.

The 'garagistes' had different ideas. Rather than road cars, how about building and selling low-priced racing cars to satisfy the mushrooming post-war explosion in motorsport that had been spurred on by the wide availability of 500cc motorcycle engines?

As opposed to bearing the enormous design and development costs of an in-house engine (as Ferrari,

BRM and Vanwall), how about outsourcing engine build to a company that could spread the costs across its core businesses in fork-lift trucks and fire-pumps (Coventry Climax) and achieve further cost synergy by supplying multiple teams?

Rather than largely relying on horsepower to win races, how about paying greater attention to balance, traction, roadholding and aerodynamics?

One of the 'garagistes' also fathered another genre of Grand Prix entrant, the driver/constructor. Jack Brabham, an Australian, and Bruce McLaren from New Zealand were team-mates at Cooper between 1959 and 1961. Their partnership with the Coopers, father and son Charles and John, was highly successful, delivering two World Championships to Cooper and Brabham, and a special place in history for 22-year-old Bruce as the youngest ever Grand Prix winner, an accolade that stood for almost 44 years. Jack left Cooper to set up the Brabham Racing Organisation in 1962 and, after a further four loyal years, Bruce took the same decision, forming Bruce McLaren Motor Racing.

Almost from the start, Jack Brabham was more than just a driver – he was also an engineer, a car builder and developer. His long and distinguished career had three distinct phases, starting with the Cooper Car Company and its rear-engine revolution, followed by the formation of his own racing team. He and his lead driver, the American Dan Gurney, were invariably competitive, although Gurney could only win twice over their three-season partnership. Success

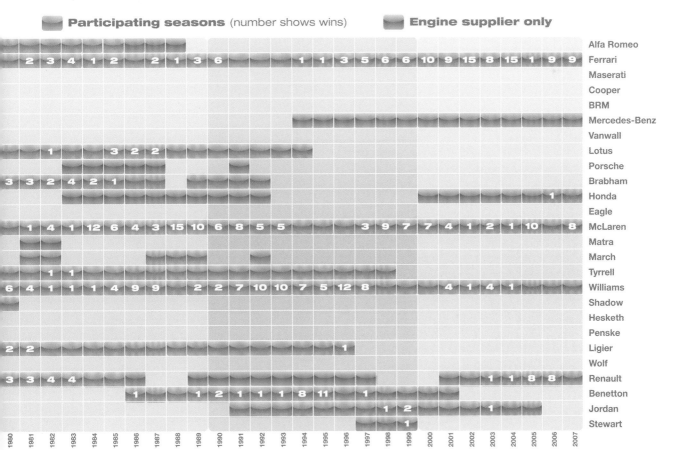

Participating seasons (number shows wins)   **Engine supplier only**

difficulties with the Eagle Grand Prix project ensued and Dan's focus increasingly turned to his parallel USAC Eagle project. Indeed, Gurney finished the 1968 season not even driving his own car for the final three races. The car he drove was... a McLaren. This was not entirely surprising bearing in mind that the previous year, when Bruce's own team was suffering growing pains, Bruce had accepted a offer from Dan to drive an Eagle-Weslake in three races.

The final twist is that, in the aftermath of the death of Bruce McLaren in 1970, his beleaguered team needed someone to step into the breach left by its owner/driver. Although he had not participated in a Grand Prix for more than a season, Gurney once again drove a McLaren in three races until a more permanent arrangement could be made.

At the time of his death, McLaren had built a winning team on the circuits, and an organisation strong enough to withstand the loss of its founder and leader. Given time, the team prospered. With title sponsorship initially from Yardley and then from Marlboro, it produced two Drivers' titles and one Constructors'. The first of these was with Emerson

on a major scale came at the start of the third and greatest phase when Brabham led his team to back-to-back titles in 1966–67, ironically after the loyal Gurney had departed – to set up his own racing team! The 1966 season was the first of the new 3-litre Formula One and Jack's car design strategy was to go for technical simplicity. It worked superbly with a spate of four successive wins over that summer's campaign.

Denny Hulme won the championship for the Brabham team the following year, after which success was harder to come by. Increasing chassis and engine sophistication meant that Brabham had to first ditch his Repco V8 for the ubiquitous Ford Cosworth DFV, and subsequently build his first full monocoque chassis for the 1970 season, having been faithful to spaceframe construction long after rival manufacturers. Not that Brabham, and his designer and fellow Australian Ron Tauranac, were not right there in other directions, notably in the development of aerodynamic wings during the 1967 season. In his final season as a driver in 1970, Brabham was still a force sufficient to mount a significant challenge for the title. One of the great names in motor racing, three-times World Champion Jack Brabham will long be remembered as the first man to drive and to win with a car bearing his own name, when he took the chequered flag at the French Grand Prix of 1966.

And only 20 World Championship races later, at Spa-Francorchamps in 1968, Bruce McLaren became the second winner in a car bearing his own name – although he was not the second driver to win in his own car! That feat was claimed by... Dan Gurney, who chose not to use his surname for either his own team, All American Racers, or his own car, the beautiful Eagle-Weslake with which he also triumphed at Spa, one year before McLaren's victory.

Another curiosity regarding this Brabham/McLaren/ Gurney triumvirate of 1960s driver/constructors is that Gurney, who had driven for Brabham for three seasons, drove for him again in 1968 on a one-off basis as mounting

Fittipaldi in 1974 and the second the famous James Hunt versus Niki Lauda saga of 1976. There is some irony in the fact that Hunt only got the seat at McLaren because Fittipaldi had left the team high and dry with a late decision to join… his own racing team!

Fittipaldi strove for five long years to join Brabham, Gurney and McLaren as the three drivers who have won in their own machinery. There is a surprisingly long list of other drivers who struggled but, for different reasons, failed in the attempt: John Surtees, Chris Amon, Graham Hill, Arturo Merzario and Hector Rebaque in the 1970s, all using the Ford Cosworth DFV 'kit-car' engine. With 118 Grand Prix appearances, Team Surtees exceeded the 104 accumulated by the Fittipaldi brothers' team. Each finished second in a Grand Prix, but that was as close as they ever got to realising their dream.

So, of that special genre of team owners, the driver/constructors, the names of Brabham and McLaren are outstanding – and, as things turned out, doubly so as they each had a triumphal 'second coming' under new management. Bernie Ecclestone acquired Brabham in 1971

and, over the following decade and a half, ran a team that was never dominant but invariably in the hunt for wins, accumulating 22 in those 16 years. As might be expected, he introduced some out of the ordinary sponsorship in the shape of the Italian companies Martini, Parmalat and Olivetti, and interesting engine suppliers in Alfa Romeo and BMW.

Possibly Ecclestone's greatest asset was his designer, Gordon Murray, who penned a succession of winning cars. Murray will probably be best remembered for the outrageous, flat-12 Alfa Romeo engined Brabham BT46B 'fan car', which won on debut at Anderstorp in Niki Lauda's hands, after which it was banned.

But the driver always associated most closely with the Ecclestone years is Nelson Piquet. The Brazilian won two Drivers' World Championships in Ecclestone's Brabhams although the Constructors' title eluded them on each occasion. However, the Ecclestone package of Brabham, Murray, Piquet, BMW and Fila became the first team to take a title with a turbocharged car and, in so doing, reintroduced the fuel-stop to Grand Prix racing.

Team founder Bruce McLaren with his McLaren M5A-Ford in the 1968 British Grand Prix at Brands Hatch. Forty years on, the team bearing his name is still winning races… and making headlines.

A glance at the all-time winners list for marques (Graphic 6.5) reveals two main features. First, across 58 years, a mere 26 marques have been successful. Second, four have been far more successful than the rest. Regrettably, one of these four is moribund. The others, the 'Big Three', will be discussed more fully later. Focusing therefore on the higher reaches of the lower echelons of the all-time winners list, it is important to consider just a few other World Champion Constructors which have not yet received due recognition.

The most recent name to be added is Renault with back-to-back titles in 2005–06. Renault has made a highly significant contribution to Grand Prix racing, particularly with engine developments, since the Regie entered the modern era in 1977. Not only the turbocharged engine but also the V10/pneumatic valves configuration both sprang from Viry and became *de rigueur* with other engine manufacturers (and briefly, indeed, mandatory). Renault as a constructor materialised on two occasions, first in

the 1970s through organic development, and second in 2002 through acquisition. The team it acquired was Benetton which itself had entered Grand Prix racing when Alessandro Benetton bought Ted Toleman's eponymous team back in the mid-1980s. Unlike so many such teams, Benetton broke into the winner's circle and continued to enjoy modest success for some years before scaling the heights with Michael Schumacher and landing the Constructors' title in 1995.

Renault was the supplier of the engine that contributed to that success, and its connection was maintained during Benetton's rather barren post-Schumacher period. The engine was branded 'Playlife' when Renault withdrew full factory support in the late 1990s. Benetton was always regarded as the likely springboard should Renault decide to re-enter Grand Prix racing, and many of the people involved with the Schumacher success years were also very much part of Fernando Alonso's Renault triumphs, notably Flavio Briatore and Pat Symonds. Indeed, the

6.5 Just 26 winning marques in 58 years

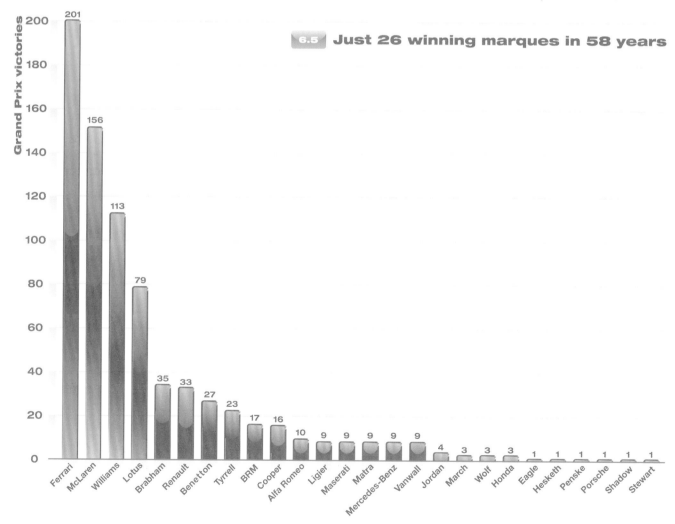

Renault team HQ remains at the former Benetton premises in Enstone, Oxfordshire.

The other Constructors' champion team which has not received attention appropriate to its success also had a French connection. Ken Tyrrell's first entry into Formula One was with a chassis built by Matra. The French weapons manufacturer had entered motorsport to showcase its technological capabilities to a wider audience and Formula One was a logical next step. During their highly successful two-year partnership over 1968–69, using DFV engines, the Tyrrell Racing Organisation operated as Matra International, because the French chassis provider needed a visible profile to achieve its commercial aims. Together they won the Constructors' title in 1969, but the relationship ended when Matra finished development of a V12 for its own team.

Tyrrell was convinced that the Ford V8 was the better bet, and how right he was. The Matra chassis never won again and, over nine seasons, the V12 saw the chequered flag only three times, in the back of a Ligier.

Tyrrell was forced to start the 1970 season with a customer chassis from March, a newly established Formula One team and constructor (the 'M' in the name stands for Max Mosley, the president of the FIA since 1990). Tyrrell recognised that customer chassis supply would not give him the command and control necessary for ongoing

Grand Prix success and embarked on an ambitious plan which also happened to be one of the best kept secrets in Formula One history.

Tyrrell 001 took shape in modest premises situated at the Tyrrell brothers' timber yard in Ockham, Surrey, and made a sensational World Championship debut at the 1970 Canadian Grand Prix in September. Jackie Stewart put it on pole position and led for the first third of the race until a stub axle broke.

With Stewart, the Tyrrell marque became an immediate force in Grand Prix racing, winning two Drivers' titles and one Constructors' before Stewart's retirement at the end of 1973. Tyrrell campaigned for another 25 years, manufacturing his cars in-house including the extraordinary P34 six-wheeler project of 1976–77. But there were to be no more championships and, in the final 15 seasons, no more race victories. This is why Tyrrell ends up at the blunt end of the Graphic (6.6) which records the average number of races (18.7) it took Tyrrell to deliver each of their 23 precious wins, having at one time shared the sharp end with such as Ferrari, McLaren, Williams and Lotus. With such a magnificent heritage, blighted somewhat by the team's disqualification in 1984, it was almost a relief when Tyrrell's place on the grid was acquired by British American Racing. The final Grand Prix for a Tyrrell came at Suzuka in 1998.

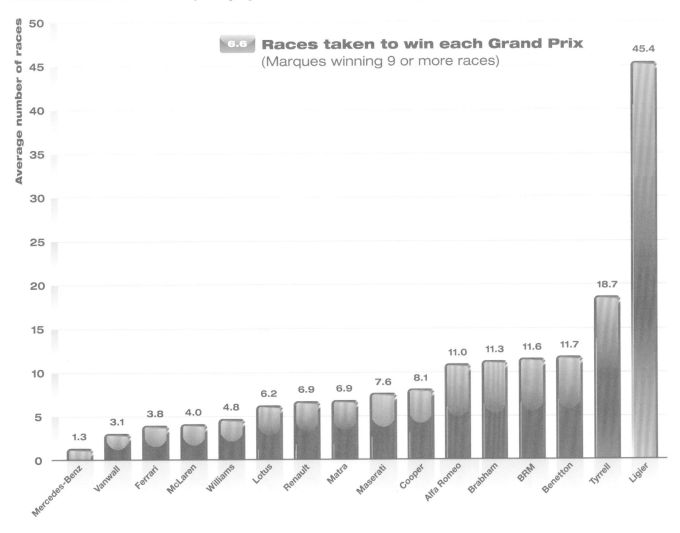

6.6 **Races taken to win each Grand Prix**
(Marques winning 9 or more races)

Average number of races

Mercedes-Benz	1.3
Vanwall	3.1
Ferrari	3.8
McLaren	4.0
Williams	4.8
Lotus	6.2
Renault	6.9
Matra	6.9
Maserati	7.6
Cooper	8.1
Alfa Romeo	11.0
Brabham	11.3
BRM	11.6
Benetton	11.7
Tyrrell	18.7
Ligier	45.4

The big three

The demise of teams such as Tyrrell, Lotus and Brabham accentuates the immense challenge of achieving sustained success in the Formula One crucible. For this reason, the 'Big Three' (Graphic 6.7) vividly demonstrates the season-by-season impact of three teams that have won then lost, but have invariably returned to win again, and that together have dominated Grand Prix racing over the past 20–25 years. It is apparent that there has been a relentless tendency over time for more and more winning to be accomplished by these three teams. From 1984, this trend became even more acute as McLaren and Williams took team domination to heights unprecedented since Alfa Romeo and Mercedes-Benz in the 1950s. It is easy to see why Ferrari took the strategic decision to bring back Luca di Montezemolo in order to reassert Ferrari's winning pedigree against the unremitting onslaught from Williams and McLaren, and how brilliantly this was achieved over the decade ending 2004. The cessation of Ferrari's run of championship supremacy was abrupt. But it was not carried out by McLaren or by Williams, either. The executioner was Renault which, having committed to Formula One until at least 2012, might yet become the team making it the 'Big Four' – or, like Benetton before it in the mid-1990s, to have been just a flash in the pan in the stakes for long-term supremacy.

In many ways, it was sponsorship which gave Formula One two of its most successful team owners, Sir Frank Williams and Ron Dennis. Although he had been trying for rather longer, Williams became a genuine force a little sooner than Dennis's team, breaking into the winner's circle in 1979 with the Patrick Head designed FW07 and primary sponsorship from Saudia and Albilad, an essential ingredient to the success. Fifteen race wins from 64 races produced two Drivers' and two Constructors' World Championships between 1979 and 1982.

The catalyst for the second coming - or maybe it should be the third – of the McLaren team under Ron Dennis was his title sponsor, Marlboro, which had also supported Ron's Project Four Formula Two team. Brand owner Philip Morris helped to engineer a merger – as with all mergers, effectively a takeover – of the then floundering McLaren concern by Dennis, and the rest, as they say, is history.

What this episode also illustrates is the significance of the active role that the Formula One sponsor was prepared to take by 1980. No longer was a company bankrolling a team willing to take a passive, uninvolved position.

A few short years after the Marlboro brokered takeover, Dennis brought together the Lauda, Prost, Barnard, TAG Porsche 'superteam' that put McLaren International on the map in a big way with a spate of exceptional successes

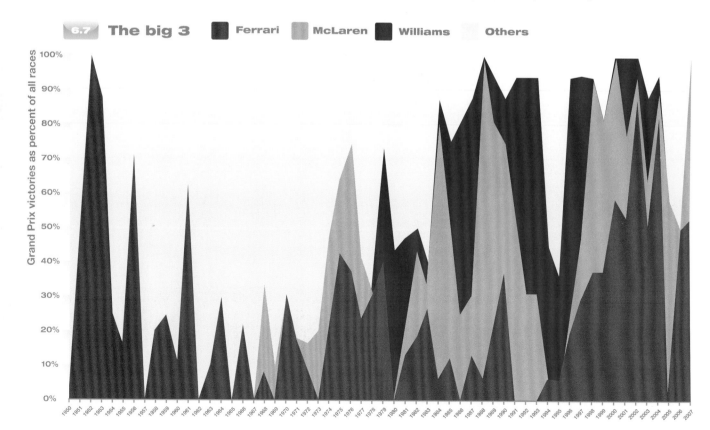

6.7 The big 3   ■ Ferrari   ■ McLaren   ■ Williams   Others

between 1984 and 1986: three Drivers' and two Constructors' World Championships, involving 22 wins from 48 races.

And Williams and McLaren have been slugging it out ever since! The superiority of these two teams grew through the 1980s and, by the 1990s, it almost became the case that if Williams was not dominating the race tracks, McLaren was. This pattern has been briefly interrupted by the Benetton/Schumacher successes of 1994–95 and the more sustained Ferrari/Schumacher supremacy since the millennium. It was Renault that finally broke that monopoly and, until 2007, when McLaren engineered a magnificent resurgence, there was a feeling that we might have seen the best years for these two exceptional teams.

And great years they were. Frank's response to McLaren dominance in 1984–85 was the Canon-Williams-Honda package with which Nigel Mansell and Nelson Piquet reigned supreme in 1986-87. But Williams lost Honda to McLaren. That allowed Dennis's team to come back with a vengeance in 1988, creating the most dominant force yet seen in Grand Prix racing at that time, and giving new meaning to the term 'superteam' with Ayrton Senna and Alain Prost as drivers. In 1988, McLaren won 15 of the 16 Formula One World Championship rounds and became World Champions with Honda in that year and for the next three, winning 39 times from 64 races!

Williams had not been wasting time during those four comparatively fallow years. A new engine supply deal with Renault, keen to return to Grand Prix racing, was one key component of its new package, as was the recruitment from Leyton House of Adrian Newey, a designer who was to become a highly influential Formula One figure in his own right. Highly sophisticated electronics and the return of Nigel Mansell as lead driver completed the picture and the beginning of a six-year spell of Williams in the ascendancy. World Championships for four different drivers - 1992 and 1993 Mansell and Prost, 1996 and 1997 Damon Hill and Jacques Villeneuve – is testament to the car superiority Williams enjoyed over that period. If Senna, in his third race for Williams, had not been killed at Imola, it is conceivable that Williams would have enjoyed even greater success with Renault, but 63 wins in their nine-year partnership was a magnificent achievement.

Renault's withdrawal from Grand Prix racing at the end of 1997 left Williams in the wilderness – a locality with which McLaren had become familiar since Honda's similar departure in 1991. By now, Dennis had rebuilt the team around Mercedes-Benz engines and a new sponsor, the West cigarette brand, breaking the longest sponsorship relationship in Grand Prix history (Marlboro-McLaren). He had also enticed Adrian Newey from Williams and, by 1997, McLaren was back to winning ways. With Mika Häkkinen, it was strong enough to beat an increasingly rampant Prancing Horse to the 1998 and 1999 Drivers' World Championships.

McLaren seem fully committed to a long-term relationship with Mercedes-Benz – indeed the German car manufacturer owns a 40 percent stake in the team, By contrast, Williams appears intent on retaining its independence.

Mercedes-Benz has been Team McLaren's engine partner since 1995. Their first World Championship together came in 1998, and Mika Häkkinen is seen on his way to the title that year with a win at the Monte Carlo circuit.

Dominators

n the top 10 most dominant performances for a marque over a season (Graphic 6.8), Scuderia Ferrari registers five times, the next highest being McLaren with two entries. Most tellingly, two of those five were as recently as 2002 and 2004 – clear evidence, if it were needed, that the five successive World title 'doubles' with which Ferrari entered the new millennium were the most dominant period for car and driver in the history of the World Championship.

In the Graphic, there are numerous other entries portraying dominant Ferrari seasons, but none of comparable stature. Those of 1952, 1953 and 1961 may be put down to good fortune, being in possession of the right equipment when a change in the regulations was made, while 1956 was aided and abetted by the donation to Ferrari of the Lancia D50 cars. Later periods of success for Jody Scheckter, Gilles Villeneuve and Alain Prost were all highly laudable, but not in the same league – except one, 30 years earlier.

The first of the two golden periods for the Prancing Horse occurred in the mid-1970s and, just as the second period is associated with Schumacher, it owed much to the contribution from Niki Lauda. But in each phase there were other figures of massive significance to the collective team success, and extraordinarily one individual associated

with both triumphal periods those many years apart… Luca Cordero di Montezemolo.

He was drafted in from FIAT in 1973, becoming Enzo Ferrari's personal assistant, and the following year was appointed as the sporting director, overseeing Formula One racing activities. Although Montezemolo returned to FIAT in 1977, between 1975 and 1979 Ferrari achieved three Drivers' and four Constructors' championships. Critics might argue that, on this occasion, Montezemolo was in the right place at the right time, that at the heart of Ferrari's 1979 success was the chemistry between designer Mauro Forghieri and driver Lauda and their relentless testing together at the new Fiorano test track adjacent to the Maranello factory. Such an opinion would be selling short his influence and involvement over that period, and his subsequent record confirms his immense talent for bringing together the essential ingredients and creating environments that breed success.

Typical of this was the leading role he took in putting on the 1990 football World Cup in Italy, a massive undertaking requiring five years of work and planning. After that success, FIAT Group chairman Gianni Agnelli made Montezemolo president of Ferrari the following year, with the personal goal of returning the Prancing Horse to its rightful place as Grand Prix champions after so many years in the wilderness.

6.8 **Dominators** Most wins by one marque in a season (over 50%)

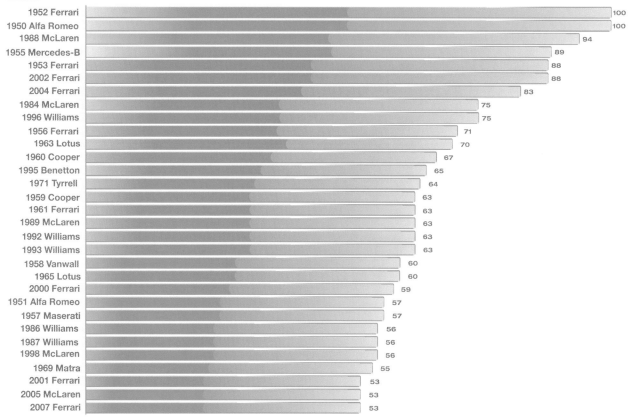

1952 Ferrari	100
1950 Alfa Romeo	100
1988 McLaren	94
1955 Mercedes-B	89
1953 Ferrari	88
2002 Ferrari	88
2004 Ferrari	83
1984 McLaren	75
1996 Williams	75
1956 Ferrari	71
1963 Lotus	70
1960 Cooper	67
1995 Benetton	65
1971 Tyrrell	64
1959 Cooper	63
1961 Ferrari	63
1989 McLaren	63
1992 Williams	63
1993 Williams	63
1958 Vanwall	60
1965 Lotus	60
2000 Ferrari	59
1951 Alfa Romeo	57
1957 Maserati	57
1986 Williams	56
1987 Williams	56
1998 McLaren	56
1969 Matra	55
2001 Ferrari	53
2005 McLaren	53
2007 Ferrari	53

138 **Analysing Formula 1**

It was not easy. It took the best part of a decade, but it was accomplished… and how!

Another measure of team dominance is the 1–2 finish. Beating the opposition with both or all of your team cars is the ultimate statement of crushing superiority, and was first demonstrated by Alfa Romeo in the very first World Championship Grand Prix at Silverstone in 1950. If Juan Fangio's 'Alfetta' had finished, it could have been a team 1–2–3–4, a feat first accomplished by Mercedes-Benz at Aintree in 1955 and emulated by Maserati (Buenos Aires 1957) and Ferrari (Spa 1961) – albeit that Olivier Gendebien's fourth placed 156 was painted yellow, representing the national colours of the driver and, of course, the venue.

Graphic 6.9 again ranks the most dominant seasons for a marque but additionally shows the proportion of those victories which were converted into 1–2 finishes. For example, Alfa won all six Grands Prix in 1950 (100 percent), and of those four (66.6 percent) were 1–2 finishes.

The trend lines have been added to the Graphic to illustrate the correlation between the proportion of wins and the incidence of 1–2 results for a given marque in a season. It is not perfect – that would hardly be expected – but it is a very strong relationship.

At conflict with the correlation, three seasons are prominent – 1958, 1963 and 1965 – where a substantial proportion of wins is recorded but no 1–2 finishes. Further analysis suggests rather different interpretations, whereby in 1958, both Stirling Moss and Tony Brooks each won three races for Vanwall, suggesting that the car was highly effective but other factors, such as reliability, prevented team

dominance. By contrast, all the Team Lotus victories in 1963 and 1965 were won by one driver, Jim Clark, and can be deciphered rather differently and in at least two ways: Lotus was unable to run a two-car team effectively, or Clark's driving flattered its car's genuine winning potential. In reality, it was probably a little of each, but the analysis provides food for thought regarding Clark's contribution to the Lotus success story.

No discussion of team domination can pass without reference to Ron Dennis who, in 1984, introduced an almost blitzkrieg approach to winning! Designer, engine, drivers, tyres and reliability were all brought together under Marlboro sponsorship to create a winning machine, technically and organisationally. In 1984 it was Barnard, TAG Porsche, Lauda, Prost and Michelin, producing 12 victories (75 percent) including three 1–2 finishes (25 percent). Four years later he upped the ante to the astonishing levels of 15 wins (94 percent) with ten 1–2 finishes (67 percent). Designer Gordon Murray, Honda, Senna, Prost and Goodyear were so very nearly victorious in all 16 rounds of the 1988 World Championship.

Infamy haunts the one race at Monza where Senna, under pressure from the Ferraris, tripped over Jean-Louis Schlesser's Williams in the chicane while leading and just two laps away from the chequered flag. It is said that Dennis experiences genuine pain when his team fails to win. What his emotions were that day in Italy is hard to imagine, but that is the level of intensity which drives him and those of similar calibre: there is no deep satisfaction in merely winning – true fulfilment comes through supreme domination.

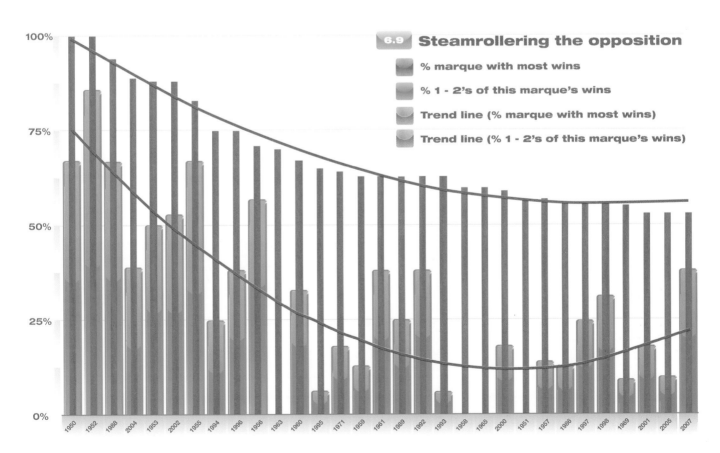

6.9 **Steamrollering the opposition**

- % marque with most wins
- % 1 - 2's of this marque's wins
- Trend line (% marque with most wins)
- Trend line (% 1 - 2's of this marque's wins)

Any chapter entitled 'cars and teams' must devote space to two components fundamental to the performance of the Formula One machine: the engine that propels it and the tyres that grip the track.

The foundation of any good car is a good engine. It represents the jewel in the crown of the Formula One racing car. A strong, flexible, reliable motor lies at the heart of numerous Grand Prix victories. With mediocrity in the horsepower department, success has been rare, but maximum power is not everything. The delivery of that power, enabling the driver to balance the car and optimise his own skills, is of no less significance.

The relentless quest for yet more horsepower is nicely portrayed by the Graphic 'Power Crazy' (6.10). This traces the BHP developed by Ferrari engines over its unprecedented 58-year participation. Despite numerous changes in the swept volume and configuration of the motors, provoked in the main by regulatory requirements, the power curve has moved inexorably upwards from a mere 73bhp/litre in 1950 to in excess of 300bhp/litre today. Every attempt by the FIA to restrain power has resulted in an assiduous year-by-year advance as the designers and engineers find the next series of improvements.

By way of example, there have been two separate periods for 3-litre engines in Formula One. At the end of the first, in 1980, the Ferrari 'boxer' engine generated 515bhp. By the end of the second 3-litre phase in 2005, its V10 had

reached 915bhp. A simple linear projection indicates an annual increment of 16bhp, or 3 percent per annum – a net growth rate any investor would be more than glad to accept over 25 years!

The second Graphic (6.11) expresses brake horsepower per litre of engine swept volume, as well as on a power-to-weight basis, emphasising the prodigious power of Ferrari's turbocharged engines between 1981 and 1988. They were also relatively slow-revving, the third line-graph (engine revolutions) clearly dipping as the power lines rise. Since the turbo era, the soaring RPM of the F1 engine is as perceptible from the chart as it has been to the eardrums of the spectators. The banshee shriek of the modern Formula One car has been made possible through mechanical (pneumatic valves) and metallurgical (use of titanium and other alloys) means, as well as developments in miniaturisation and heat dissipation. Today's Formula One engine is more than ever a technological jewel.

Over time, 61 engine 'makes' have been brought to the line at the start of a Grand Prix: from the diminutive (1.1-litre V-twin JAP) to the vast (4.5-litre Ferrari V12), from the simple (four-cylinder Coventry-Climax FPF) to the complex (V16 BRM), from the obscure (H16 BRM) to the bizarre (Pratt & Whitney gas-turbine), all sizes types and configurations seem to have been tried at one time or another (although the Life W12 never made the grid). The recent FIA decision to mandate the use of 2.4-litre V8s,

6.10 **Power crazy** 58 Years of Ferrari horsepower

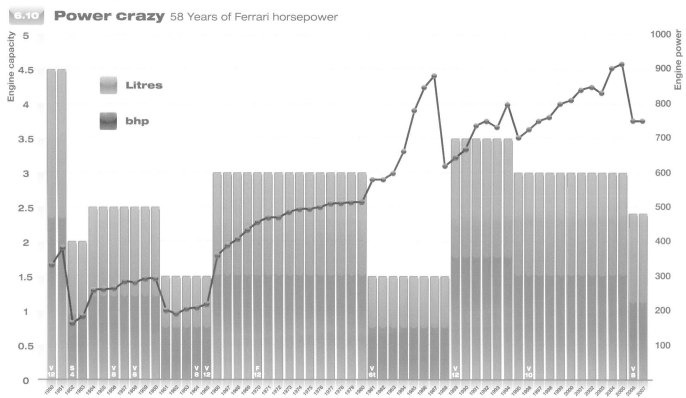

rpm   bhp/tonne   bhp/litre

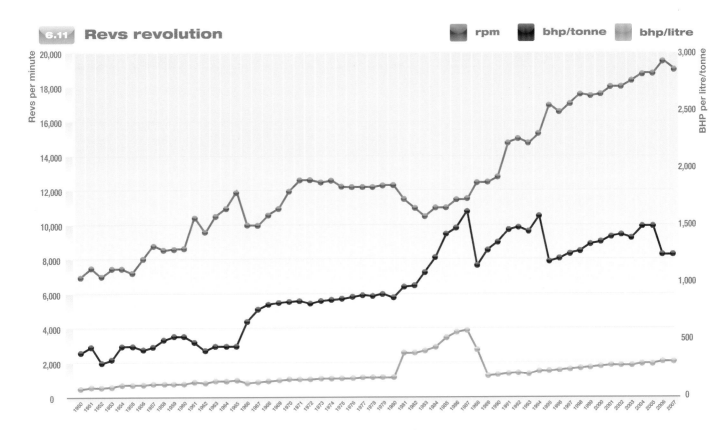

now capped at 19,000rpm, suggests that the golden age of perfecting and honing the F1 internal combustion engine – which lasted more than half a century and even enjoyed accelerated development in the last decade – is finally over. As it observes the future of Formula One through green-tinted spectacles, this is the precise outcome the FIA was attempting to provoke.

This means that the V8 will forever epitomise the optimal (or at least the most successful) engine configuration, having caught and passed the ubiquitous V10 since the FIA's 'V8s only' regulation (see 6.12). The V6 weighs in a strong third, having been the preferred configuration during the turbo era, but the surprise is that the 12-cylinder format, in either V or 'boxer' configuration – perhaps the most charismatic of the multi-cylinder designs because of the Ferrari connotation – finishes some way down the list.

6.12 **Winning engine configurations**

V8	260
V10	240
V6	112
S4	54
V12	41
F12	37
S8	19
S6	9
F8	1
H16	1

Of the 60 or so engine makes to have been used across virtually the same number of Grand Prix seasons, the maximum to have participated in any one year is 11, approximately half the maximum number of chassis marques (Graphic 6.13). The engine versus marques comparison visibly illustrates the Formula One 'kit-car' period when, during a 15-year span from 1968, numerous constructors (about 50) used the Ford-Cosworth DFV as their entry ticket to Formula One. In 1974, the engine supported 16 of the 18 teams that participated (only Ferrari and BRM excepted). For the record, these were: Lotus, Tyrrell, McLaren, March, Brabham, Shadow, Surtees, Ensign, Williams (Iso Marlboro), Hesketh, Maki, Lola, Lyncar, Token, Parnelli and Penske (plus Amon and Trojan, which both failed to qualify). A similar pattern was evident for Grand Prix winners of the period, the Ford DFV completing a clean sweep in 1969 and 1973 in the back of respectively four and three winning constructors. In 1982, more constructors were successful (seven) than at any time before or since. The extraordinary DFV equipped five winning teams with Ferrari and Renault also featuring, while Brabham won with both DFV and BMW turbo power during that season.

It is apparent from Graphic 6.13 that, during the turbo era, there was a steady increase in the number of engine makes participating. BMW had demonstrated that a simple four-cylinder engine block of fairly humble origins could become an effective turbo winner. Disregarding Megatron, a rebadged BMW unit, a total of 10 turbocharged engines were built and raced as follows:

S4	Hart, BMW, Zakspeed
V6	Renault, Ferrari, TAG, Porche, Honda, Motori Moderni, Ford Cosworth
V8	Alfa Romeo

The inclination to rebadge engines with names such as 'Megatron', 'Petronas', 'Acer' and 'Asiatech' tends to cloud the issue regarding engine suppliers. Should a Petronas V10 be considered separately from a Ferrari V10? When is a 'Playlife' or a 'Mecachrome' or even a 'Supertec' simply a Renault with a fancy name, or otherwise?

Another radical change is the attitude of the manufacturers. No longer do they appear to consider that the required return on their Formula One involvement can be achieved simply in their traditional role as engine suppliers. Despite considerable past success as suppliers to Formula One teams, Renault, Honda and BMW have each decided to follow Toyota's lead with a bespoke team, and Mercedes-Benz looks to be set on a similar course. Renault's results in 2005–06 may encourage the others that success is

The ubiquitous Ford-Cosworth DFV engine in the back of a Lotus 78. Between 1967 and 1983 this essentially unchanged engine design won 155 Grands Prix.

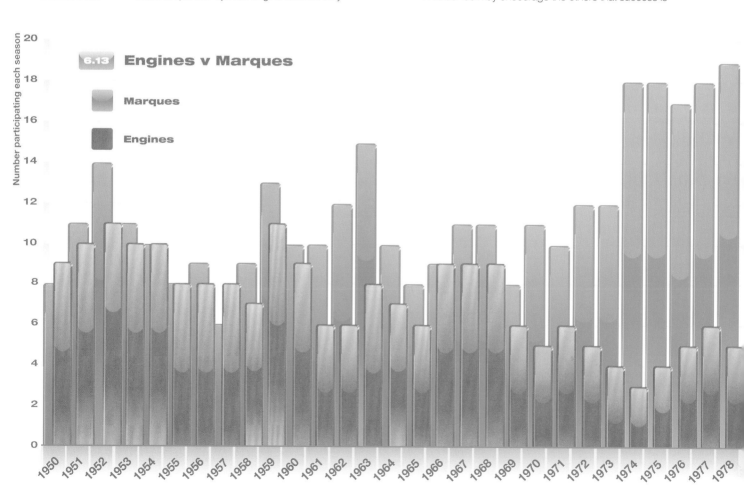

6.13 Engines v Marques

■ Marques

■ Engines

Number participating each season

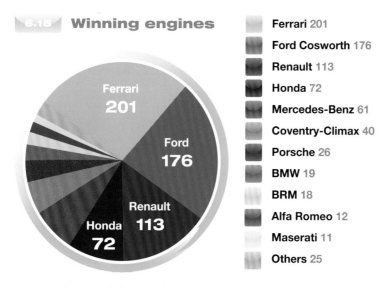

Ferrari 201
Ford Cosworth 176
Renault 113
Honda 72
Mercedes-Benz 61
Coventry-Climax 40
Porsche 26
BMW 19
BRM 18
Alfa Romeo 12
Maserati 11
Others 25

Ferrari 201 / Ford 176 / Renault 113 / Honda 72

Race Victories

The Ferrari 312 V12 engine of 1969. Despite the legendary connotation, the V12 configuration was not that successful for the Prancing Horse.

attainable but, besides Mercedes-Benz in the 1950s, there is scant evidence that manufacturer teams can cut the mustard. Just ask Jaguar (Ford)!

And to a large extent it works both ways. The relationship that the Formula One team owners are required to cultivate with the manufacturers which supply their engines is both fascinating and important. Williams will tell you. Their post-Renault relationship with BMW was disappointing on and off the track, and Toyota, its new engine partner, will hope for something better. As will Williams which must be only too aware that, after the heydays of the DFV, the four years it has raced without manufacturer engine support (1988 Judd, 1998–99 Mecachrome, 2006 Cosworth) realised exactly 10 podiums – but zero wins!

Toyota, WilliamsF1's new partner, is the most recent manufacturer to join Formula One, entering in 2002 with a team built from scratch. Toyota had long been involved in rallying and sports car and US single-seater racing, but still felt it necessary to tackle Formula One. As one of the world's largest and most successful volume car producers, Toyota must believe in the value that a Formula One programme can bring, considering that its enormous corporate success to date is proof enough that it does not actually need to be in Formula One! It would be too simplistic to believe that the decision is purely based on the mantra, 'Win on Sunday, sell on Monday'. But involvement in what is widely regarded as the pinnacle of motorsport does help to create an image generating a positive emotional response to the Toyota name and logo in the mind of the car-buying public worldwide.

If it changes perception to the extent that Toyota at least comes into consideration, in the car-buying decision process of potential customers who were previously unattainable, then the association with Formula One will have paid out handsomely.

For whatever reason, Ford rarely capitalised on its involvement and achievements in Formula One but, as a distinct engine design, the Ford DFV V8 from Cosworth surpasses the success of any other individual motor with 155 race victories. However Ferrari, with its recent spate of winning, has pulled well clear of Ford in the overall statistics for engine victories (6.15). Renault, too, has now moved firmly ahead of Honda and Mercedes-Benz, whereas BMW, another current contender for honours, remains stuck on 19. But this is still 19 more than Toyota – the world's largest car manufacturer.

It has always been tough at the top, but it is even tougher to become a winner in Formula One!

6.14 **Winning engines** ■ **Participating seasons** (number shows wins)

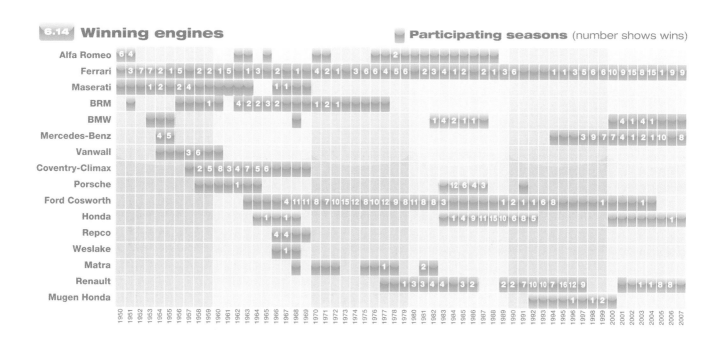

A war within a war: in many ways, competition between the Formula One tyre suppliers has been exactly that. Just as the racing teams have been in a technological 'arms race' to make another performance step with their chassis, aero or engines, so the tyre companies have indulged in their own form of warfare involving tyre design, structure and compound. As tyres are the medium through which car performance is transmitted to the track, the relationship between racing team and tyre supplier has to be close to be effective. More than any other ingredient in the Formula One package, tyres have invariably been a make-or-break factor between success and failure.

'Indygate' presents a perfect case history for the power of the tyre in Formula One. The media gave it that name because it was a scandal that brought Grand Prix racing into disrepute – the farce that was the running of the 2005 US Grand Prix. In front of 100,000-plus spectators and millions of TV viewers, just six Bridgestone-shod cars took part in the 73-lap, 90-minute race and the two Ferraris

alone completed the full race distance. The 14 runners using Michelin rubber withdrew following the parade lap. They did not take up position on the grid because the French company could not guarantee the safety of the available tyres, which had shown a tendency for catastrophic failure during practice.

After a 15-year interlude, in 2001 Michelin re-entered Formula One to challenge Bridgestone, the Japanese company having enjoyed a supply monopoly for the two prior seasons. As teams staked their allegiances in this new outbreak of tyre wars, Ferrari, still in the early stages of achieving six successive Constructors' World Championships, remained a Bridgestone customer. With its own test tracks at Fiorano and Mugello, Ferrari worked with Bridgestone and tested relentlessly together to the gradual exclusion of the rest. Other leading runners felt they could no longer influence Bridgestone's line of development to meet their own specific requirements, and switched to Michelin. Effectively Ferrari ended up with an

6.16 Tyre wars

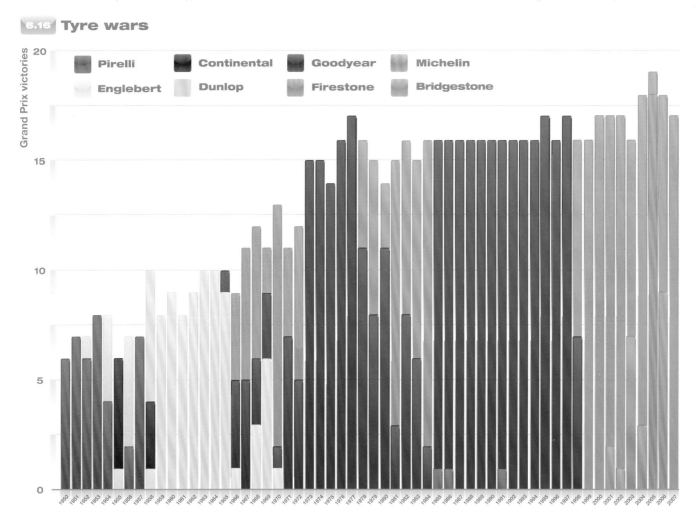

exclusive supplier providing bespoke tyres. Car and tyre development was in perfect harmony, and to devastating effect. In 2004, Ferrari and Bridgestone won 15 of the 18 rounds of the World Championship.

Tyre wars, then, had taken on a perspective very different from that of the past. It was now much more akin to an exclusive partnership or strategic alliance with much greater exclusivity in design and manufacture on offer to a leading team. But the highly successful Ferrari/Bridgestone exploitation of this corporate closeness, with its resultant domination, did nothing for 'the show'. With TV viewers beginning to turn off the predictable fortnightly Ferrari fest, the governing body – in the name of safety, naturally – threw a spanner in the works for the following season. In 2005, two- or three-stop sprint racing, with fresh rubber at each pitstop, a strategy which Ferrari, Bridgestone and Schumacher had made their own, would be no more. Tyres would need to last the full race distances.

So after a season of dominance in 2004, Ferrari and Bridgestone endured a season of débacle in 2005, winning just one race, and that was the fiasco they called 'Indygate'! Suddenly, with a whole Grand Prix distance to contend with, Michelin was (normally) the rubber to have.

In terms of tyre structure and compound, Michelin and Bridgestone could not have been further apart in the black art which is tyre design. Michelin had introduced radial ply tyre construction into Grand Prix racing almost 30 years earlier and, along with this, had perfected high 'chemical' grip, the way the tyre interacts with the track surface. Bridgestone's strength was through mechanical grip, the means by which the tyre contact patch is presented to the track. Michelins enjoyed high track temperatures, Bridgestones did not. Bridgestone could put heat into tyres more quickly and used this advantage in qualifying. Once up to temperature, Michelin tyres suffered less degradation and graining than Bridgestone, and so it goes on…

The upshot was that Michelin held all the aces for the 2005 season with the notable exception of the US Grand Prix at the Indianapolis Motor Speedway. The Grand Prix track there incorporated part of the legendary oval circuit, and it was here that high and sustained levels of downforce and lateral and longitudinal g-loadings combined to wrinkle Michelin's more flexible sidewalls, with disastrous consequences.

This illustration of the importance of tyre technology to Formula One car performance and success is not complete without fast-forwarding 12 months to the same race in 2006. Here, Bridgestone trounced the Michelin opposition totally against the prevailing run of results. To avoid even the slightest possibility of a repeat 'Indygate', it was widely recognised that Michelin went very conservative for the 2006 race.

In the 1950s and early 1960s, racing tyre development was slow and their proportions changed little, having a 'skinny' appearance by today's standards. The dominance of Italian teams and cars – Alfa Romeo, Ferrari and Maserati – had led to Pirelli being the initial tyre of choice. Engelbert and Continental from Germany also competed fruitfully, the latter enjoying success with the Mercedes-Benz 'Silver

Arrows'. As British teams, led by Vanwall and Cooper, became successful in the late 1950s, so Britain's Dunlop monopolised the Formula One scene. Of the others, only Pirelli would attempt a comeback in the 1980s and 1990s, and then with only moderate commitment and even less success.

In the early 1960s, tyres were still not regarded as offering the competitive edge they would later exert. Indeed, it is reported on good authority that in 1963 Jim Clark's all-conquering Lotus completed four races on the same Dunlop tyres. These tyres had actually been developed for Le Mans sports-racing cars, much heavier and more powerful than the diminutive 1.5-litre Lotus 25 Climax. In fairness, Dunlop was progressing along certain significant development paths, particularly rain tyres using high-hysterisis compounds. To this day, the uncanny performance of a Formula One car in the wet is something to marvel at.

Of much greater consequence to 1960s tyre development was the challenge by Team Lotus to take the honours in the Indianapolis 500-mile race, traditionally run on Commemoration Day since 1911. Jim Clark triumphed in 1965 and was the runner-up in both 1963 and 1966. The design of the Lotus was to revolutionise Indy Car racing in the USA, but in tyre technology there was some useful transference in the opposite direction via Firestone.

The US tyre giant Goodyear first won in Grand Prix with Honda, with victory in the final race of the 1.5-litre formula, but it was with the new 3-litre Formula One regulations from 1966 that Goodyear, Firestone and Dunlop truly competed head-to-head and the expression 'tyre war' took on new meaning.

The 2007 season was, in effect, the first in which a control tyre was adopted for F1. Regulations require two compounds to be used in each race, the white line identifying the option tyre.

As the three companies battled it out over the Grand Prix circuits of the world, the years that followed witnessed the most dramatic changes in racing tyre design and technology at any time before or since. The catalyst for such rapid development was not only competition-inspired, it was also the result of race car innovation. In 1968, Formula One cars sprouted wings which brought a new and crucial constituent to the performance mix – aerodynamic downforce. This altered the fundamentals of racing car design forever and with it tyre design. By the early 1970s, the tread width was such that wheels and tyres had become drum-shaped as designers tried to maximise the downforce-enhanced grip under acceleration, braking and cornering.

Then treads themselves were dispensed with as Goodyear and Firestone introduced 'slicks' in 1971. With no tread patterns to deform, slick tyres could use yet softer and stickier compounds and deliver ever more grip. From there, it was just a short step to special 'sticky' qualifying tyres, utilising rubber so pliant that they lasted just one flying lap!

Treaded tyres were introduced on the grounds of safety in 1998.

As with all aspects of racing car evolution, the need to curtail ever-rising speeds on the grounds of safety has led the Formula One administrators to invoke specific regulations controlling tyres. Qualifying tyres were seen to create an especially dangerous environment, tragically exemplified through the death of Gilles Villeneuve in 1982, and were banned, as too were slicks from 1998. The introduction of grooved tyres was intended to limit performance in two ways. First the grooves would reduce the size of the contact patch between tyre and track. Second, because the grooves were required to maintain their integrity throughout the life of the tyre, this would place certain limits on the softness of the compounds used.

Despite this, the 'marbles' – those little balls of tyre rubber slivers evident at corners off the racing line – indicate that, even with these restrictions, today's race rubber remains comparatively malleable.

As it was by far the largest corporation, it was perhaps inevitable that Goodyear would vanquish the other contenders in the tyre war that brought the withdrawals of first Dunlop and then Firestone by 1974. Goodyear's next serious challenger came from France in the cheery and familiar shape of 'Bidendum' (the Michelin man). Michelin partnered Renault in its 1977 incursion into Grand Prix racing and brought new thinking to the traditional crossply construction of Formula One tyres. Gradually, as the aspirant from Europe enjoyed increasing success and attracted more teams to its stable, Goodyear had to grasp the nettle and in 1981, after a short withdrawal, switched to radial tyre construction itself. This significant undertaking should be seen as part of Goodyear's unequalled commitment to

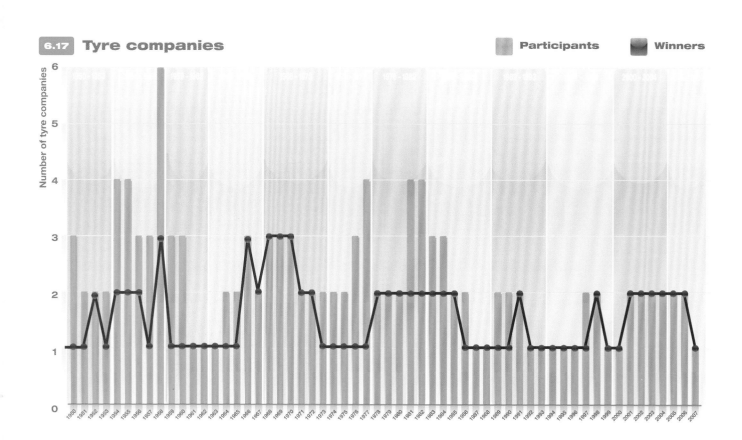

6.17 Tyre companies   ■ Participants   ■ Winners

Grand Prix racing over a period of more than three decades, during which it equipped more than 350 winners – as many as the next three tyre companies together. Goodyear made many friends over that time and its strategic withdrawal after 1998 left a gap difficult to fill. By then, the Japanese tyre company Bridgestone – also the current owner through acquisition of the Firestone brand – had entered the fray and, with Michelin's withdrawal after a fairly short second campaign, became the sole supplier from 2007.

This has effectively brought forward by one year, for the very first time in Formula One, provision of a 'control tyre' from an appointed single supplier. This was to have been part of a raft of revised regulations for implementation from 2008, coinciding with fresh commercial agreements between the rights-holder, the teams and the organisers in the new Concorde Agreement. Safety and cost were behind this move: removing the competitive element in tyres should appreciably reduce testing, one of the major contributors towards increased track performance and ever higher costs. Bridgestone won the first tender and will be the sole tyre supplier to Formula One for the first five-year period.

So, no more tyre wars. No more a war within a war.

6.18 Tyre triumphs

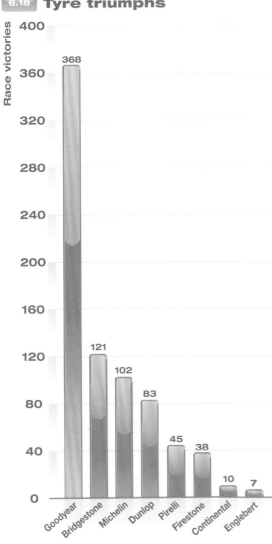

CHAPTER 7
Drivers
and danger

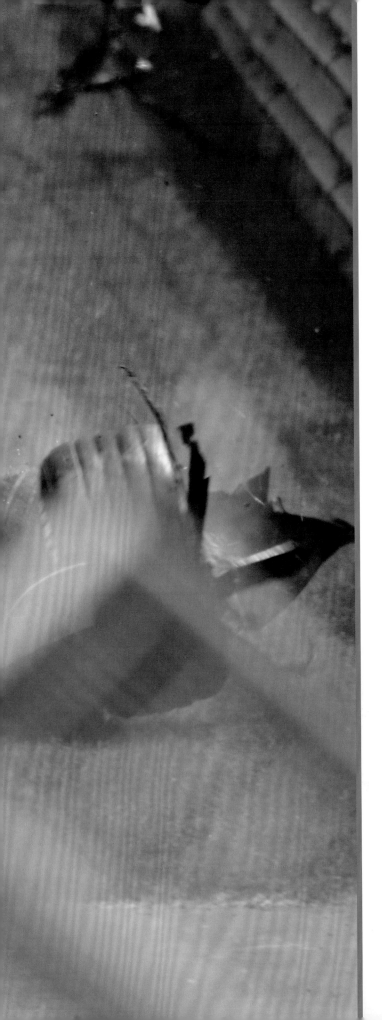

For 2008, 11 teams entering 22 drivers were invited to participate in the FIA Formula One World Championships.

It was not always thus. There have been times when more or fewer teams and drivers vied for places on grids that have ranged from as many as 34, to as few as 10. This chapter reveals the changing Grand Prix landscape from the perspective of the drivers... and the danger they expose themselves to in pursuit of their chosen sport.

We have previously identified the composition of the 1950s grids in terms of the manufacturers and constructors at one end of the scale, and the independents or privateers at the other. The drivers at that time reflected this same divide, apparent in most walks of sport during the first half of the 20th century, whether described as gentlemen versus players in cricketing parlance, or more accurately, amateurs and professionals in the realms of tennis and motor racing.

Professionals, who could live from their earnings as paid drivers, were comparatively few and far between and usually drove for the works teams. They had built reputations for ability and talent that could command retainers for their services. Their access to some of the better-equipped works teams and cars tended to perpetuate their status although, in most cases, this was deserved. Such drivers in 1950 were the three 'Fs', Farina, Fangio and Fagioli, entrusted with the works Alfa Romeos that swept the board in the first World Championship, with Farina and Fangio winning three races apiece and Fagioli ensuring 1–2 finishes on four occasions.

Robert Kubica's terrifying accident in his Sauber BMW during the 2007 Canadian Grand Prix at Montréal was a stark reminder of the perils of Formula 1 racing.

Drivers and danger 151

E ven though there were just six championship races (excluding the Indy 500), and the average grid size was around 20 cars, almost 50 drivers took part in the Grands Prix scheduled for that inaugural season (Graphic 7.1). Expressed another way, as few as nine drivers participated in five or all six races and as many as 28 entered just one or two. Many of these were the true amateurs, participating for sheer joy, the thrill of taking part, but usually because their circumstances also allowed it. Many had the time and the wealth to indulge in a sport that, from its very inception, has had something of a society lifestyle surrounding it.

One such was Prince Bira from Siam (Thailand) who competed over five seasons and in 19 Grands Prix, winning a creditable eight World Championship points driving mainly privately entered Maseratis, his team nomenclature including Ecurie Siam.

The motor trade was another source for aspiring teams and drivers. HWM (Hersham & Walton Motors) is a celebrated example of the 'grey area' that existed between enthusiastic amateur racers and fully professional operations. In 1946, George Abecassis and John Heath

bought a garage at Walton-on-Thames in Surrey. A natural extension of the venture was to enter Grand Prix racing in cars designed by Heath and, on two occasions, driven by Abecassis. Using Alta engines, HWM competed in Grand Prix races mainly when they were run to Formula Two regulations in 1952–53, providing opportunities for drivers such as Lance Macklin, Peter Collins and Duncan Hamilton to cut their Grand Prix teeth. Indeed, at Bremgarten in 1951, a young Stirling Moss made his Grand Prix debut behind the wheel of an HWM.

During this period, the number of participating drivers in Grand Prix racing reached levels never to be exceeded – more than 70 in both 1952 and 1953 (Graphic 7.1). Formula Two was already a flourishing racing category and the adoption of these regulations for the Drivers' World Championship made Grand Prix participation even more accessible. In countries where post-war motor racing was flourishing, notably Italy, Germany and Great Britain, the local Grand Prix attracted numerous one-off entries. One of these was Jimmy Stewart, Jackie's elder brother, whose one and only venture into Grand Prix racing was at Silverstone in 1953 driving a Cooper-Bristol, the car made

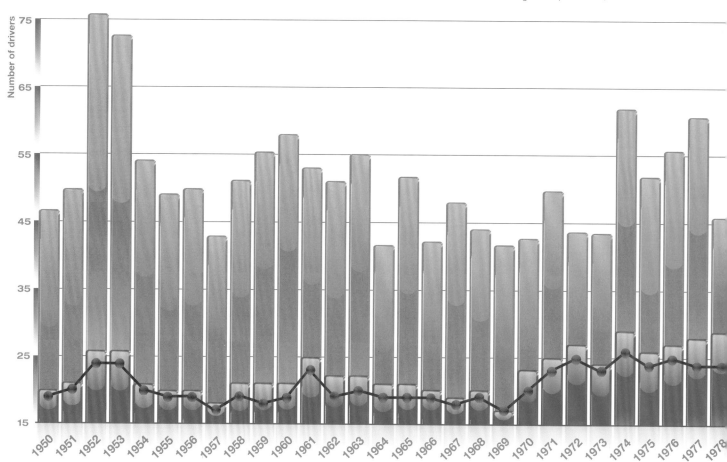

famous through the exploits of a youthful Mike Hawthorn the previous year.

The precept that any driver could enter a Grand Prix on an ad hoc basis continued throughout the 1960s and 1970s. Typical of such drivers was Yorkshire-born Dave Charlton, participating in 11 Grand Prix races over nine seasons between 1965 and 1975. A South African resident, he was a regular at Kyalami over these years with ex-works Lotus, Brabham and McLaren cars, campaigning in 1972 with a state-of-the-art Lotus 72D with which he took in three additional Grands Prix in Europe. In only three of his 11 career starts was he a classified finisher. He typified the amateur driver, having no high expectations of genuine success, his participation for love rather than money.

Speaking of love, this was the surname of the one amateur or, more accurately, semi-professional driver, who nearly pulled off the impossible in 1967. John Love from Rhodesia (Zimbabwe) was, along with Charlton, one of a clique of African based occasional drivers including such as Lederle, Johnstone, Keizan, Pieterse, Serrurier, de Klerk, Botha, Blokdyk, van Rooyen, Niemann, Tingle, Pretorius and, fittingly, Driver. Thirteen drivers with 27 Grand Prix starts between them. Their Grand Prix racing was largely restricted to their home race, some building their own Formula One specials and others occasionally hiring the spare car from the works teams in order to take part. John Love usually drove under the Team Gunston

banner but in 1967, the very first running of the South African Grand Prix at Kyalami, he was in a privately entered Cooper T79 equipped with a 2.7-litre Coventry-Climax engine, a car developed for the 1965 Tasman Cup series for and by Bruce McLaren.

Remarkably, albeit at the start of only the second year of the 3-litre formula, Love claimed P5 on the grid and, in a race in which the fancied runners foundered, wound up leading and pulling away at three-quarter distance! Sadly there was no fairy-tale ending. With just seven laps remaining, Love had to make a splash-and-dash pitstop because his Tasman Series fuel tankage was not quite up to seeing him through the full 200-mile Grand Prix distance. However, second place behind the works 3.0-litre V12 Cooper T81 Maserati of Pedro Rodriguez was still an astonishing result for a private entry up against the might of the full works teams. Love further enhanced his reputation driving works Mini-Coopers in the British Saloon Car Championship with considerable verve and success.

Another privateer who met with some success was Carel Godin de Beaufort, although his encounter with Grand Prix racing was to end tragically. His vivid orange Porsche, colours signifying his Dutch homeland, entered under Ecurie Maarsbergen, the name of his home town, became a regular feature of Grand Prix racing for many seasons until his death while practising at the Nürburgring in 1964. As a 23-year-old, de Beaufort's first taste of Grand Prix racing had been at this same circuit seven years earlier. His

7.1 **Driver participation in Grand Prix**

Drivers entering per season

Driver entries per race (average)

Drivers starting per race (average)

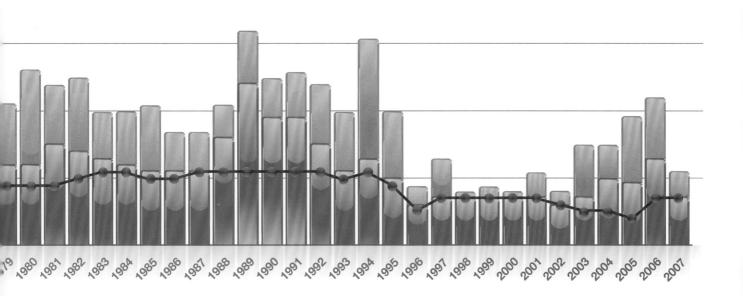

1.5-litre Porsche finished third in the Formula Two section of the race. The following year, he raced in his home Grand Prix at Zandvoort for the first time and by 1961 – the first year of the new 1.5-litre formula, in which the Porsche factory first entered Formula One – de Beaufort was running a works-spec car on a regular basis. Four sixth-place finishes over the following two seasons, worthy of four World Championship points, was no mean feat with what was increasingly outmoded equipment. His death added to the ominous reputation of the 'Ring and confirmed that even a privateer, driving more for the fun than the glory, was not invulnerable to the ultimate sacrifice to his chosen sport.

These cameos, which are in sharp contrast to the total professionalism required of today's super-fit, media savvy team drivers, are illustrative of the changing landscape for the Grand Prix driver over almost six decades. There have been two main agents of such change. The first was the increased commercialism of Formula One. This resulted from the easing of sponsorship restrictions (1968) and the developing technological potential for global television coverage (c1979). The response to this opportunity, first by FOCA and subsequently the FIA but in each case through the common denominator of Bernie Ecclestone, was to bring more structure and formality to Formula One which has evolved into today's race 'package'. Each race promoter is guaranteed up to 12 two-car teams and a three-day programme timed to the last second to meet television schedules worldwide.

The second agent of change for the Grand Prix driver relates to safety. This too, at least in part, may be linked to commercialism. In the politically correct 21st century,

the board of a Formula One sponsor company or a TV company transmitting a Grand Prix does not want its brand or its channel associated with the media frenzy that would follow death or serious injury of a driver during Sunday afternoon viewing. The advent of the FIA 'Superlicence' in 1982 was a way to regulate who could or could not participate in a Grand Prix. Put another way, it was a method of saving from himself any driver who had more money than sense, or most certainly more money than talent! To this day, the 'pay-driver' (as opposed to the paid driver) is still not totally eliminated from Grand Prix racing, but these days self-funding through personal wealth is a thing of the past. Where funding is through sponsorship, there is usually at least some correlation with driver competence, if not genuine talent.

By the beginning of the 1980s, these various measures culled the numbers of drivers annually participating in Grand Prix racing. By the end of the 1990s, the grids were confined to a constant 20 or so drivers competing in each and every Grand Prix throughout each Formula One World Championship. Today, achieving Grand Prix driver status is the province of a comparatively elite few, fortunately governed more by merit than probably at any time before. The advent since 2003 of the official third team driver, responsible for general testing and Friday practice testing sessions, has tended to produce once again slight disparity between the number of participants and the number of Grand Prix entries or starters. This is because there are able understudies in the wings, actually present on race day if required, who can provide a ready substitute in the event of the nominated drivers being indisposed or underperforming.

At Kyalami in 1967 (facing page), local privateer John Love, seen leading Dan Gurney's Eagle, almost accomplished the impossible in his Cooper-Climax (see text).

Sporting the vivid racing colours of his homeland on his Porsche 718, Carel Godin de Beaufort captures the true spirit of the privateer as he comes in ninth at his home Grand Prix at Zandvoort in 1963.

As the widely regarded pinnacle of motorsport, Grand Prix racing has needed to protect its standards on the one hand and ensure adequate levels of safety on the other. A procedure was called for designed to sort wheat from the chaff for both driver and car. Qualifying provides a process not only to establish the formation of the starting grid, but also to limit the number of cars allowed on track during the race and the extent of the disparity in performance levels at each end of the grid. For many years, a 107 percent rule operated, whereby all drivers had to qualify their cars within seven percent of the pole position lap-time. Although seven percent does not seem to be much of an allowance, in practice it translates into the fastest cars lapping the slower ones twice, maybe three times during the duration of a typical race distance. Anything much slower than that could not only heighten on-track danger but might also be regarded as not a serious contender.

The first race where the letters NQ (for non-qualifier) appeared on the timesheets was the Italian Grand Prix of 1952. This left 11 disappointed men, including all three HWM drivers! The organisers, for reasons of safety, restricted the grid to 24 starters. The 24th and final qualifier was Gino Bianco's Maserati with a lap-time not seven, but

nine percent slower than Alberto Ascari's pole-winning Ferrari. Even with the blue flag alerting slower drivers to the leaders bearing down on them, it was unquestionably very sensible not to allow any wider on-track performance differential at such a high-speed power circuit.

The Italian Gabriele Tarquini holds the record for the most failures to qualify. His 40 abortive attempts exceeds by two the number of races he did start! In fairness, despite driving for Osella/Fondmetal, Coloni and AGS, he did bring home a single championship point.

In 1965, a new term entered Formula One nomenclature. NPQ stood for non-prequalifier. Ironically in view of what so nearly happened for John Love two years later, the race at which it was introduced was the South African Grand Prix. This was the final year of the 1.5-litre formula so the grids could be expected to be well populated and with the latest machinery. The regulars were joined by as many as a dozen local drivers, many of whom were using spaceframe Lotus or other chassis first raced four years earlier. Equipped with Coventry-Climax engines, such cars were perfectly adequate for their owner/drivers to give a reasonable account of themselves in the South African Championship. But the Grand Prix? A somewhat informal approach was taken

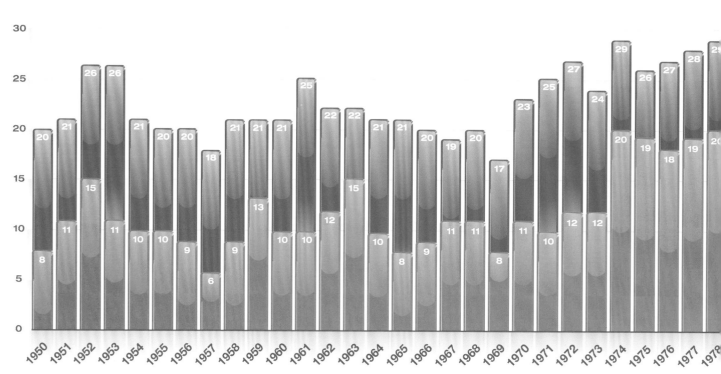

towards this first case of prequalifying. It was decided that, the day before official practice began, there would be a free-for-all. Those drivers who could lap in 1min 37sec would be invited to take part in official practice, the fastest four to complete the 20-car starting grid. It therefore fell to Dave Charlton, Jackie Pretorius and Clive Puzey to become the first drivers not to come through a prequalifying session, although they were joined by a further five NQs after official practice had been completed. For the record, the speed differential between Jim Clark's pole lap and that of Sam Tingle in 20th and last place on the grid was eight percent, once again demonstrating good sense and judgement by the organisers.

During the 1970s and early 1980s, when entries exceeded permitted starters with regularity, NQ and occasionally NPQ operated with some frequency. However, it was the popularity of Grand Prix participation in the latter half of the 1980s and on into the early 1990s (Graphic 7.2) that caused prequalifying to become a regular part of race weekend procedure. The 1987 season was the first of a three-year transition heralding the end of the turbo era. The 3.5-litre naturally aspirated cars were encouraged to race alongside the turbos and, by 1989, with turbo engines now banned, as many as 20 teams planned to race to the new Formula One regulations.

For teams new to Grand Prix and those at the wrong end of the Constructors' Championship table in the previous season, a special one-hour session was set aside at the unholy hour of 6.00am on the Friday morning. With grids and official practice sessions limited to 26 and 30 cars

respectively, numerous drivers and their teams were going to end up disappointed. And so it proved. Over a 16-round season, a full quota of 39 cars took part in all the races bar three that fielded just one fewer. Over the season, a staggering 200 qualifying attempts ended in failure, the usual pattern being nine eliminations in prequalifying and a further four during official qualifying. What wasted effort for the unlucky many. How demoralising for some teams and drivers to have to pack up and go home by 7.00am on the opening day of the race meeting!

That is, on many occasions, exactly what happened to an assortment of teams and drivers with somewhat obscure names. The leading hard-luck story must go to Rial Racing. On 12 occasions, it got both drivers through prequalifying… only to fail each and every time during qualifying proper. EuroBrun made a strong play for most dismal performance award with a full-house of prequalifying failures, but at least it could claim that it was a one-car team. Rightfully the award should go to the Yamaha powered West Zakspeed Racing team which registered NPQ for both its entries no fewer than 14 times, one of its drivers completing a full 16-race season of NPQs. The name of Zakspeed never graced Grand Prix entry lists again, but the unfortunate driver with the blank starting record returned with a vengeance 17 years later. His name? Aguri Suzuki, the founder of today's Super Aguri Formula One team. Some might heartlessly comment that, as a team chief, he is continuing where he left off as a driver – making up the numbers – but others would give him the credit that he has done rather better than that.

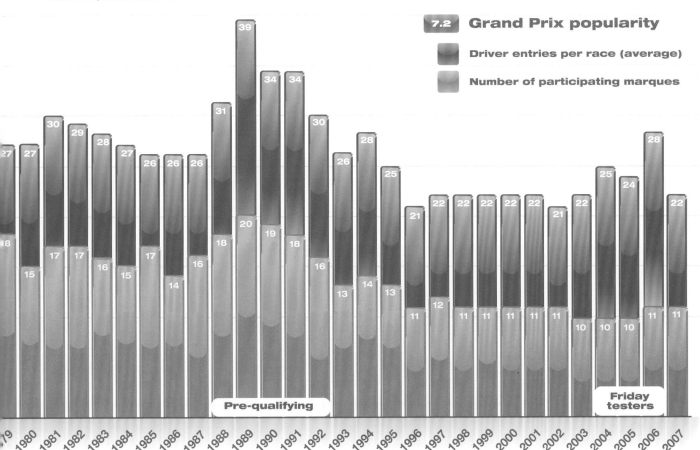

7.2 **Grand Prix popularity**

Driver entries per race (average)

Number of participating marques

ust making the starting grid for a Grand Prix may be counted as some form of achievement, but even then it does not follow that a race will ensue! Nine drivers have succumbed to maladies on the dummy grid, another 22 never managed to complete the parade or formation lap, and these must be joined by the 14 drivers who withdrew their Michelin-shod cars at the end of the 2005 US Grand Prix parade lap leaving just six cars to take the grid proper! Even World Champions have suffered the exasperating indignity of failing to take the start-line flag or lights – Alain Prost, Michael Schumacher, Mika Häkkinen, Jacques Villeneuve and Damon Hill – but only two drivers have endured it more than just the once. Jarno Trulli has twice failed to complete the parade lap and Rubens Barrichello has failed to leave the dummy grid on two separate occasions. What makes this quite extraordinary, in the case of Barrichello, is that he was at the wheel of a Ferrari and the year was 2002.

This was the season when Ferrari failed to win only two of 17 rounds, Barrichello himself having contributed four wins. That season, Schumacher's Ferrari was totally bulletproof, finishing every single race in the points, all bar

two of these on the podium including 11 on the top step. No dummy grid failures for Michael.

Although almost always in his shadow on the track, Barrichello has overtaken Schumacher in one respect. At the close of the 2007 season, he had completed 250 Grand Prix starts, one more than Michael, although he remained behind Riccardo Patrese's astonishing 256. Of the currently active drivers, David Coulthard was on 228, then Giancarlo Fisichella on 194, so Barrichello was on course to establish a new record that might last some time. He is already holder of the dubious distinction of making the most starts (124) before registering his first win but, with nine victories in his pocket, he will probably be at ease with that.

The 2005 US Grand Prix débacle apart, the smallest starting grid to assemble was at the Grand Prix of Argentina on 19 January 1958 (Graphic 7.3). Because of financial difficulties for the organisers, there had been on-off-on rumours circulating about the race. Its early date in the season also meant that the Vanwall and BRM teams were still struggling to find a solution to running their engines reliably using the newly initiated fuel regulation, requiring the use of Avgas (high-octane aviation fuel). The sparse

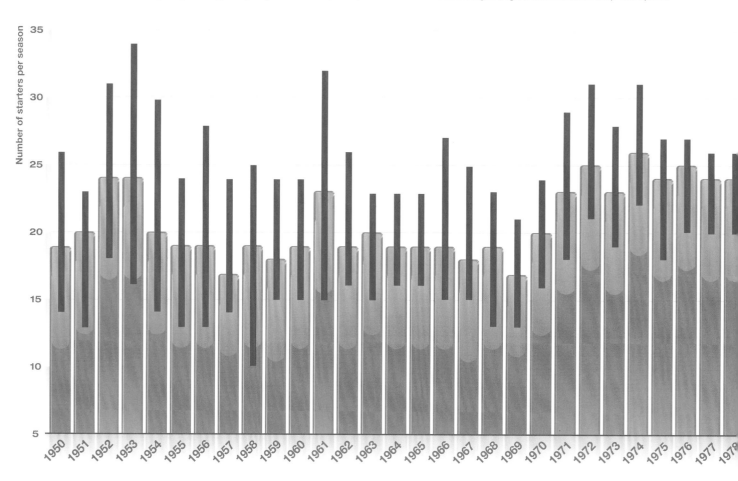

grid comprised six Maserati 250Fs, three Ferrari Dino 246s and a lone Cooper T43 Climax, entered by the independent R.R.C. Walker Racing Team for Stirling Moss. History was made that day when Moss brought home the diminutive Cooper ahead of the rest to register the very first victory for a rear-engined car since the inception of the World Championship.

Politics could also play havoc with the starting grid. In 1982, at the height of the 'FISA–FOCA War', most of the FOCA-aligned teams boycotted the race at Imola, and only 13 cars took the start after Derek Warwick's Toleman had expired on the parade lap.

At the other extreme, no fewer than 34 cars set off to complete the 18 tours of the 14-mile Nordschleife circuit at the Nürburgring for the 1953 German Grand Prix, the largest number of eligible cars ever to accelerate away from a World Championship grid. Considering that grids of more than 30 have happened on only three other occasions, this must have made an awe-inspiring sight. But there is a caveat to this record: at that time, Grand Prix racing was being run to Formula Two regulations. This had also applied to the 31-car grid in 1952, while the 32 car grid of 1961 was the first year of the Formula Two based 1.5-litre Formula One. For the imposing sight of more than 30 full-blooded Formula One cars making a grid start, it is necessary to look to the 1970s and the popularity of Formula One fostered by the 3-litre Ford-Cosworth DFV engine. The 1972 US Grand Prix and

the 1974 Belgium Grand Prix each released grids of 31 Formula One cars. As a spectacle, there was probably very little to choose between them, but aurally the Watkins Glen event almost certainly was the one to have attended. At the leafy circuit in upstate New York, the howl of the 24 V8 DFV engines was not only spiced up by the screams of two flat-12 Ferraris and three V12 BRMs, but also the shrieks of a sole V12 Matra and a flat-12 Tecno!

With the exception of the three years highlighted earlier, average grid sizes in the seasons in the 1950s and 1960s never exceed 20 cars, close to the minimum number for a viable World Championship. The 1970 season represented the beginning of 25 years of plenty for Formula One with an excess of entrants and the number of starters averaging between 24 and 26 (Graphic 7.3). Although tighter control between most and fewest alleviated the problem, significantly fewer starters in the mid-1990s reflected a decline in the fortunes of some teams, no longer able to secure the financial resources necessary to participate.

The disappearance of such teams as Pacific, Simtek and Forti did not cause too much anguish, particularly when better funded teams such as Stewart, BAR and Toyota were preparing to enter the World Championship. It was the collapse of Prost and Arrows in quick succession in 2002, soon followed by the withdrawal of Ford's Jaguar team, which sent a cold recessionary shiver through Formula One as grids tumbled back to just 20 cars.

7.3 **Number of Grand Prix starters**

Season average

Most drivers - Least drivers

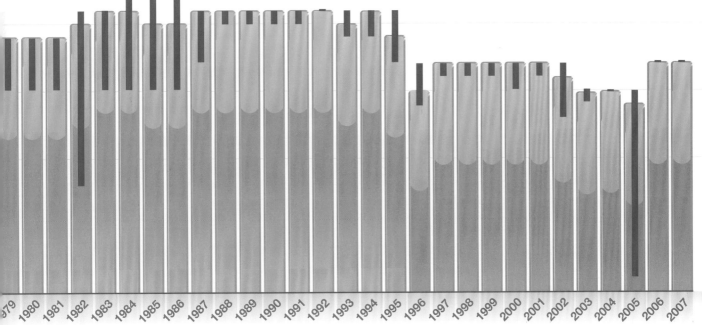

With the average all-time finishing record for Grand Prix starters standing at little more than half – 56 percent to be precise (Graphic 7.4) – it follows that the problem with small grids is the race organiser's worst nightmare – the fear that, as the final laps wind down, not even one car would be running to take the chequered flag!

It has never been quite that bad, but there is one venue that figures prominently in the list of fewest race finishers. It is Monaco. This is partly because, for many years, the number of starters at Monte Carlo was capped, usually to 20, and partly because the race was a renowned car breaker and driver destroyer. Even Ayrton Senna, a six-time winner at the street circuit, when leading the 1989 race with just 12 laps remaining, lost the 100 percent concentration required to master the round-the-houses course and stuffed his McLaren into the Armco.

The record for the fewest finishers lies between the 1966 race, when just four cars were running and were classified when the chequered flag dropped, and as recently as 1996 when only three were still circulating – although four others were classified as finishers having already completed the required minimum distance before they became *hors de combat*.

As for worst nightmares, the organisers of the 1956 German Grand Prix at the 14-mile Nürburgring circuit must have been close to apoplexy towards the end when only five cars completed the course – and one of those was subsequently disqualified. With a lap taking close on 10 minutes at that time, the spectators must have had to endure long periods of silent inactivity on track during a race lasting over three and a half hours. Fangio led from start to finish, all 22 laps.

On the other side of the coin, the 1961 Dutch Grand Prix at Zandvoort is still revered as the only race on record where not only were there no retirements – but there is no record of any pitstops, either!

Extraordinarily, in the history of Grand Prix racing, only eight drivers have finished every race in a season. Reference has already been made to Michael

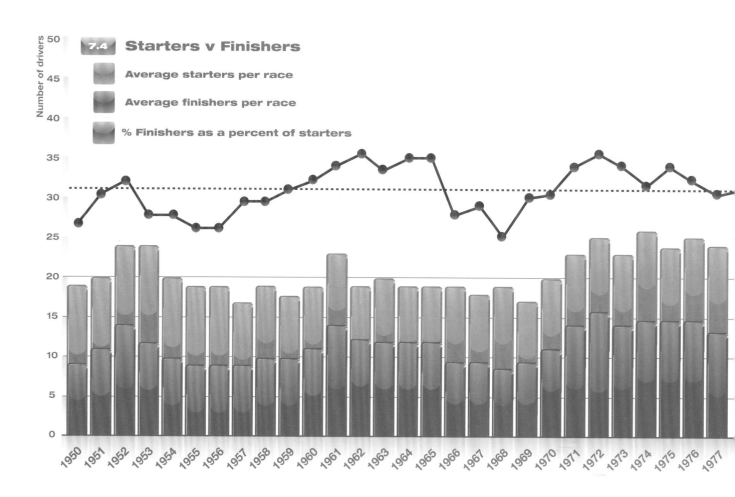

7.4 **Starters v Finishers**

- Average starters per race
- Average finishers per race
- % Finishers as a percent of starters

Schumacher's remarkable 2002 finishing record but, although he was by no means the first to achieve this feat, he was the first for a very long time – 38 years.

DATE	DRIVER	MARQUE	WINS
1953	M Hawthorn	Ferrari	8
1954	JM Fangio	Maserati & Mercedes	8
1959	M Trintignant	Cooper-Climax	8
1961	D Gurney	Porsche	8
1962	G Hill	BRM	9
1963	J Clark	Lotus-Climax	10
1964	R Ginther	BRM	10
2002	M Schumacher	Ferrari	17

With an all-time average figure of 56 percent for finishers as a percentage of starters, it is not surprising that the Grand Prix community coined the adage: "To finish first, first you have to finish!" This overall average figure hides some seemingly significant peaks and troughs over the decades. To obtain any understanding of these changes, it is necessary to examine more closely the reason why drivers have been forced to retire from races.

The 1961 Dutch Grand Prix remains a unique race – there were no retirements!

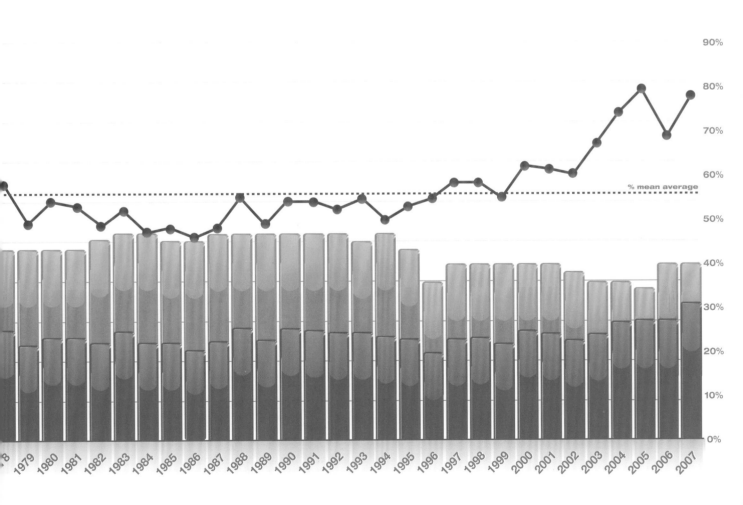

Unfortunately the available records that provide the reasons for race retirements contain such vagueness and potential ambiguity that the interpretation of any deep analysis might well be unsound. That said, probably the most interesting distinction in the analysis of race retirements is the division between those accounted for by car failure and those that may be put down to driver error. Even here, because of the chicken-and-egg situation as to whether the primary cause for retirement was car or driver, there is a potential for misclassification: was a car breakage caused by driver abuse, or did mechanical failure cause the driver's accident?

A perfect example is Kimi Räikkönen's last-lap accident at the Nürburgring in 2005: the vibration that caused a tyre to let go and destroy the suspension was caused by Räikkönen flat-spotting his tyres earlier in the race.

A third common cause for race retirement adds yet another level of complexity to the subject. This is when a driver is inadvertently taken out of the race due to another's difficulties or miscalculation.

All these caveats suggest that, although examination of the trends for total race retirements may be instructive, perhaps not too much credence should be given to the causal information. This data has been separated between that where the primary reason given is 'spin' or 'accident' (surrogate statistics for driver error) versus the remainder, which may be regarded as approximating to car failure, and which accounts for three-quarters of all race retirements.

Encouragingly, some corroboration of the trustworthiness of this seemingly rough and ready division is provided by the data taken from recent history (Graphic 7.5). This shows that finishing records (the reciprocal of retirements) have improved massively since the mid-1990s and, by 2005, had reached the unprecedented level of almost 80 percent of starters. Furthermore, during a period of increasing freedom of use and effectiveness of 'driver aids' – notably fully and semi-automatic gearboxes and traction control – there does seem to have been less emphasis on driver-led retirements. Until, that is, the introduction of 'long-life' engines in 2004 produced a significant reduction in retirements caused by car failure, adding further plausibility to the robustness of the analysis.

7.5 Retirements as percent of starters

All retirements

Car-led retirements

Driver-led retirements

Even so, perhaps data which may be dubious should not be pushed much further than to suggest some broad indications over time.

As for conclusions, those which may be drawn regarding car-led retirements are that, apart from the three exceptional periods, reliability has steadily improved and now, encouraged by the regulations, is at record levels. The periods of exception were the 1950s, when the word 'magneto' became a popular term given for failure; second, the early years of the 3-litre formula in the late 1960s; and finally the turbo era when cars were not only far more susceptible to run out of fuel, but expressions like 'boost pressure', 'wastegate' and 'compressor' were added to the non-finishers' lexicon.

From the data available, conclusions regarding driver-led retirements are much more difficult to draw and probably ask more questions than supply clear answers. Why was there a steadily rising trend in driver-led retirements throughout the 1970s? Was it that cars of the ground-effect period and of the subsequent flat bottom/solid suspension variety were less forgiving for the driver? Or did it have much more to do with the fierce competition engendered by the closely matched cars of that time?

Why were driver-led retirement rates at their lowest throughout the 1950s and 1960s? Was it because drivers could not afford to have the word 'accident' against their name in the retirements column – because it could just as easily have read 'fatal accident'?

Why were driver-led retirement rates at their highest throughout the 1990s? Could it be the obverse of the 1950s/1960s syndrome, brought about by a comparatively 'safe' racing environment coupled with the frustrations of being unable to overtake in 'dirty air?' Was it 'driver aids' that more recently brought driver-led retirements back down to near-average levels? In all of the above, what part have tyres played?

There are so many potential variables that, without stronger information and deeper analysis, it is better to leave the questions open, avoid speculation, and bring this subject to a more anecdotally based conclusion.

Some hard-luck stories of the underdogs deserve their own special recognition: the stories of the 'one-lap wonders' – eight drivers whose World Championship careers lasted less than a single lap; Alex Soler-Roig, who holds the 'record' for the number of Grands Prix in which he took part – six – without ever finishing; Andrea de Cesaris, who retired from every single race in the 1987 season – 16; Rubens Barrichello of Brazil who joins Riccardo Patrese of Italy as the holders of the 'record' for the number of retirements in their home Grand Prix – 10; and Barrichello again who, by virtue of his two dummy grid failures in 2002, joins de Cesaris and Jarno Trulli as the three drivers to have retired on more occasions than any other – 11 – before the completion of lap one.

And they say there is no such thing as luck!

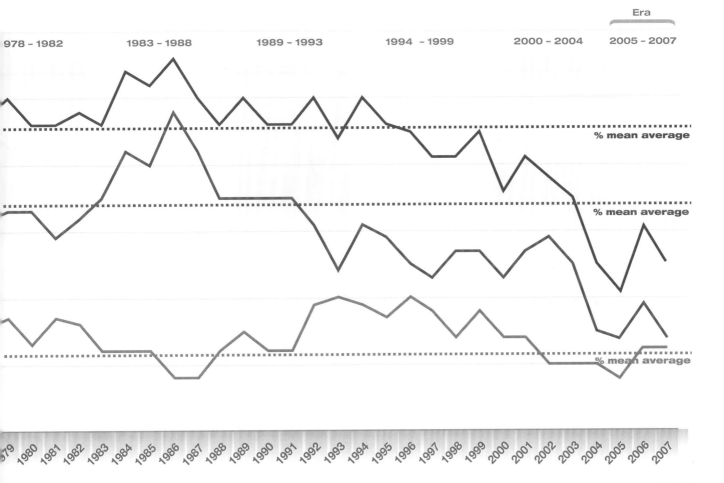

Winners

Graphic 7.6 illustrates that, across the changing Grand Prix landscape, the number of winning drivers in a given season has varied greatly. It has ranged from a minimum of two, which has happened on two occasions, to a remarkable peak of 11 in 1982. There has never been a year when one driver has won every single race in the championship, although Alberto Ascari came very close in 1952, winning all but one.

Ironically, he had not taken part in the opening round of the season in Berne. If he had, it is more than likely that he would have won in style, as evidenced by every other Grand Prix that year – particularly as, in his absence, his Ferrari team-mates lapped the rest of the field while scoring a resounding 1–2. But Enzo Ferrari had decided that he would take on the Americans and entered Ascari for the Indy 500, which at that time counted towards the Drivers' World Championship. It was an abortive attempt. Ascari's Ferrari 375 was out with mechanical ailments after covering only 100 miles.

When the unprecedented 11 drivers received the chequered flag in 1982, the number of winners per season appeared to have gradually built towards this peak. It could be argued that this was simply a function of the steadily increasing number of races counting towards the championship. To eliminate this effect, it is worth plotting the number of winners as a percentage of the number of races (Graphic 7.6).

Although the resultant statistic oscillates appreciably, it is clear that, from 1984, a significant shift in the trend is clearly discernible. From then on, apart from a few exceptional spikes (as in 2003), the level is obviously lower than before. Something had changed. A change was also evident in the number of new Grand Prix winners – three times higher in the 10 years leading up to 1984 (26 new winners in 153 races) than the 10 years following (seven new winners in 160 races). Very Orwellian!

This phenomenon is even more graphically expressed by plotting the percentage wins each season attributable to a single driver (Graphic 7.7). Despite its volatility, the trend conveys the fact that single driver dominance was a feature of the 1950s (Fangio and Ascari) before it gradually declined to the extraordinary trough of 1982. From there,

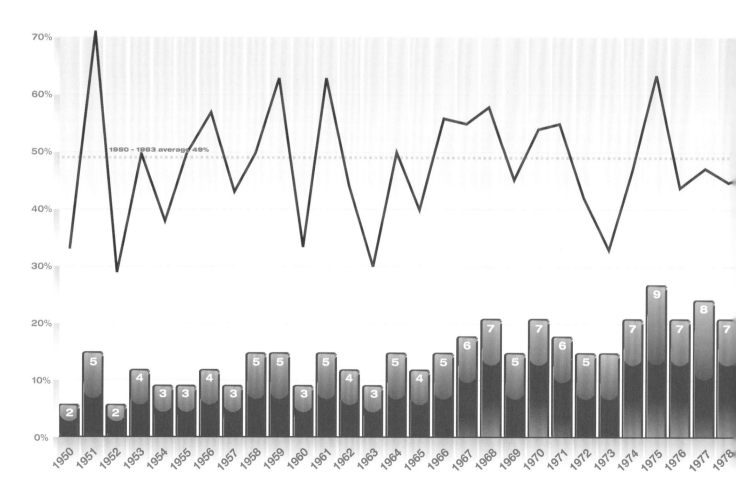

1950 - 1983 average 49%

led by the peaks of 1984 (McLaren, Prost and Lauda) and then 1988 (McLaren, Prost and Senna), the trend swings strongly upwards until 1950s-style domination returned in the new millennium (Ferrari and Schumacher).

The accompanying table lists the top 10 drivers accounting for most wins in a season. Besides Clark's intervention in 1963, it confirms that the two periods of extreme single driver domination (over 60 percent) were the 1950s and 2000s.

It is now apparent that 1982, a year when predicting

a winner became something of a lottery, represented a watershed for Grand Prix winners and Grand Prix winning. Never again would there be so many winners in one season. In fact, from that time, or more specifically from 1984, the dominance accorded to a single driver in a season simply grew and grew. What was the cause of such a drastic change in the pattern of winning?

First, what made 1982 so exceptional? The facts are extraordinary. The 16 races produced 11 winning drivers. Five drivers won two races, none more. There were seven winning marques. Two teams won four races, none more. Four teams won with both their drivers. Five teams won seven races using the Ford DFV, and three teams won nine races using turbos (Brabham won with both the DFV and the BMW turbo). Six Goodyear teams won eight races, and two Michelin teams won eight races.

As so often, a 'tyre war' made a contribution to the variety of winners, but in 1982 they were a factor, not the main reason. The primary cause was that 1982 was the watershed season between two radically different engine technologies. It was effectively the swansong season for the Ford DFV as a winning unit and the end of the 'kit-car' phenomenon which it had brought about.

The kit-car (Ferrari apart) eliminated one of the key performance variables – the engine, a scenario which theoretically will always create closer racing and a multiplicity of winners. Up against the DFV brigade in

Most Victories in a Season by a Single Driver: Top 10 Percentages

1952	A Ascari	Ferrari	86%
1954	JM Fangio	Maserati & Mercedes-Benz	75%
2004	M Schumacher	Ferrari	72%
1963	J Clark	Lotus-Climax	70%
1955	JM Fangio	Mercedes-Benz	67%
2002	M Schumacher	Ferrari	65%
1953	A Ascari	Ferrari	63%
1965	J Clark	Lotus-Climax	60%
1957	JM Fangio	Maserati	57%
1992	N Mansell	Williams-Renault	56%

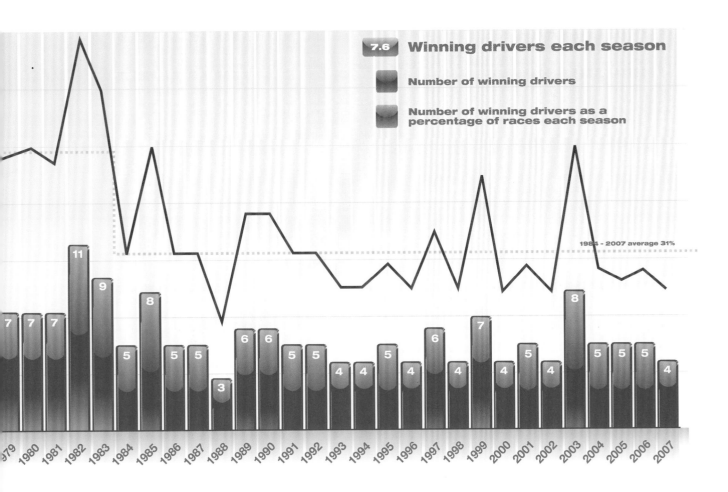

7.6 Winning drivers each season

Number of winning drivers

Number of winning drivers as a percentage of races each season

1984 - 2007 average 31%

1982 were turbo-powered cars, not just from Renault but now also from Ferrari and Brabham (BMW), but none of these three as yet had a clear advantage. With ground-effect now outlawed, the turbo was increasingly superior in all but two areas against the venerable DFV. One was reliability, the other the type of circuit. On a power circuit, the turbo would blow the DFV into the weeds, but on a 'handling' circuit, a nimble DFV-powered chassis with its progressive low-down torque curve could still be the car to have. An unusually high proportion of street circuits in the 1982 calendar – Long Beach, Monaco, Detroit, the car park at Caesars Palace in Las Vegas – plus Zolder, Dijon-Prénois, even Brands Hatch, still gave the durable DFV a good chance. Thus the turbo era did not begin until the following year when the Ford DFV managed just two wins – both on street circuits!

If variety is the spice of Formula One, as it is the spice of life, then there must be lessons from that 1982 season for the future direction of Grand Prix racing. But there was another more poignant factor that might have made a difference to the variety of that season. After just four of the 16 rounds, Gilles Villeneuve, the driver many believed would become World Champion that year and may even have dominated the season, was killed.

After that extraordinary season, the change in the pattern of winning altered completely and 1984 marked the beginning of a decade dominated by the McLaren and Williams teams and the emergence of two

exceptional drivers, locked in competition together. It was the decade of Senna versus Prost.

If it ever needed to be demonstrated, it had been proven in the 1950s. Put the best driver in the best car – Ascari at Ferrari and Fangio at Mercedes-Benz – and the consequential potency will steamroller any opposition. Ron Dennis at McLaren and Frank Williams at Williams took the concept to a new plane from 1984 until Senna's death, 10 years on.

The new way was to employ the most 'complete' driver to race for the most 'complete' team.

Creating a 'complete team' meant attending to every single facet of winning. Not only had the basic package to be strong – designer, engine, driver, finance, tyres – but the increasingly large and complex operational and environmental aspects of the team had also to reach an equivalent pitch to ensure cohesion, quality and motivation. It was recognition that a gaffe by a fabricator back at the factory could be as damaging as an on-track blunder by the driver.

Finding a 'complete driver' also represented a more analytical approach to driver selection. The acknowledgement was required that, although speed was indeed of the essence, numerous other qualities create a driver complete enough not only to win races, but to put together a sustained season of excellence to win championships. Attributes such as racecraft and concentration, mental toughness and focus, aggression

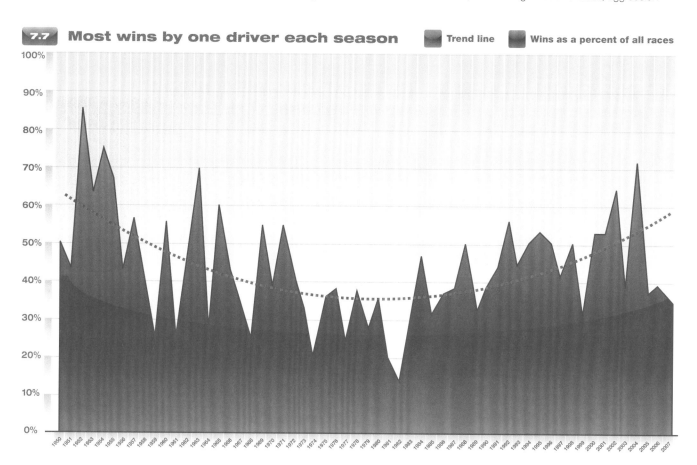

7.7 **Most wins by one driver each season**   Trend line   Wins as a percent of all races

and resilience all counted as much as raw speed and talent.

Another part of the McLaren and Williams racing philosophy was that, rather than relying on a traditional lead driver with his trusty number two, the prospect of a team conceived as a total winning machine became even closer if it was possible to attract two exceptional drivers simultaneously. The absence of any team orders added further to the intensity of performance required of both drivers, the expectation being that, if one failed to win, the other would be there to take the honours.

In actuality, there is a scarcity of drivers of such 'completeness' and virtuosity, drivers who have the capability to deliver not just one but multiple championships. They surface once every five, maybe more years. They are so extremely rare that they very seldom compete directly, at least not when they are both at the height of their powers. Prost and Senna were such drivers and that made their rivalry very special – and, for 1988–89, Ron Dennis secured the services of both, wheel to wheel, head to head! No wonder there was such immense success. And no wonder there was such intra-team fireworks.

Prost drove for Frank Williams for just the one season of 1993, and Senna made only three appearances for the team in 1994. For 1986–87, when his Honda V6 turbo powered cars had been developed to a level of performance superiority, Williams had to look elsewhere for drivers and paired Nelson Piquet with the incumbent Nigel Mansell, who had joined the previous season. Piquet, if

not a dominant force, was a proven accumulator of race wins that had brought him two World Championships. Equipped with a Williams-Honda, he was certain to find winning form, but it was Mansell who became the more prolific race winner for Williams. Twenty-eight of his career 31 victories came at the wheel of the Oxfordshire based cars during his four years with the team in the 1980s, plus his two-year return, to complete his "unfinished business", in the early 1990s.

With just one World Championship each, in many ways Mansell and Piquet provided the support act to the star attractions of Prost and Senna, who bagged seven titles between them between 1984 and 1993. But what supporting players! The upshot was that, driving for the McLaren and Williams teams, these four serial winners – Senna, Prost, Mansell and Piquet – produced such a potent mixture that they totally dominated the decade (Graphic 7.8). Of the 160 Grands Prix run over that time span, the statistics are astonishing. The two teams accounted for 128 victories (80 percent), the four drivers accounted for 126 victories (79 percent), and together they won 107 races (66 percent), leaving mere scraps for such great teams as Ferrari, Lotus, Brabham, Renault and Tyrrell to squabble over.

What Ron Dennis and Frank Williams could not have anticipated was that, during that decade of overwhelming dominanace, they had sown a wind. Come the new millennium, they would reap the (scarlet) whirlwind!

Photos from left: Ron Dennis; Ayrton Senna, Alain Prost, Nigel Mansell and Nelson Piquet; and Frank Williams.

7.8 The six who changed the face of winning across a decade: 1984–93

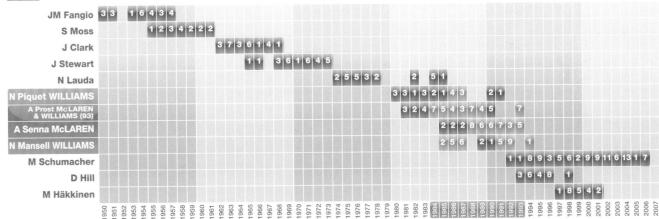

The ultimate losers

At every Grand Prix, there is a winner, but for each driver who wins, there are another 20 or more who lose. Some say it is the losing that makes the winning sweet, but there was a time when Grand Prix racing had a darker side, when losing had a much deeper meaning. Losing a race was one thing. Losing your life quite another. In what has at times been a cruel sport, it could happen to anyone on the grid, to the champion or to the journeyman (Graphic 7.9).

In the 1950s, 1960s and even on into the 1970s, the mind-set was an unquestioning acceptance that motor racing was dangerous, that injury or death was the inevitable consequence of this extreme test of human and technical endeavour (Graphic 7.10). Maybe in the 1950s this attitude was a residual from a cavalier approach necessarily adopted in World War II. Jackie Stewart must be given credit for leading a personal crusade to alter this morbid outlook. Stewart was disgusted by the slaughter and had the vision to realise that quite simple changes could lead to an improvement in survival in the event of a life-threatening accident, such as his own at Spa in 1966, the particular experience which led to his campaign for greater safety. Stewart lay trapped in his car, soaked in fuel, for at least 20 minutes before proper help arrived.

Along with burns from fuel fires, crippling leg injuries were another area of driver injury where, over time, great improvements have been made as the concept of the

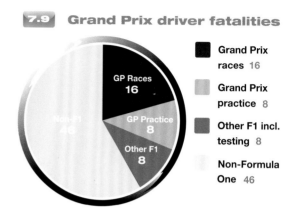

7.9 Grand Prix driver fatalities

- ■ Grand Prix races 16
- ▨ Grand Prix practice 8
- ▨ Other F1 incl. testing 8
- □ Non-Formula One 46

chassis survival cell has evolved, cocooning both a safety fuel cell and the driver in a protective shell. Wearing, as he is, a helmet and HANS device (Head And Neck System), strapped securely into a high-sided cockpit and surrounded by impact-absorbing materials, it is often a matter of amazement when a driver steps out unaided from a particularly violent accident and coolly replaces the steering wheel. At the root of the survival cell concept lies the use in chassis construction of carbonfibre – both lighter and very much stronger than aluminium and a development going way back to John Barnard's then-innovative McLaren MP4 of 1981 – which offered significant advantages in both performance and

7.10 Grand Prix driver fatalities

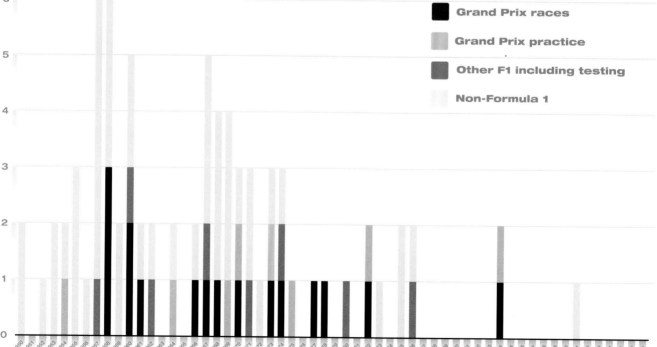

ROLL OF HONOUR Fatalities in World Championship Grand Prix Events

YEAR	DRIVER	NAT	CAR	CIRCUIT	DURING	YEAR	DRIVER	NAT	CAR	CIRCUIT	DURING
1954	Onofré Marimon	RA	Maserati	Nürburgring	Qualifying	1970	Piers Courage	GB	De Tomaso	Zandvoort	Race
1958	Luigi Musso	I	Ferrari	Reims	Race		Jochen Rindt	A	Lotus	Monza	Qualifying
	Peter Collins	GB	Ferrari	Nürburgring	Race	1973	Roger Williamson	GB	March	Zandvoort	Race
	Stuart Lewis-Evans	GB	Vanwall	Casablanca	Race		François Cevert	F	Tyrrell	Watkins Glen	Qualifying
1960	Chris Bristow	GB	Cooper	Spa	Race	1974	Helmut Koinigg	A	Surtees	Watkins Glen	Race
	Alan Stacey	GB	Lotus	Spa	Race	1975	Mark Donohue	USA	March	Österreichring	Warm-up
1961	Wolfgang von Trips	D	Ferrari	Monza	Race	1977	Tom Pryce	GB	Shadow	Kyalami	Race
1964	Carel Godin de Beaufort	NL	Porsche	Nürburgring	Qualifying	1978	Ronnie Peterson	S	Lotus	Monza	Race
1966	John Taylor	GB	Brabham	Nürburgring	Race	1982	Gilles Villeneuve	CDN	Ferrari	Zolder	Qualifying
1967	Lorenzo Bandini	I	Ferrari	Monte-Carlo	Race		Riccardo Paletti	I	Osella	Montréal	Race
1968	Jo Schlesser	F	Honda	Rouen	Race	1994	Roland Ratzenberger	A	Simtek	Imola	Qualifying
1969	Gerhard Mitter	D	BMW F2	Nürburgring	Qualifying		Ayrton Senna	BR	Williams	Imola	Race

safety. This, coupled with ever more stringent crash testing, ensures that the integrity of the survival cell is maintained and the risk of fire, or injury to the vulnerable head and legs, is minimised.

The enormous sway this macabre subject has inevitably held on Grand Prix racing has already been alluded to in Chapter 4 (see Fangio & Fatalities and Imola Implications) so there is no call to dwell excessively here. In the accompanying roll of honour, the bald facts speak for themselves.

Grimly poignant reading this may make, but whichever way the facts are examined (Graphic 7.11), injury, particularly fatal injury, has been successfully and substantially reduced since the early 1980s. In the first 32 years ending 1982,

22 drivers lost their lives during Grand Prix events. In the subsequent 25 years, the death toll is two, a comparative statistic for which the sport as a whole can be justly proud.

For the driver, the virtual absence of the spectre of death has been one of the most dramatic changes between the Grand Prix landscape of today with that of the past, the implications of which will be considered more fully in the closing chapter.

That evocative picture (previous page) of those four serial winners, Senna, Prost, Mansell and Piquet, posing together on that sunny day in Estoril in 1987, holds special poignancy in the knowledge that one of their number was to die at the wheel. He was the last Grand Prix driver to do so – it is hoped, the last ever.

7.11 Death & injury in Grand Prix events

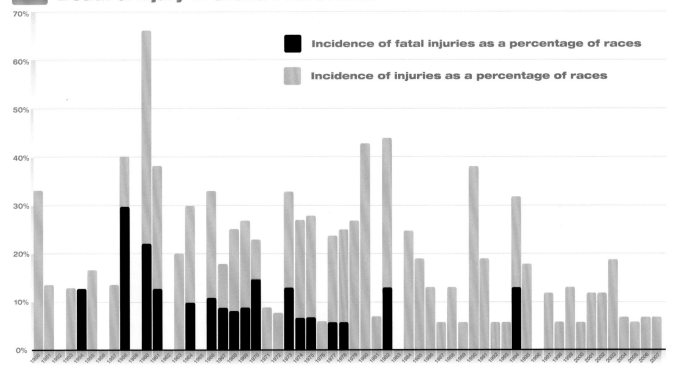

■ Incidence of fatal injuries as a percentage of races

■ Incidence of injuries as a percentage of races

The three preceding chapters have examined the changing landscape of Grand Prix racing in considerable detail. They have illustrated how, in many ways, Formula One appears to have altered out of all recognition over its 58 years. Although this is so, many of these changes are in style rather than in substance. In reality, the fundamentals of Grand Prix racing are not so very different to this day.

This is borne out in the opening section of this chapter. It is an account of a Grand Prix that took place more than 50 years ago. Its purpose is to identify the key components and dynamics of the Grand Prix race which essentially remain today as they ever were. In considering the starting grid, the start, the opening lap, the race leaders, the lead changes, the fastest laps and the victory margin, it could just as easily be Lewis Hamilton versus Kimi Räikkönen at a night race in Singapore as Juan Manuel Fangio versus Alberto Ascari at the Nürburgring in 1951.

The chapter takes a closer look at each facet of the winning process to appreciate what more can be learned about Grand Prix racing today from that of 50 years ago, and to establish whether there are distinct parallels on which to base firm conclusions.

A very special moment frozen in time. Lewis Hamilton takes his maiden Grand Prix victory, in Montréal. In 2007 the 22-year-old showed his own special brand of 'winning ways'.

Graphic 8.1 plots the essential race statistics for the fifth round of the seven-race 1951 World Championship (excluding the Indy 500), which was held over 20 laps of the Nürburgring circuit. It was the first championship race to be held in Germany since the war.

Having dominated the early part of the season, as well as the inaugural championship the previous year, Alfa Romeo had now endured its first defeat. Two weeks earlier, at Silverstone, Froilán Gonzáles had not only inflicted that first defeat but had also recorded an historic maiden victory for SEFAC Ferrari. His win had moved him up to third place in the title race: Juan Fangio (Alfa Romeo) 21 points, Giuseppe Farina (Alfa Romeo) 15, Gonzáles (Ferrari) 11, Alberto Ascari (Ferrari) nine.

With three of the seven rounds still to run, it seemed that Fangio was now set for a battle not only against his team-mate, but also against the increasing threat of Ferrari. Having lost out (because of a gearbox problem) to Farina in the final round of the previous season, he now faced the prospect that a Ferrari driver might well steal this second opportunity to claim his first World Championship.

The fact that the Alfa Romeos were beaten by the best part of a minute at Silverstone was, indeed, cause for concern. Such a margin suggested a performance advantage for the 4.5-litre V12 Ferrari of more than half a second per lap. And, as they prepared for the vastly different challenge of the 14-mile Nordschleife, even more disconcerting was that the longer race distance of the German Grand Prix would require two fuel stops to satisfy the supercharged, 1.5-litre, straight-eight Alfa. The prognosis was that Ferrari's naturally aspirated V12 might well see out the distance with just one fuel stop, which had been the case at Silverstone.

The only chance for Fangio in Germany, it seemed, was to build up such a lead advantage that he could afford two stops if, as calculated, Ferrari did indeed need just the one. Around the Nordschleife circuit, Fangio had felt confident that he could achieve this against his compatriot, Gonzáles, despite the apparent new-found speed of the V12 Ferrari through the fast, flat corners of Silverstone. But, could he shake off Ferrari team leader Ascari? Although the usual suspects occupied the four-across front row of the starting grid, the comparative qualifying times around the daunting and extensive 14.173-mile course served to diminish Fangio's highest hopes:

ASCARI	GONZÁLES	FANGIO	FARINA
Ferrari	Ferrari	Alfa Romeo	Alfa Romeo
9m 55.8s	9m 57.5s	9m 59.0s	10m 01.0s

8.1 **Anatomy of a Grand Prix victory** Ascari defeats Fangio, Nürburgring, 1951

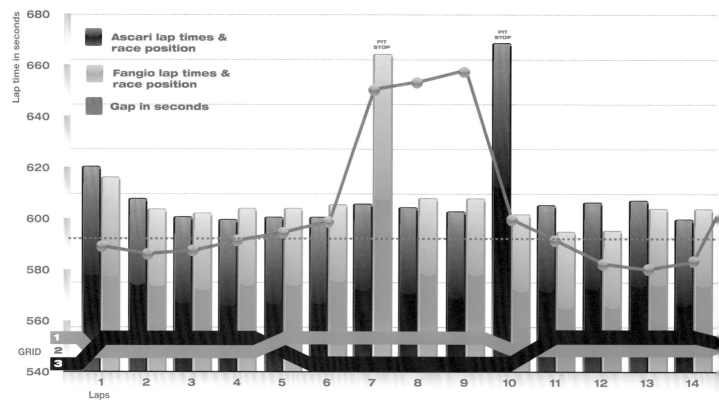

Bad news for Fangio, then: not just Ascari, but both Ferrari drivers quicker. However, a good start might just provide him with the opportunity of building the lead he so desperately needed.

Farina made the best start but, within a few hundred metres, as the pack rounded the Südkehre, Fangio assumed the lead. On the completion of the opening lap, he had a 3.4sec advantage over Ascari, who was similarly ahead of Gonzáles and Farina. Naturally, from a standing grid start and with a heavy fuel load, this would be Fangio's slowest lap of the race (10m 17.1s). It was some 13 seconds adrift of his next tour, during which he succeeded in doubling his advantage over second-placed Ascari, to 7.1sec (Graphic 8.1).

The third lap was Fangio's fastest of this, his first stint before the initial pitstops. But it was still a lap of over 10 minutes and, more significantly, it was slower than Ascari's, who pegged the lead deficit back to 5.5sec.

Ascari stacked up the pressure over the fourth lap and crossed the line a mere 1.2sec (approximately 15 car lengths) behind the Alfetta. Ascari wrested the lead from Fangio on lap five, at Breidscheid, roughly halfway round the circuit – and, by the completion of the lap, the Ferrari had a useful 2.2sec lead. This was the time to assert superiority. Again the Italian driver put the hammer down, and his sixth lap was but a tenth of a second slower than his pressure-filled fourth lap and only two-tenths shy of the 10min mark. The lead was now 8sec ahead of… Gonzáles. With a dwindling fuel load, Fangio had made his pit call for the first of two planned stops, taking on a churn of fuel and having all four tyres changed. The operation cost a precious minute.

Worse still, despite the fresh tyres, Fangio's fuel-filled Alfa was now running in third place and losing yet more time to Ascari – even though the Ferrari driver could now afford to ease off a little relative to the frenetic pace that had been required to take the lead and pull away (Graphic 8.1). When Ascari made his scheduled pitstop, at the end of lap nine (half-distance), his lead over Gonzáles was up to 75sec. Gonzáles, scheduled to make a later stop than his team leader, led lap 10. But, while at a standstill in the pits, he was passed by Fangio.

When Ascari resumed, having also spent at least a minute in the pits, he found that Fangio was still very much in touch on the road. Now it was Ascari's turn to be hampered by the extra weight of a brimmed fuel tank, and he was overhauled on lap 11. Once in front again, Fangio knew that this could be the final chance to make a telling break, while Ascari burned off fuel. Although it was somewhat futile, knowing he still had to make his second stop, there was always a chance that he could force a mistake or provoke tyre or mechanical problems which might yet give him victory.

This effort, on lap 11, produced a lap-time 3sec faster than his qualifying time. On the next tour, Fangio set the fastest lap of the race – matching Ascari's pole position time of 9m 55.8s – and extended the lead to nearly 15sec. But that was as far as it went. Even Fangio could not sustain such speeds and, when he re-emerged from the pits for the second time, Ascari had sailed past to build up an advantage of almost a full minute.

Back in control, Ascari upped the ante to ensure his victory and, most likely, with the intention of snatching fastest lap along with the extra World Championship point at that time awarded for this accomplishment. He duly posted a couple of sub-10min laps but his best, on lap 16, was still 1.5sec slower than his adversary's new lap record. By then, the tyres on the Ferrari were the worse for wear but, with a lead of nearly 80sec (Graphic 8.1), he could afford the luxury of a second pitstop, this time a shorter one for tyres alone. He resumed still almost half a minute ahead.

After three hours and 23 minutes of racing over 283 miles, that was how it ended. Ascari's winning margin to Fangio was a comprehensive 30.2sec.

Before examining each of the 'winning ways' in turn, there is a postscript to this account of the 1951 German Grand Prix. The next round at Monza brought Fangio yet more anguish. Because of an engine fault, he failed to finish and Ascari led Gonzáles to a Ferrari 1–2. The race for the championship had closed up: Fangio (Alfa Romeo) 27 points, Ascari (Ferrari) 25, Gonzáles (Ferrari) 21, Farina (Alfa Romeo) 17. Neither Gonzáles nor Farini were now in contention.

Pedralbes, a 3.9-mile street course near Barcelona, in Spain, hosted the final, deciding round. To secure the World Championship, Ascari needed to finish strongly and ahead of Fangio. After a hat-trick of Ferrari victories, this appeared to be more than just a possibility, particularly when Ascari secured pole position. However, the challenge fizzled out due to tyre problems because of a wrong wheel choice made by his team, and he could only finish a distant fourth. Fangio was victorious and lifted his first World Championship title. Despite this success, Alfa Romeo saw the writing was on the wall for its thirsty pre-war supercharged engine technology and withdrew from the competition at season's end.

The standing start is one of Grand Prix's greatest attractions. Of the three generally accepted ways to start a motor race – the others being the rolling start (Indy 500) and the echelon start (Le Mans, now defunct) – the grid start is superb in its formation and spectacular in its execution.

It is formed from one of the great collective 'macho' events in the world of sport – qualifying. It asks a fundamental question of its 20-plus participants: which of you can drive the fastest over a single flying lap of the track? The majority of us can surely relate to that, some in the belief that, given half a chance, they would come out on top!

Then there is the execution of the standing start: 20-plus of the fastest cars and drivers in the world form up in close proximity… the tension, anticipation, colour and excitement… the red lights on the gantry blink on one by one, the engine revs soar to a shrieking crescendo of sound and power, pulverising the senses… the ground trembles, the air pulsates as nearly 20,000bhp is held for those final long, long moments, ready to be unleashed…

Suddenly all the lights go off and the cars blast away, gathering pace at an astonishing rate towards the horizon of the first corner, jinking and weaving to find a gap as they descend en masse towards turn one… knowing that as they leave that corner – if they leave that corner – they will soon enough be extolled as idol or derided as idiot… while leaving those back at the startline inhaling a haze of oil and rubber smoke and marvelling at the violent, explosive scene they have just witnessed.

The grid start remains an integral part of a 21st century Grand Prix, albeit somewhat neutered by 'launch control'. However, what has fundamentally changed (with effect from the 2003 season) is the way the grid is formed. Traditionally, prior to every race, grid order was determined by a qualifying session(s), with the fastest driver/car combination gaining the advantage of pole position. Inevitably, such a sporting model, with faster drivers starting ahead of those slower, frequently can, and often does, result in the pole man leading the race from start to finish, with a procession in grid order of those following.

It is perhaps because of this that the fascination and excitement of Grand Prix racing has never been wholly dependent upon wheel-to-wheel dicing (let alone overtaking), especially for the lead. The sporting model always tended to militate against such eventualities. Noise, colour, speed and unpredictability are also essential ingredients of the theatre of the Grand Prix motor race. Unpredictability can come in many forms due to driver error, car failure, or rain. As a result, even the best driver in the best car could rarely keep a winning streak going for too long. And, whisper it, in the good old, bad old days, the intrinsic danger for drivers often curtailed a dominant career well before its time.

But in the 2002 season, the monotony of Michael Schumacher's 11 wins from 17 races was felt to be killing the

8.2 ## Racing is becoming more processional

Percent podiums filled by grid 1, 2, 3 positions each season

- ■ Grid 1, 2, 3; finish 1, 2, 3
- ■ Grid 1, 2, 3; finish 1, 2, 3 but in any other order

essential element of unpredictability and variety. This had a bearing on a number of changes, and among them was an attempt to mix up the grid and introduce greater volatility for the sake of 'the show'. The fact that Schumacher's 2002 strike rate of 65 percent had been exceeded by Ascari's 100 percent from six starts in 1952, and Jim Clark's 70 percent from 10 starts in 1963, was of little consequence. In the 1950s and 1960s, dominance was far easier to accept with fewer races during a season and when 'the show' did not need to satiate a multi-million global TV audience.

After more than 50 years, the traditional multi-lap, multi-car free-for-all on 'empty' tanks was replaced for the 2003 season by single-lap qualifying for individual cars, each fuelled ready to race. The theory went that, because of their predetermined fuel strategy, the cars would carry differing quantities and therefore weights of fuel into qualifying. The appreciable performance effect of dissimilar fuel weights would mix up the starting grid, and so unpredictability and even on-track overtaking would be restored. Regrettably, it also meant that the fabled pole position lap was gone, along with it that 'macho' opportunity for a driver, regardless of the outcome on race day, to demonstrate his raw speed, his superiority over one flying lap.

What would Ayrton Senna have said?

Graphic 8.2 offers certain evidence in an attempt to place a measurement on the charge of processional racing that has been levelled at Grand Prix racing of late. It shows, as a percentage of races each season, the incidence when the first three on the grid also finished 1–2–3 on the podium. It is designed to provide a balanced opinion and so deliberately excludes the additional occasions when the first two on the grid have finished that way, of which there have been many. It is merely an indication that, when the top three on the

grid finish on the podium, the likelihood is that the race had become largely processional.

Assuming 17 to 19 races a year, an incidence of 10 percent is bearable, 20 percent unfortunate, and more than that unacceptable. It is not difficult to judge the problems faced by the FIA – and nor whether its measures have been successful in alleviating the problem. The graphic certainly confirms that there is an issue to be addressed. Indeed, some might even conclude that the introduction of fuel strategy to the starting grid might have even promoted the Ferrari/Schumacher supremacy.

Qualifying has since been enhanced by the return, in 2006, of the multi-car format in 'knock-out' form, but the retention of fuel strategy as an element of the top-10 shoot-out is convoluted. Burning off fuel to receive fuel credits adds nothing but complexity and removes the immediacy of knowing who has put in a truly great lap, and whether Lewis Hamilton is faster than Fernando Alonso, Alonso faster than

How is it possible to win a Grand Prix from 22nd on the grid? John Watson knows, as he did just this at Long Beach in 1983 in his McLaren MP4/1C.

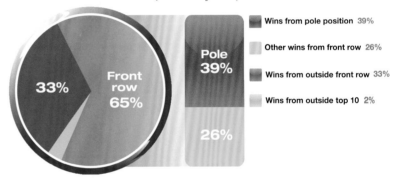

8.3 ## Percent winner's grid position
All Grands Prix (excl. Indy 500)

- 33%
- Front row 65%
- Pole 39%
- 26%

- Wins from pole position 39%
- Other wins from front row 26%
- Wins from outside front row 33%
- Wins from outside top 10 2%

Kimi Räikkönen, or Felipe Massa faster than all of them. Making fuel-adjusted estimates later is not quite the same!

In view of the sporting model for grid formation – fastest at the front – Graphic 8.3 holds few surprises. Of the first 774 Grand Prix races held (excl. Indy 500), two in every five (39 percent) have been won from pole position, and two in every three (65 percent) from the front row of the grid. The corollary is, of course, that one in every three races – a significant proportion – have been won by drivers from further down the grid.

The chances of victory outside the top 10 starters are an infinitesimal two in 100. It has only happened 18 times! The adjoining panel shows the top 10 of these 18 who therefore deserve a very special place in Grand Prix history, particularly John Watson, who not only holds the record but also features twice in the top three.

At Long Beach in March 1983, from a grid of 26 cars, John Watson started the race in 22nd spot – by modern standards, dead last! Just over 1 hour and 53 minutes of racing later, he took the chequered flag almost 30sec ahead of his McLaren team-mate, Niki Lauda, who had started 23rd. During the race, the attrition rate had been high, but half of the large field had recorded a finish and the McLarens were followed home by cars from the first and second rows of the grid. Winning from 22nd is truly exceptional – indeed, unique, as no driver before or since has won from outside the top 20 qualifiers. A further startling revelation is that, until quite recently, Watson was the runner-up to his own record, having won from 17th on the grid at another street circuit, Detroit, barely 10 months earlier!

Although the prevalence of winning from pole position is high (39 percent), there has been enormous variation season to season. The lowest at 6 percent (one race from

16) is again that exceptional season of 1982 when 11 different drivers won a Grand Prix. The highest at 75 percent, nearly twice the average, are the two seasons 1959 and 1991; in the latter year, Senna accounted for six of the 12. Because of this wide year-to-year variation, it is more effective to look for any meaningful differences over time by using groups of consecutive years. Graphic 8.4 plots the percentage of wins from pole (39 percent average) versus the percentage from outside the front row (33 percent average) but this time not by year, but by era (see Chapter 4).

The variations are marked but crystal clear. Pole position has featured more strongly for winners in the early and late Grand Prix eras. Pole position was of least significance to winning during the era 1978–82 when, as revealed in Chapter 4, two radical technologies, ground-effect (chassis) and turbocharging (engine) fought wheel-to-wheel for ascendancy.

Pole position dominance became most prominent during the 'gizmo Grand Prix' era of 1989–93, when highly sophisticated racing cars from Williams and McLaren left the rest of the field struggling to keep up. This is borne out by Graphic 8.5, which indicates the competitiveness of grids over time and in 1992 peaks as the highest differential in recent history, the gap between the pole and 10th place on the grid reaching over 4 percent.

This analysis into the depth of competition of the Grand Prix field was undertaken to assist understanding of the extremely low levels of winners from outside the front row during the 1950s and 1960s (Graphic 8.4). One obvious factor was that, with starting grids normally comprising four front-row cars up to 1967, and three up to 1973, wins from grid positions three and four were largely excluded prior to 1973.

However, Graphic 8.5 suggests that there was far more to

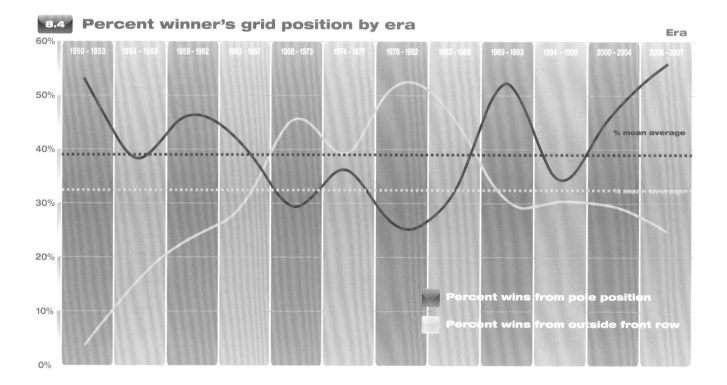

8.4 Percent winner's grid position by era

Era

| 1950 - 1953 | 1954 - 1958 | 1959 - 1962 | 1963 - 1967 | 1968 - 1973 | 1974 - 1977 | 1978 - 1982 | 1983 - 1988 | 1989 - 1993 | 1994 - 1999 | 2000 - 2004 | 2005 - 2007 |

% mean average

Percent wins from pole position
Percent wins from outside front row

it than that. It shows that the depth of competition on 1950s starting grids was generally much weaker than the normal differential of between 2 and 4 percent. This was particularly the case in my 'phoney formulae' years of 1950–53, although it does not necessarily follow that competition between the team-mates of those superior performing teams was not fierce. It just meant that the lower order teams were not particularly competitive and therefore highly unlikely to pull off a surprise win from outside the front row.

Quite clearly, the 1970s was the most consistently competitive period (Graphic 8.5) for the top half of the grid, and 1975 the most prominent year when Lauda was taking on the combined might of the Ford DFV teams… and winning. During that particular season, the top 10 on the grid were covered by less than a second on five separate occasions, but the most closely bunched grid during that period was at Kyalami in 1974, when 0.6sec separated the top 10 and just 4.2 percent covered the performance differential for all 27 starters.

While on the subject of tight grids, mention must also be made of the Grand Prix of Europe in 1997. This was the infamous occasion when, during that title-deciding race, Michael Schumacher made a deliberate attempt to punt his title rival, Jacques Villeneuve, off the track. The portents that an unusual event was to unfold were strong when, during qualifying, the top three on the grid posted identical times to one thousandth of a second.

The grid order was decided in the traditional manner – the first driver setting the time received grid position precedence. The top three thus formed up with Villeneuve on pole, Schumacher beside him on the front row, and Heinz-Harald Frentzen, Villeneuve's Williams-Renault team mate, leading row two. The watching world was fully aware that one or other

WINNER	GRID POSITION	VENUE/YEAR
John Watson	22nd	Long Beach 1983
Rubens Barrichello	18th	Hockenheim 2000
John Watson	17th	Detroit 1982
Kimi Räikkönen	17th	Suzuka 2005
Jackie Stewart	16th	Kyalami 1973
Michael Schumacher	16th	Spa 1995
Alan Jones	14th	Österreichring 1977
Johnny Herbert	14th	Nürburgring 1999
Bruce McLaren	13th	Buenos Aires 1960
Alain Prost	13th	Mexico City 1990

of the two with identical times on the front row would become the World Champion, but not that Schumacher was on the verge of actions that would disqualify him (but not his team) from the 1997 Formula One World Championship.

For the record, Gerhard Berger, 10th on that grid, was separated from pole by 0.584sec and the whole 22-car grid was covered by 3.98 percent, both measures an improvement over Kyalami some 27 years before.

It is a shame that Graphic 8.5 is curtailed after 2002. It seems more than likely that, with so many big-money manufacturer teams competing together currently, competition within the top 10 has once again become highly intense. Fuel strategy has served its purpose. It is time for Grand Prix racing to recapture that raw edge of excitement only possible from that most 'macho' of sporting occasions, the balls-out unfettered shot at pole position.

8.5 Grid competitiveness

Annual average percent that P10 is slower than pole position

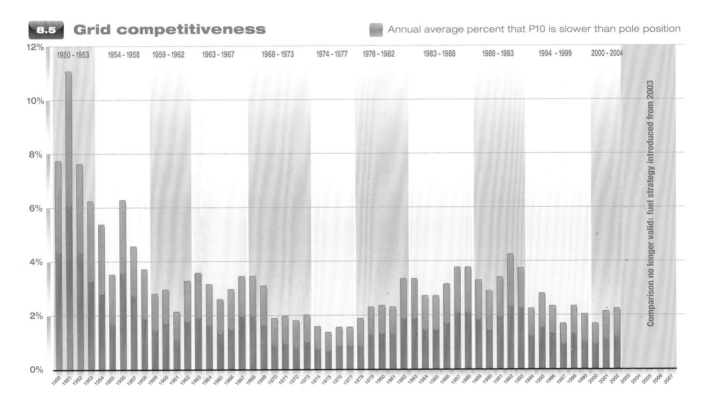

Opening lap

The opening lap is a continuation of that wonderful sequence which begins the moment the lights are 'go'. The drivers are still tightly bunched and jockeying for position, particularly those who have lost out on the grid or at the first corner and are now hell-bent on reasserting track position.

Graphic 8.6 is less notable for the statistics for pole position and the front row, but for the one-in-eight (12 percent) of occasions on which the first-lap leader did not have the benefit of a front-row grid position. Over the decades, this has happened on approximately 100 occasions, but within that figure only seven times from a position lower than the second row (see panel)!

Clay Regazzoni is the only driver to lead lap one from the fourth row, although his unique achievement in 1971 was somewhat tarnished by massively jumping the start: "The Ferrari was moving quite fast before the start was given." Indeed, it was in the lead within a few hundred metres of the grid but, for some unaccountable reason, was not penalised!! Maybe there was a similar explanation as to why Carlos Pace, in a Brabham, went similarly unpenalised at Interlagos in 1977: "With a couple of seconds to go, he dropped the clutch of the Brabham-Alfa and, by the time

the rest were pulling away from the line, Pace was looking for a way past the leaders."

The other five all seem to be legitimate and most usually down to devastating starts where revs, clutch, wheelspin and traction were fed-in and synchronised to perfection. None, therefore, as a racing lap, compare with Senna's ascension at Donington in 1983 from seventh at the first corner (albeit row two on the grid) to the lead by the end of the lap. Moving from the sublime to the abysmal, and to the other extreme, Schumacher's opening lap to lead from the third row of the grid at Indianapolis in 2005 has been excluded: the four cars ahead of him were absent!

Graphic 8.7 completes the first-lap leader analysis on a season-by-season basis, remembering that, before 1973, the front row would have comprised up to four cars. Without attempting to extract more conclusions than the data can reasonably support, there is evidence that, in the past 15 years or more, pole position has become even more significant to track position during the opening laps. With electronically controlled start procedures and electronically controlled starting (launch) procedures, this is not entirely surprising.

Clay and Carlos would find it all highly frustrating!

Starting from the fourth row, Clay Regazzoni managed to get his Ferrari 312B2 into the lead by the first corner at Monza in 1971 – but no jumped-start penalty for Ferrari resulted! Here he leads fellow Swiss Jo Siffert's Yardley-BRM P160.

8.7 Grid position of first lap leader % grid position

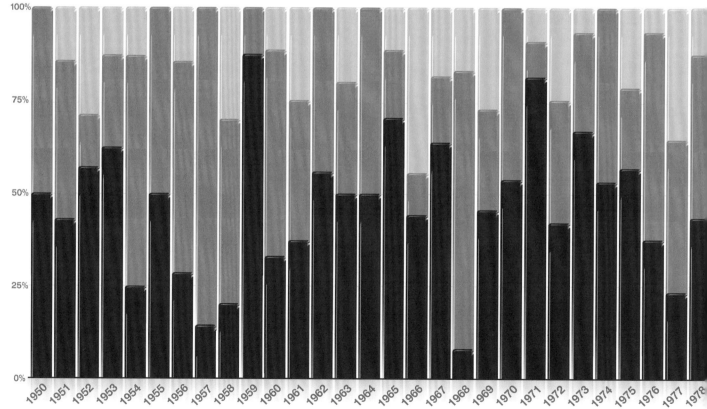

8.6 **The importance of pole position**
First lap leaders as a percent of all Grands Prix

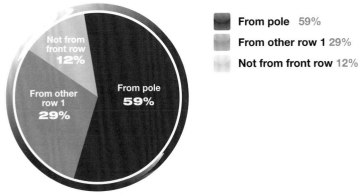

- From pole 59%
- From other row 1 29%
- Not from front row 12%

GRID SLOT	GRID ROW	DRIVER	CAR	RACE	YEAR
8	4	Clay Regazzoni	Ferrari	Monza	1971
8	3	Jim Clark	Lotus	Spa	1963
6	3	Jackie Stewart	Matra	Nürburgring	1968
6	3	René Arnoux	Renault	Monza	1982
5	3	Carlos Pace	Brabham	Interlagos	1977
5	3	Gilles Villeneuve	Ferrari	Österreichring	1979
5	3	Jean Alesi	Tyrrell	Estoril	1993

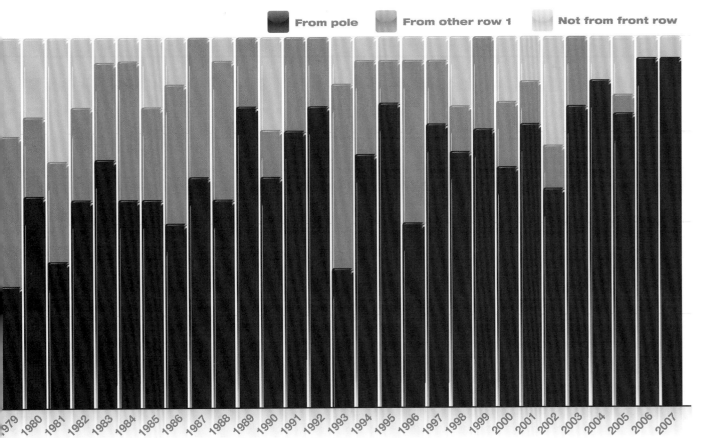

From pole　　　From other row 1　　　Not from front row

1979 1980 1981 1982 1983 1984 1985 1986 1987 1988 1989 1990 1991 1992 1993 1994 1995 1996 1997 1998 1999 2000 2001 2002 2003 2004 2005 2006 2007

A great deal is spoken about overtaking in today's Grand Prix racing – or, rather, the lack of it. This section should confirm the worst or bust the myth wide open!

The definition of a motor race is anything that involves two or more cars racing each other. All forms of racing, whether cars, horses or athletics involve speed, and the fastest competitor over the distance takes victory. Racing can be exciting without one competitor overtaking another for the lead, but the expectation is that the lead (and therefore victory) will be disputed by two or more participants, making it into a genuine contest and heightening the excitement for onlookers.

To evaluate the quality of the racing component in Grand Prix racing, a starting point is to obtain an overview that Graphic 8.8 effectively accomplishes. It shows that, of all the 774 Grand Prix races run between 1950 and 2007 (excl. Indy 500), two-thirds had two or three leaders – a favourable initial finding. The term 'race leader' applies to the car and driver leading at the end of each lap according to the official lap chart, and therefore ignores any other leader or lead change at any other point of the circuit during each lap. Likewise, one lap in the lead is enough to register as a race leader.

Graphic 8.9 studies the issue from a different standpoint. This time-series plots the number of race leaders each season from two perspectives. The first, the average number of race leaders per race, has hardly changed, rooted between two and three each year with very few exceptions. The second, the number of race leaders per season, varies considerably and differences coincide closely with changes in regulation, strikingly so in the 1950s and 1960s. Towards the centre of the graphic (1968–82) there is a period when there is quantifiable evidence of greater variety in race leadership over a season. This coincides with the period when the Ford Cosworth DFV engine was prolific and Formula One came close to being a single-engine formula.

Graphic 8.8 also showed that four or more leaders per race has been a comparatively rare occurrence. In fact, the largest number of leaders during a single Grand Prix race is eight (Graphic 8.10) and in total only 12 races have been run involving more than five leaders. Interestingly, the 1950s and 1980s are the only two decades not represented in this list, which includes some well-known weather-affected 'lotteries'. But perhaps most noteworthy is that one particular track features on numerous occasions: Monza.

The reason for this phenomenon is largely explained by

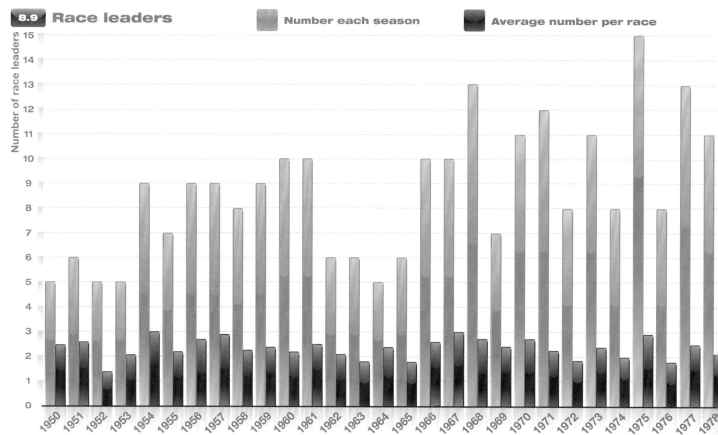

8.9 Race leaders   Number each season   Average number per race

the next Graphic (8.11), listing the races that have produced lead changes of more than 10, in which Monza again features repeatedly with no fewer than nine entries. The explanation for this, as well as the presence of tracks such as Reims, the AVUS and Hockenheim, is that these were high-speed circuits with long straights which lent themselves to the technique known as slipstreaming, where a following car can pick up a tow from the slipstream of the car ahead.

The lead car is effectively doing all the work of punching a hole in the air, allowing the car sitting tightly behind to be drawn along at the same speed for less work, saving some engine power and revs. The following driver then ducks out of the slipstream and uses his residual revs to make a pass towards the end of the straight. Slipstreaming races could involve numerous cars, and as many as eight diced for the lead at Monza in 1971. Because of the chopping and changing between race leaders and the uncertainty over the eventual outcome, they were invariably exciting events. This driving technique pretty much disappeared as Monza and other tracks were emasculated by chicanes in the early 1970s, change forced upon them for reasons of safety.

Graphic 8.12 traces the average number of lead changes per race over time. At first glance, the 1950s and 1960s look far busier than later decades. The very last Monza 'slipstreamer' was in 1971 and, for years before that, the passing and repassing there and at other slipstreaming circuits does inflate the incidence of lead changes very significantly. To account for this, a second set of figures is provided which excludes the slipstreaming races with 10 or more passes as listed in Graphic 8.11.

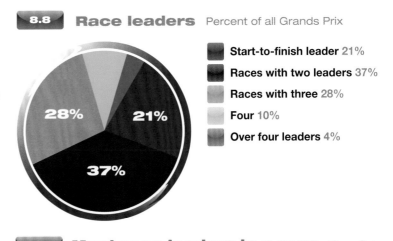

8.8 **Race leaders** Percent of all Grands Prix

- Start-to-finish leader 21%
- Races with two leaders 37%
- Races with three 28%
- Four 10%
- Over four leaders 4%

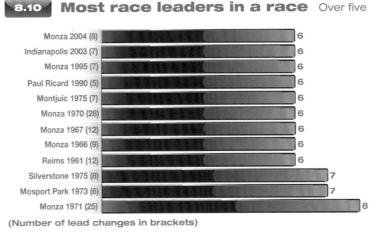

8.10 **Most race leaders in a race** Over five

Monza 2004 (8) — 6
Indianapolis 2003 (7) — 6
Monza 1995 (7) — 6
Paul Ricard 1990 (5) — 6
Montjuic 1975 (7) — 6
Monza 1970 (28) — 6
Monza 1967 (12) — 6
Monza 1966 (9) — 6
Reims 1961 (12) — 6
Silverstone 1975 (8) — 7
Mosport Park 1973 (6) — 7
Monza 1971 (25) — 8

(Number of lead changes in brackets)

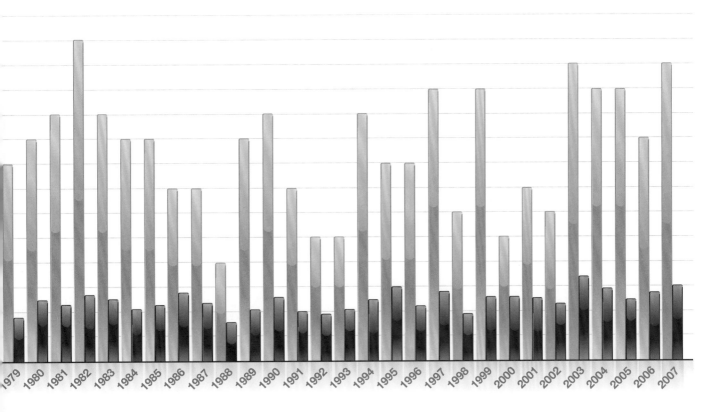

8.11 Most lead changes in a race 10 or more

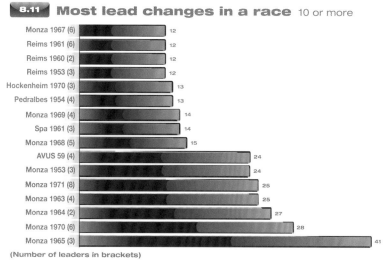

Monza 1967 (6)	12
Reims 1961 (6)	12
Reims 1960 (2)	12
Reims 1953 (3)	12
Hockenheim 1970 (3)	13
Pedralbes 1954 (4)	13
Monza 1969 (4)	14
Spa 1961 (3)	14
Monza 1968 (5)	15
AVUS 59 (4)	24
Monza 1953 (3)	24
Monza 1971 (8)	25
Monza 1963 (4)	25
Monza 1964 (2)	27
Monza 1970 (6)	28
Monza 1965 (3)	41

(Number of leaders in brackets)

The 1971 Italian Grand Prix – the greatest Monza slipstreamer of all time. There were eight race leaders, 25 lead changes and the first five were just a second apart, Peter Gethin's BRM in front.

Even after this adjustment, lead changes remain more pronounced in the earlier decades, although it does not follow that this is always due to bone fide on-track overtaking for the lead. Lead changes can occur for numerous reasons including unreliability (more prevalent in the 1950s) and also routine pitstops. The latter largely account for the rise in the incidence of lead changes from 1994, when pitstops were reintroduced having been banned since 1983.

The most recent upturn, in 2003, can be traced to the measures introduced by the FIA to mix up the grid using fuel strategy and penalties for a lack of engine reliability. Experimentation of this sort, as with attempts to find an

improved qualifying format, is laudable and worthwhile, as long as measures which do not work, or are no longer effective, are axed without compunction.

It is easy to sound critical when comprehension is the objective, but the rule mandating 'long-life' engines, required to last over two (or more) consecutive race meetings, reduces further the thrill of unpredictability in Grand Prix racing. Introduced primarily as a cost-cutting measure, it also creates bulletproof reliability, so removing engine failure as a source of uncertainty. Indeed, the constructors expend massive resources attempting to eliminate all forms of unpredictability, not only from the cars but also from the drivers through electronic 'driver aids' and pit-to-car communications that remind them constantly to warm up their brakes and tyres and so forth.

All of which makes the trend depicted in Graphic 8.13 hard to comprehend. It suggests that, despite all the measures to eliminate mechanical unreliability and driver error, the phenomenon of the lights-to-flag race winner is, against all expectations, actually declining. There have been only 15 instances across the eight seasons of the new millennium.

However, deeper investigation into the 139 races that have been run over that period reveals something rather different (Graphic 8.14).

The pie-chart shows that, although wins by a start-to-finish leader account for just 12 percent (appreciably less than the 21 percent for all Grand Prix races shown in Graphic 8.8), a further 34 percent of races would have been start-to-finish wins apart from the laps that the predominant leader failed to lead due to routine pitstops.

8.12 Changes of race leadership Average per race for each season

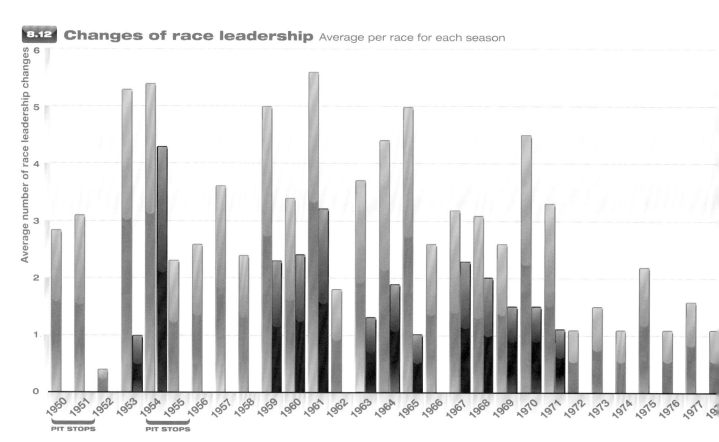

All races   All races excluding slip streamers

1979 1980 1981 1982 1983 1984 1985 1986 1987 1988 1989 1990 1991 1992 1993 1994 1995 1996 1997 1998 1999 2000 2001 2002 2003 2004 2005 2006 2007

PIT STOPS   PIT STOPS

This is usually for just a handful of laps, in many instances just the one, but it can be up to as many as a dozen or so depending on how the pitstop strategies unwind – particularly when the winner is on a totally different strategy from P2. Setting aside these normally short interruptions caused by routine pitstops, the effective proportion of lights-to-flag victories has virtually doubled against the mean since the nineties became the 'noughties'.

Of the 54 percent of races in which a meaningful change of leadership took place (Graphic 8.14), approximately half were due to a pass during a pitstop – leaving, of the 139 races this century, only 12 percent attributable to on-track overtakes. This figure would fall to 9 percent if four 'artificial' passes were excluded: two contrived Ferrari overtakes, and two when the leader was outdragged following a safety car period. But because of its rarity value, when it comes, the full-blooded overtake for the lead sears the memory forever. The best of the bunch since the turn of the century, to my mind, came on lap 41 at Spa in 2000. Approaching Les Combes, leader Michael Schumacher overtook the backmarker Ricardo Zonta on the left, while the hard-chasing Mika Häkkinen overtook the pair of them on the right: opportune, brave and skilful, such brilliance should always be a rare commodity.

Lead changes accomplished during routine pitstops create some level of excitement… will he, won't he come out ahead?… but it does not conjure the essential meaning of the word 'racing' in the same way as the on-track overtake. This ingredient explains the popularity of MotoGP, but to expect something similar from Formula

One racing every fortnight is unrealistic. Setting aside the obvious design and dimensional differences between the two types of vehicle, dynamically the MotoGP bike has far more in common with a Grand Prix car of the 1950s… skinny tyres, no aerodynamic downforce, low cornering power, longer braking distances… than any Formula One car since the Lotus 49B of 1969. This also applies to track performance, the bike being far inferior to the car. Formula One and MotoGP share a few tracks in their respective series and the comparative lap-times in 2006 make interesting reading:

FASTEST LAPS	FORMULA ONE	MOTOGP	PERCENT DIFFERENCE
Barcelona	1m 16.648s	1m 43.048s	34%
Sepang	1m 34.803s	2m 02.127s	30%
Istanbul	1m 28.005s	1m 52.877s	28%
Shanghai	1m 37.586s	1m 59.318s	22%

The percentage differences show how much slower a MotoGP bike is against a car over a racing lap: even Valentino Rossi would be lapped at least five times by a Formula One car during the course of a typical MotoGP race of 45 minutes. The majority of this performance differential will not be found on the straights but in the braking and cornering sections of the circuit. It is here

8.13 **Race leading variations by season** Percent of all races each season

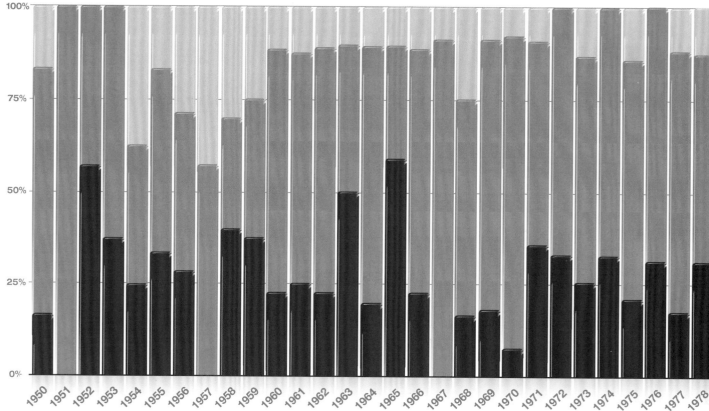

that the mistakes and accidents more usually occur and, in MotoGP, there are many unpleasant and painful-looking crashes.

A recent crash in Formula One that created a violent release of immense energy forces came during the 2007 Canadian Grand Prix at Montréal, when Robert Kubica suffered an enormous accident in his BMW Sauber. The development of Formula One aerodynamics and tyre technology since the late 1960s, with its commensurate and massive increase in cornering and braking power, put Grand Prix racing on an evolutionary path which can never emulate the form of racing seen in MotoGP, nor recapture the Formula One dicing of the 1950s.

If 21st century Grand Prix racing is felt not to offer enough spectacle for the onlooker, in the grandstand or on the TV sofa, only radical restructuring can truly address this issue. The FIA is currently engaged in juggling this in conjunction with its other key imperatives: safety, cost, environmental impact and manufacturer participation. For a transition period of three to five years, the solution might well be to operate a two-tier Formula One.

The better-funded manufacturer teams, willing and able to invest in the pursuit of 'green' technologies, could compete against the more cost-conscious teams (independents, 'customer' and B-teams) running traditional Formula One equipment. Competitive balance between these parallel technologies could be achieved through weight or fuel restrictions. A two-tier formula would not be new, operating at the beginning and towards the end of the turbo era… and producing some very effective racing.

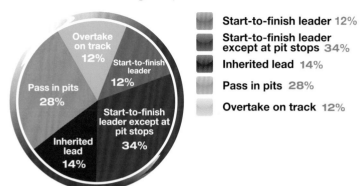

8.14 Overtaking versus passing!
Percent of all grand prix held from 2000

- Start-to-finish leader 12%
- Start-to-finish leader except at pit stops 34%
- Inherited lead 14%
- Pass in pits 28%
- Overtake on track 12%

Overtake on track 12%
Start-to-finish leader 12%
Start-to-finish leader except at pit stops 34%
Inherited lead 14%
Pass in pits 28%

Michael Schumacher, Ross Brawn and the Ferrari pit-crew perfected the 'pass in the pits', but not on this particular occasion (Spain 2005).

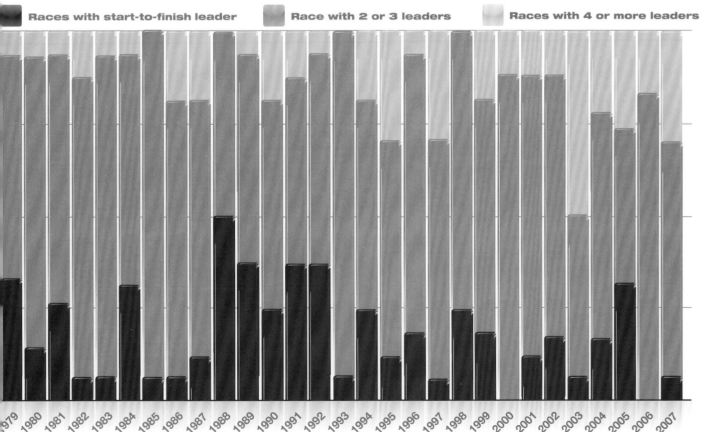

Races with start-to-finish leader   Race with 2 or 3 leaders   Races with 4 or more leaders

1979 1980 1981 1982 1983 1984 1985 1986 1987 1988 1989 1990 1991 1992 1993 1994 1995 1996 1997 1998 1999 2000 2001 2002 2003 2004 2005 2006 2007

A long with the eye-ball popping pole position lap, the cacophony of the grid start, the frenetic opening lap and a heart-stopping on-track overtake, another component of the Grand Prix race which makes the blood pump faster is a close finish… particularly if the hunted has been chased down by the hunter.

Although the on-track overtake for the lead may have become something of a rarity, finishes are generally far closer these days than at any time before. Before extolling the virtues of this trend, it is useful to define what constitutes 'a close finish' in Grand Prix parlance.

If we assume a 'typical' lap distance to be 5 kilometres, and a 'typical' lap-time to be 90sec, then a representative lap-speed is 200kph (120mph). At such a speed, a Formula One car is covering more than 50 metres in one second, equivalent to about 12 car-lengths. So if the winner crosses the finish line one second or 12 car-lengths ahead of the next, is that a close finish?

Not really!

As a 0.5sec winning margin is still an advantage of five car-lengths, it follows that a close Grand Prix finish does not really become electrifying until it is down to 0.1sec – around one car-length. Anything under that, and the cars are overlapping as they cross the line.

Now that is exciting!

But there have been precious few of them, as revealed by the tabulation opposite. This lists every Grand Prix race to finish within 0.3sec, commencing with that final Monza 'slipstreamer' when five cars crossed the line within 0.61sec, and Peter Gethin's BRM won by about 70cm (a couple of feet)!

This list contains some wonderful Grand Prix moments and memories, but there are some cuckoos in the nest, four of them painted red and relating to the 2002 season. Further comment would be superfluous!

Graphic 8.15 looks at Grand Prix win records in fuller detail, with more than 100 races (16 percent) finishing within a second or two. At the other extreme, with a not dissimilar number of 10 percent, the winning margin has been a minute or more!

These results also have their place in Grand Prix folklore. On 22 occasions, the winning driver has lapped the entire field, up to and including the second-place finisher. The names of drivers performing this feat contains the usual suspects, Fangio leading the way with three, this having been a far more frequent occurrence in the 1950s and 1960s.

The following tabulation gives the largest recorded winning margins. Only two drivers have ever lapped the entire field twice, Damon Hill being responsible for the most recent occurrence of this unusual happening.

8.15 Winning margin

Number of all Grand Prix finishes
<10 seconds by one second increments

Percent of all Grand Prix finishes by 10 second increments

YEAR	CIRCUIT	WINNER	VICTORY MARGIN
1958	Porto	Stirling Moss	5m 12.75s
1968	Nürburgring	Jackie Stewart	4m 03.2s
1958	Nürburgring	Tony Brooks	3m 29.7s
1957	Pescara	Stirling Moss	3m 13.9s
1969	Montjuïc	Jackie Stewart	2 laps
1995	Adelaide	Damon Hill	2 laps

Due naturally to their extreme lap distances, Pescara and the Nürburgring staged three of the longest winning margins on record, Jackie Stewart again to the fore. Stewart is only topped by the bizarre happenings at the 1958 Portuguese Grand Prix when Mike Hawthorn, almost a lap behind Stirling Moss but immediately ahead on the road, spun his Ferrari while completing his final lap, taking many minutes to regain the track.

Graphic 8.16 confirms that the winning margin has closed up massively and continually over the decades. In the first era of Grand Prix racing (1950–53), the time from winner to P2 was over a minute on average (62sec), and this happened in almost two-fifths of all the races (39.2 percent). Close finishes of less than 1sec were also a rarity – just two in fact (3.6 percent), and one of those was a team formation finish!

In the fourth era (1963–67), Jim Clark was virtually wholly responsible for bucking the steep trend down towards closer finishes, but since then it has gradually come down to under 10sec on average, and winning by a minute or more is virtually extinct. Not that winning by less than 1sec is that prevalent either (3.6 percent), and don't be fooled by the upturn in 2000–04 to 16.5 percent for close finishes.

From the evidence already provided in this chapter, the Ferrari family were toying with their opposition as much as they were toying with the punters who had laid down good money to watch them pretend to race. This was a dire era for Grand Prix racing and the FIA was right to curb team orders. Whether your delight is Grand Prix or gastronomy, a varied menu is normally preferred, and if not achievable race-to-race, then certainly year-to-year!

YEAR	CIRCUIT	HEADLINE	SEC
1971	Monza	Gethin edges out gang of four	0.01
2002	Indianapolis	Barrichello–Schumacher in staged dead-heat	0.011
1986	Jerez	Senna holds off Mansell's late charge	0.014
1969	Monza	Four-car slipstreamer to Stewart	0.08
1954	Reims	Formation Silver Arrows finish by Fangio & Kling	0.1
1961	Reims	Debutant Baghetti beats Porsche pair	0.1
1982	Österreichring	de Angelis holds nerve and racing line to deny Rosberg	0.125
2000	Montréal	Schumacher wins as Barrichello obeys orders	0.174
2002	A1-Ring	Schumacher's undeserved win from Barrichello	0.182
1955	Aintree	Fangio donates home win to Moss…or did he?	0.2
1967	Monza	Surtees outdrags sideways Brabham from Parabolica	0.2
1981	Jarama	Gilles Villeneuve leads five-car convoy across the line	0.211
1992	Monte Carlo	Mansell ducks and dives but Senna resists to win	0.215
2005	Imola	Alonso easily holds off closing Schumacher	0.215
1985	Zandvoort	Lauda and Prost play racing team tag	0.232
2002	Monza	Barrichello wins as 'Schu' makes amends for Austria	0.255
1990	Hungaroring	Boutsen frustrates Senna's challenge all the way	0.288
2002	Nürburgring	Barrichello wins as 'Schu' makes amends for Austria	0.294

8.16 Winning margin by era

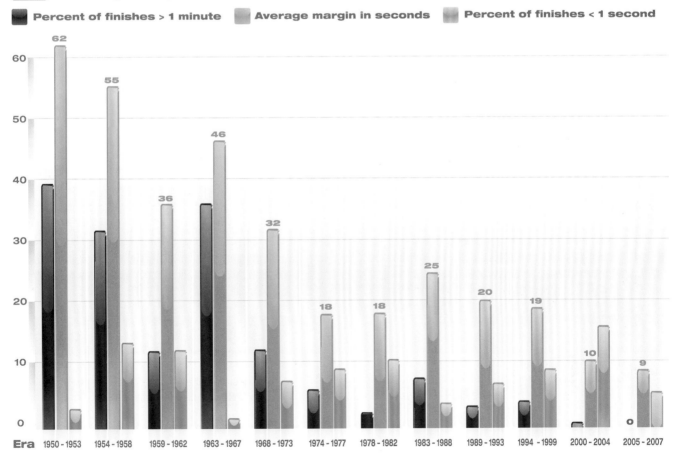

Percent of finishes > 1 minute   Average margin in seconds   Percent of finishes < 1 second

Era 1950 - 1953 1954 - 1958 1959 - 1962 1963 - 1967 1968 - 1973 1974 - 1977 1978 - 1982 1983 - 1988 1989 - 1993 1994 - 1999 2000 - 2004 2005 - 2007

Fastest lap

The Pampas Bull, Froilán González, streaks into a lead he is never to lose. At the 1954 British Grand Prix at Silverstone, his Ferrari 625 shared fastest lap with six others in 1min 50.000secs precisely!

Setting the fastest lap of the race has always held a certain cachet in Grand Prix racing. In part, this is because it received a significant weight of importance within the scoring system first adopted for the World Championship of Drivers. Between 1950 and 1959, an extra point was awarded to the driver achieving this, but not to each driver should two or more post the same time – the point had to be shared. Which is why, at the 1954 British Grand Prix at Silverstone, seven drivers were attributed with the fastest lap and each received 0.14 of a championship point!

It should be remembered that, back then, lap-timing was not electronic and to thousandths of a second, but by clockwork hand-held stopwatches – 'official' times agreed between multiple timekeepers, their thumb reflexes and their consciences! This still makes Silverstone 1954 hard to understand until the grid times are scrutinised. They are all to the nearest full second!

Either this was a pervading sense of realism of the limitations of the contemporary timing technology by the boys in blue blazers, or a complete cop-out. Wretchedly, it must be the latter. The grids for every other race that season were timed to one-tenth of a second. A good analogue stopwatch in the right hands could split seconds like peas!

Five pole positions, seven races led and three fastest laps – but never a winner. Chris Amon hustles the V12 Matra at the Nürburgring in 1972.

Most of the dozen instances of shared fastest laps inevitably occur in the 1950s and 1960s but the penultimate one was during the 1973 Brazilian Grand Prix, when timing was still being measured to one-tenth of a second. There is then a gap of 11 years until the next one, when Michele Alboreto and Nelson Piquet were both given identical times… to one-thousandth of a second. On lap 62 of 67, they both recorded the same time as they fought over second place, the former's Ferrari snatching the position on the final lap and finishing 1.011sec ahead of the Brabham-BMW.

As well as the championship point benefit, the fastest race lap has always been the opportunity for a driver to make his mark on a Grand Prix race meeting. The dominant can add the fastest lap to complete the grand slam: pole position, leading every lap, winning. The fancied runner out of the race prematurely due to some repaired mechanical malady can at least fire a warning of future intent. The dilettante or rookie can lay down a pointer for future reference.

The fact is that the fastest lap is not as conclusive a statistic as pole position – at least before fuel strategies intervened. There have been winning drivers who considered driving the fastest lap as a sign of lack of discipline, the mentality being that winning at the slowest speed, with its corresponding improvement in reliability, is the more intellectual, as well as the more challenging path to winning.

But the fastest race lap is the province of the Grand Prix winner. Over the 58 years of the sport, only 25 non-winners have posted the fastest lap, the most significant contributors being Chris Amon and Jean-Pierre Jarier – each with three! Seventy-five Grand Prix winners have amassed 96 percent of all fastest laps, but not necessarily when they were winning themselves.

Only 39 percent of the fastest laps have been recorded by the actual race winner (Graphic 8.17). This tallies with the example that opened this chapter, the anatomy of the 1951 German Grand Prix. Fangio, an inveterate race winner, could not win the race but, in his attempts to do so, he pushed hard enough, on lap 12 of the 20, to record the fastest lap of the race (Graphic 8.1). It follows therefore that, as its significance totally depends on the given circumstances, there is little merit in generalising any further about the statistic of fastest lap, although more will be added in the following chapter in relation to specific drivers.

8.17 Fastest laps

Fastest laps (including shared) as percent of all Grands Prix

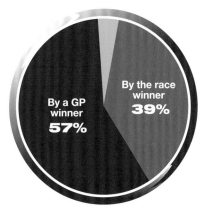

- **By the race winnner** 39%
- **By a GP winner** 57%
- **By a non-GP winner** 4%

By a GP winner **57%**

By the race winner **39%**

The next chapter – the final chapter – contains the culmination of this analytical journey across 58 years of results and information to discover the holy grail of Grand Prix racing: who is the greatest of all time?

Before this, there is one more important step to make. This is to focus in on facts and figures specific to the short-list from which the greatest will be chosen – the 'Magnificent Seven' (see Chapters 2 & 3). This penultimate chapter applies the 'winning ways' of the preceding chapter to these seven all-time greats to ascertain what can be learned about the way they went about their profession of winning.

How do their victory profiles contrast and compare? Is it possible to observe why Prost was 'the Professor', and Fangio 'the Maestro'?

To begin at the beginning: how early did these seven reveal their exceptional talents? And, if there are relevant ways to measure this, can the criteria be applied to the drivers of today to see if we already have a new phenomenon in our midst?

French driver (Alain Prost) in a French car (Renault RE30) at the 1981 French Grand Prix (Dijon-Prenois). It is also Prost's maiden victory – no wonder he looks elated as he sprays the French champagne.

hapter 7 revealed how elusive that first Grand Prix victory can be. Even serial winners such as Nigel Mansell (72 starts) and Mika Häkkinen (96 starts) served long, hard apprenticeships before they broke through and joined the winner's circle. So how about the magnificent seven? What can be learned from their record of early achievement that can establish the benchmark of signs of greatness for future Formula One generations?

The tabulation below examines a list of firsts for the magnificent seven – not just that initial race win, but also other primary indicators widely accepted as signalling something special: the first point, podium, pole and so on.

Although numerous caveats might be applied to the average figures, it is evident, taking them initially at face value, that the first World Championship point normally takes only a handful of races, and that the first time the podium is mounted is normally halfway through the first season (assuming a 16–19 race season).

On average, the first fastest lap, first race lead and first victory all come around the same mark – shortly before the completion of the first full (virtual) season. It should be noted that the average for fastest lap is from a far more scrabbled series of figures and that, in the past, the first race lead could happen ahead of the first win. The first pole position averages appreciably later but is highly influenced by a couple of inflated figures. In modern times a World Championship is unlikely to be landed much before the fourth or fifth season.

Setting aside Fangio's achievements as atypical on this occasion, the outstanding statistic across this comparison between the seven greats is Jackie Stewart's victory in only

his eighth Grand Prix start. What is more, he registered win number two just three races later, still sooner than any of the other five who took between 16 and 22 starts to win their first! In fairness to the others, Stewart did land a number-two seat with a team (BRM) of proven winners at the start of his career, rather like Lewis Hamilton, his stock sky-high as he made the transition to Grand Prix racing from the lesser formulae.

How do the similar credentials of 2007's leading lights compare?

It has taken the new World Champion a comparatively lengthy seven years to land his first world title, his two previous late-season challenges thwarted by Michael Schumacher (2003) and Fernando Alonso (2005). In most other respects Alonso shades Räikkönen in these early indicators of potential greatness, remembering also that each spent a learning season with one of the lesser teams on the grid, Alonso at Minardi and Räikkönen with Sauber. Neither enjoyed quite the level of schooling and grooming that Lewis Hamilton's closely managed career development has received, but Hamilton still had to deliver on the opportunity presented, and deliver he did.

Hamilton's figures speak for themselves, but few will ever forget the nine podiums in a row, starting with his F1 debut, and the achievement of winning from pole position on his sixth and seventh attempts! In his first F1 season, he held the Grand Prix world spellbound as he led the championship fight from round four in Spain right through the summer until the title shoot-out in Brazil five months and 13 races later. As it turned out, his destiny was not to become the first rookie World Champion, but in making claim to his own special niche in the record books, few will argue that Lewis Hamilton, with panache and style, repeatedly displayed true signs of greatness.

Few will argue that Lewis Hamilton, in an unprecedented rookie season, displayed the signs of true greatness.

NUMBER OF RACES TO ACHIEVE:

	FIRST POINT	FIRST PODIUM	FIRST FASTEST LAP	FIRST POLE	FIRST RACE LEAD	FIRST VICTORY	FIRST TITLE
JM Fangio	2	2	2	2	1	2	13
S Moss	11	11	12	22	18	22	N/A
J Clark	2	5	8	16	15	17	30
J Stewart	1	2	35	42	2	8	47
A Prost	1	14	27	21	19	19	71
A Senna	2	5	5	16	16	16	77
M Schumacher	2	8	18	42	18	18	52
AVERAGE	3	7	15	23	13	15	48
F Alonso	18	19	25	19	19	30	68
K Räikkönen	1	28	18	43	35	36	121
L Hamilton	1	1	2	6	1	6	N/A
F Massa	2	42	43	51	18	51	N/A

The tabulation that follows shows that there was some degree of overlap between the illustrious careers of the magnificent seven.

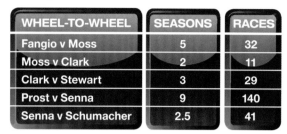

WHEEL-TO-WHEEL	SEASONS	RACES
Fangio v Moss	5	32
Moss v Clark	2	11
Clark v Stewart	3	29
Prost v Senna	9	140
Senna v Schumacher	2.5	41

For at least three of the five pairings, any detailed comparison, while amusing, would be academic rather than truly revealing. Generally speaking, when the former of the pair was at his zenith, the latter was negotiating the nursery slopes. But comparison for two of them is far more plausible, with one pair the most riveting of any on-track rivalry: Senna versus Prost.

Graphic 9.1 provides an extensive head-to-head comparison of the 140 races over nine seasons during which these two giants of the sport battled each other for supremacy. It may be a surprise to discover that the comparison is almost too close to call. There are many expected advantages for one over the other as well as some unexpected ones. But net–net, the difference is not great, and for wins – surely the conclusive arbiter – Prost is just ahead in the 140 races they both started, but vice versa in the 78 in which they both finished. However, within those 78 races, Senna and Prost, or Prost and Senna, finished 1–2 on 23 occasions.

The importance of this last statistic is that it discloses that Senna deprived Prost of victory on 16 occasions, whereas Prost denied Senna seven wins. Without Prost, Senna's win tally would have risen from 41 to 48, upping his strike rate from 25 to 30 percent. Similarly, if Senna had not turned up to spoil the party, Prost would have won an absolute minimum of 67 races (34 percent strike rate) and most probably many more had he remained at McLaren in 1990 – and so on.

When Senna began in Grand Prix racing, he was five years Prost's junior. Prost had already completed four seasons and was an established race winner and budding World Champion. Their nine seasons in direct competition lasted between 1984 and 1993, the one exception being Prost's sabbatical year of 1992. Essentially, there were three phases across the time that their two careers

9.1 Wheel-to-wheel: Prost v. Senna

Started 140 races together; both finished 78

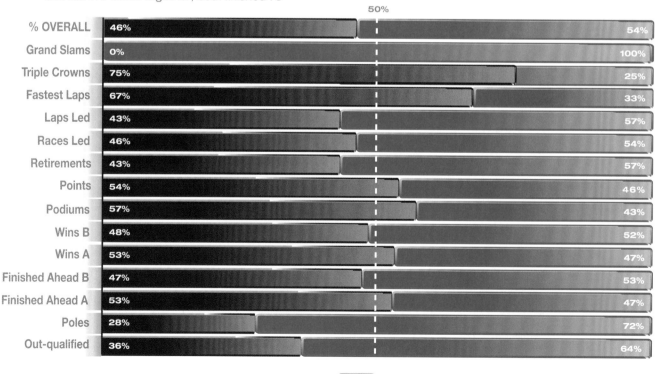

A = when both started   B = when both finished   **Percent Prost**   **Percent Senna**

corresponded. The first had Prost at McLaren while Senna completed his brief initiation on the nursery slopes with Toleman before moving to Lotus. The last was with Senna now ensconced at McLaren and with Prost switching to Ferrari and finally Williams. But the meat in this career sandwich was the two years they jointly spent as team mates at McLaren, when each won a World Championship.

Over those two seasons of 1988 and 1989, they started 32 races together in identical machinery, both finishing in 20 of them – the purest basis for assessment between two of the greatest drivers which has ever been possible before or since. Graphic 9.2 presents this very comparison and confirms, if there was any doubt, that although Prost was a worthy adversary, Senna creamed him. Graphic 9.2 shows that Prost was ahead only in terms of three incidentals: podiums, points and fastest laps.

Once again, the comparison of their Grand Prix victories is most telling, particularly in that, of the 20 races in which they both finished, Senna won 13 (72 percent) and Prost five (28 percent). When Senna beat Prost to the World Championship in 1988, he won seven times to Prost's five. But, remarkably, when Prost regained the title in 1989, only once did he beat Senna in a race in which they both finished! In all four of Prost's 1989 wins, Senna failed to finish, whereas Prost finished in all six of Senna's, next on the road in four of them. Such are the vagaries of a points-based championship, but the injustice of the system as it played out that year may in part explain why their relationship became so fractious.

As for the second pair who deserve comparison, it will be

of no surprise, particularly as Stirling Moss is on the record in acknowledging Juan Manuel Fangio's supremacy, that Fangio holds the upper hand. However, closer inspection suggests that it is by no means a one-sided verdict. One of their five seasons in competition must be discounted simply because Moss was just getting started in such machinery as HWM, ERA and Connaught, whereas Fangio enjoyed competitive machinery throughout.

Then, as team-mates at Mercedes-Benz in 1955, Moss certainly acquiesced to Fangio's number one status at least once, which would have made their wins ratio as team-mates 3–2 rather than 4–1. But perhaps most compelling is this statistic: Fangio and Moss started 32 races together but only both finished in 19 of them. Of those particular 19 results, the score for Grand Prix victories was… seven apiece.

Following Fangio's retirement, Moss made a highly successful transition to the rear-engined Formula One car. Over three seasons driving privately entered machinery, he frequently demonstrated his mastery of this format against superior works opposition from Cooper and Ferrari. However, wheel-to-wheel against Fangio, it has to be acknowledged that Moss was Fangio's equal at best, never truly his master. Likewise, although the overlapping careers of Prost and Senna are difficult to separate overall, their two seasons wheel-to-wheel at McLaren place Senna well ahead in this bitter rivalry.

On which evidence, in the final evaluation of the magnificent seven, it would be surprising to find Moss above Fangio, or Prost ahead of Senna.

9.2 **Wheel-to-wheel at McLaren: Prost v. Senna**
Started 32 races together; both finished 20

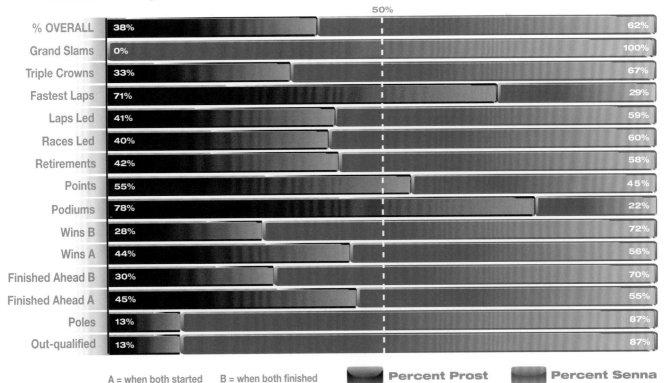

	Prost	50%	Senna
% OVERALL	38%		62%
Grand Slams	0%		100%
Triple Crowns	33%		67%
Fastest Laps	71%		29%
Laps Led	41%		59%
Races Led	40%		60%
Retirements	42%		58%
Points	55%		45%
Podiums	78%		22%
Wins B	28%		72%
Wins A	44%		56%
Finished Ahead B	30%		70%
Finished Ahead A	45%		55%
Poles	13%		87%
Out-qualified	13%		87%

A = when both started   B = when both finished   **Percent Prost**   **Percent Senna**

f you want to witness pole dancing at its finest, the place to visit is Monte Carlo for the Monaco Grand Prix. The topography and narrowness of that iconic race track, surrounded by unforgiving barriers, brings out something utterly spell-binding in just a handful of drivers: they make their cars dance. With a Monaco master at the wheel, that mesmerising 'body language' of a car on a quick lap turns into a salsa of speed.

Briefly down on its haunches, squirming under braking, then up on tip-toes to flick through a corner seeming to defy all rules of adhesion, the rear-end stepping out just a fraction to almost brush the barrier, skimming, wriggling, darting – all perfectly choreographed in a continuous blur of speed.

The greatest Monaco mambo was not actually a pole dance. It was Jochen Rindt's pursuit of Jack Brabham in 1970, when he pressurised the great Australian into an error in the final corner of the final lap, then sweeping through to a famous victory. During those closing laps, as Rindt began to scent an improbable victory, a panel of ballroom dancing judges would each have held up the 6.0 board for Rindt's display out of Casino and into Mirabeau, the Austrian and his Lotus dancing a quickstep of such lightness of touch as to make Fred and Ginger practise still harder.

The Monaco Grand Prix was not held between 1951 and 1954, so Fernando Alonso's 2007 pole was the 54th. It was his second pole, adding his name to the 'dirty dancing' dozen who have won the Monaco pole more than once:

MONACO GP	POLES	WINS
Juan Manuel Fangio	4	2
Stirling Moss	3	3
Jim Clark	4	0
Graham Hill	2	5
Jackie Stewart	4	3
Niki Lauda	3	2
Alain Prost	4	4
Ayrton Senna	5	6
Nigel Mansell	2	0
Michael Schumacher	3	5
Mika Häkkinen	2	1
Fernando Alonso	2	2
TOTAL	38 of 54 (70%)	33 of 54 (61%)

The eminence of the names on this list confirms that, first, pole position at Monaco is a very special achievement, and second, winning more than one pole marks out drivers of exceptional calibre. It seems uncanny that, over the 54 years of the Monaco Grand Prix, just 12 drivers account for 70 percent of all those pole positions. Inevitably, the magnificent seven feature strongly and the other five are all serial winners… bar just two.

The two serial winners who did not make the cut are still, nevertheless, Monaco pole men: Nelson Piquet (1981) and

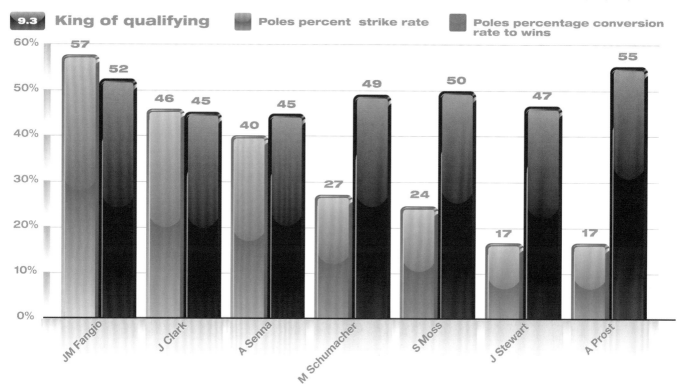

9.3 King of qualifying — Poles percent strike rate — Poles percentage conversion rate to wins

57 · 52 · 46 · 45 · 40 · 45 · 27 · 49 · 24 · 50 · 17 · 47 · 17 · 55

JM Fangio · J Clark · A Senna · M Schumacher · S Moss · J Stewart · A Prost

Damon Hill (1995). As for the two who usurped these serial winners with more than one pole apiece, one is Damon's dad, Graham, very much the Monaco specialist with two poles (and five wins!), the other Fernando Alonso, surely a serial winner in the making.

In the final analysis, if Monaco poles and Monaco wins mean something special – and clearly they do – then Ayrton Senna reigns supreme with more poles (five) and more wins (six) than any other. I repeat: than any other... And to think Senna handed one win to Prost in 1988 when he dropped it at Tabac with only 12 laps to go! But it is in those singular moments – when the near-superhuman exposes a human frailty – that the truly great show their true greatness.

So who is the king of qualifying? Surely Senna? Graphic 9.3 ranks the magnificent seven by their pole strike rate – the number of poles as a percentage of their number of race starts. But it is not Senna, nor even Jimmy Clark, in the 'pole position' of pole positions: it is Juan Manuel Fangio. Over his seven- to eight-year career, competing in 51 Grands Prix, Fangio stuck it on pole better than once every second race, 57 percent of the time. Clark comes next and Senna third, with Michael Schumacher and Moss around the one in four mark. Stewart and Prost complete the ranking but very much at the opposite extreme, taking pole roughly every sixth start (during which time Fangio, Clark or Senna might have snatched two or even three).

For these three, Fangio, Clark and Senna, even more astonishing are the margins by which pole position was won. The following tabulation lists each of their top 10 poles, led by the one with the greatest time gap to the driver beside them on the front row:

In 1950, Monaco was the second round of the new FIA World Championship. Fangio planted his Alfa Romeo 158 on pole a remarkable 2.6secs ahead of the next man. Skill or courage, or both? Take a look at the picture and decide!

TOP 10 POLE POSITIONS

JUAN FANGIO			JIMMY CLARK			AYRTON SENNA		
YEAR	CIRCUIT	MARGIN	YEAR	CIRCUIT	MARGIN	YEAR	CIRCUIT	MARGIN
1957	Pescara	10.1sec	1967	Nürburgring	9.4	1989	Suzuka	1.730
1956	Spa	4.9	1965	Nürburgring	3.4	1988	Monte Carlo	1.427
1954	Nürburgring	3.2	1967	Spa	3.1	1989	Phoenix	1.409
1951	Spa	3.0	1963	Reims	1.7	1991	Hungaroring	1.232
1957	Nürburgring	2.8	1963	Mexico City	1.7	1985	Detroit	1.198
1950	Monte Carlo	2.6	1966	Nürburgring	1.5	1989	Monte Carlo	1.148
1956	Buenos Aires	2.2	1968	Kyalami	1.0	1991	Phoenix	1.121
1953	Spa	2.0	1963	Nürburgring	0.9	1989	Monza	1.014
1950	Reims	1.9	1965	East London	0.9	1991	Spa	1.010
1951	Bremgarten	1.9	1964	Mexico City	0.86	1989	Hockenheim	1.006

Inevitably the respective 10sec and 9sec margins by Fangio and Clark catch the eye but, the Pescara and the Nordschleife lap distances being so much longer than Suzuka's, calculations are called for to ascertain how they each really compare. Fangio's Pescara pole was 1.758 percent quicker than the next man. At Suzuka, Senna went 1.76 percent faster – whereas Clark's margin at the Nürburgring was 1.98 percent. What a lap! In their fifth race together, Clark and the Lotus 49 really got into their stride. Despite the addition of the new Bremskurve (chicane), Clark's lap-time was fully 12.4sec faster than his own pole time from the previous year, which had been set in a 2-litre Lotus 33.

That pole lap of Clark's was his most dominant actually and proportionately, as was Senna's at Suzuka in 1989. Diligent digging divulges that Fangio posted three pole laps proportionately superior to his Pescara lap, two of which were also superior to Clark's best: 1950 Monaco (2.36 percent), 1956 Buenos Aires (2.146 percent on his home circuit), and 1956 Spa (1.96 percent). Therefore, from whichever approach, Fangio emerges as the qualifying king. Fangio and Clark mainly excelled on long road courses when inborn ability stood for everything compared with the '90-second circuits' which required a more passionate, aggressive, rhythmic approach.

Many of Senna's great poles were recorded during the 1988–89 seasons when, it seems, he was attempting to demoralise or humble Prost who was driving an identical car. Indeed, Prost was alongside on the starting grid in all except one of these occasions. They included two

of his six Monaco poles and, in contrast to Fangio and Clark, Senna's street-fighter qualities are apparent, with Phoenix and Detroit featuring with Monaco in many of his big 'pole' laps.

In 2006, his final season, Michael Schumacher relieved Senna of one of the few statistics not yet in his formidable haul. This was the longstanding record for the number of pole positions. Senna had made this record his own at Mexico City in 1989, when he had first edged ahead of Jim Clark's 33, which had been established way back in 1968. Senna had needed 10 more Grand Prix starts to reach Clark's record, but this was nothing compared with the additional races required by Schumacher to match Senna's.

Senna's 65 poles were accumulated over 161 Grand Prix races, whereas Schumacher took 235. Here again was proof positive that volumetric records have their place, but are potentially misleading unless qualified by other related information.

The second column in Graphic 9.3 shows the percentage conversion rate of poles to wins. To explain, although Prost only has a 17 percent strike rate (33 poles from 199 starts) compared with Senna's 65 poles from 161 starts (40 percent strike rate), Prost made slightly better use of the advantage, winning 18 times from his 33 poles (55 percent conversion) compared with Senna's 29 wins from 65 poles (45 percent). The percent pole-to-win conversion rate is very similar for all seven drivers at around 50 percent – confirming that starting from pole position by no means guarantees victory, but it sure helps!

The very different victory profiles for Prost and Stewart

Sadly the yellow helmet would not become a familiar sight in a Williams. But in Ayrton Senna's three outings for the team, he stuck the FW16 on pole every time. Here, at Imola, he takes his 65th and final pole.

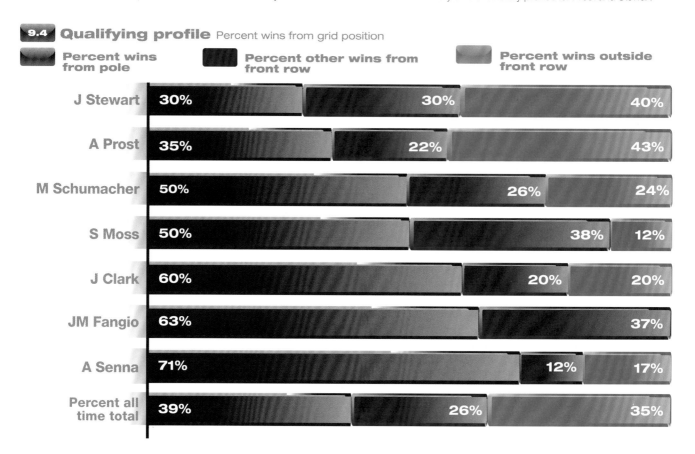

9.4 **Qualifying profile** Percent wins from grid position

	Percent wins from pole	Percent other wins from front row	Percent wins outside front row
J Stewart	30%	30%	40%
A Prost	35%	22%	43%
M Schumacher	50%	26%	24%
S Moss	50%	38%	12%
J Clark	60%	20%	20%
JM Fangio	63%		37%
A Senna	71%	12%	17%
Percent all time total	39%	26%	35%

are reaffirmed in Graphic 9.4, which compares each of the seven drivers with the all-time average of wins achieved from pole, the front row or elsewhere on the grid. The latter is remarkable in the cases of Prost and Stewart: 40 percent of their win tallies resulted from a starting position behind the front row.

For Prost – the Professor – such a profile might well be expected. He receives much credit for the guile and racecraft often used to win races by coming from behind, not relying

solely on sheer speed, although his ability in this respect should not be underestimated. But Stewart's low pole strike rate (17 percent) and high incidence of wins from outside the front row (40 percent) is more surprising, particularly when one remembers that Prost was often denied the pole – by Senna.

So Jackie Stewart's rather unexpected qualifying profile (Graphic 9.4) deserves deeper investigation to ascertain what more can be understood about the process of winning.

Scotland the brave

t is extraordinary that the seven most magnificent Grand Prix drivers of all time should include not one, but two hailing from Bonnie Scotland. In 1973, his final season, Jackie Stewart became the leading winner in Grand Prix history, claiming that mantle from fellow-Scot Jim Clark, who in turn had exceeded Fangio's total in 1968. No doubt Clark and Stewart were both equally proud of their Scottish birthright but Stewart, far more the showman, used his as part of the Stewart image, wearing the clan tartan as a badge of honour on his racing helmet. Once behind the wheel, Clark became highly assertive, winning 60 percent of his victories from pole position, exactly double Stewart's 30 percent (Graphic 9.4).

Indeed, as already noted, 11 of Stewart's total of 27 victories, a surprisingly high proportion of 40 percent, were achieved from behind the front row. The salient details of these 11 races are summarised in the table below.

Scrutiny of this tabulation reveals that there is very little similarity in style between Stewart and Prost in their mutual accomplishment of wins from outside the front row. Indeed, quite the reverse. When dealing with a less favourable grid position, Prost's 'Professor' reputation was built on a softly-softly approach, using racecraft to read the situation as the race unfolded, keeping in the hunt and then applying pressure at the right time.

Stewart's approach towards conjuring wins from lower grid positions was far more aggressive. In complete contrast, Stewart's success is down to fast starting, getting into the groove quickly, harrying those ahead, and then executing the coups de grâce swiftly before sailing off into the distance. The tabulation confirms this: the places quickly made up from a poor grid position, often within the first lap, the pass for the lead occurring within the early laps of the race, a high proportion of the race in the lead, the significant extent of the win margin. Even in the three races where, before going on to win, he inherited the lead from his P3/P4 grid slots, he had already elevated himself to P2 in the race where he could benefit from any ailments to the leader.

Graphic 9.5 analyses the circumstances of Stewart's 27 race victories. In almost half of them, he overtook (at least one other car) on track to lead and win; in nearly another third, he led from start to finish; and in the remaining quarter, he assumed the lead when another car or driver failed ahead of him. Although it is very easy to become defensive about inherited wins, the maxim 'To finish first, first you have to finish' has always been a fundamental part of Grand Prix racing.

There are numerous scenarios that by no means make the term 'inherited win' synonymous with 'lucky

9.5 Jackie Stewart race victories

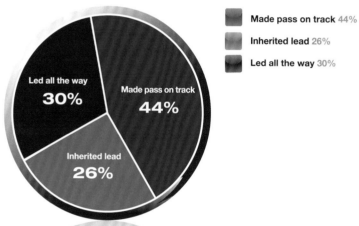

- Made pass on track **44%**
- Inherited lead **26%**
- Led all the way **30%**

Led all the way **30%**

Made pass on track **44%**

Inherited lead **26%**

Percent of all Stewart wins

YEAR	CIRCUIT	TRACK	GRID ROW	GRID POS	LAP 1 POS +/-	LAP TOOK LEAD	HOW TOOK LEAD	% OF RACE LED	FASTEST LAP?	WIN MARGIN (SEC)
1966	Monaco	Dry	2	3	+1	15	Inherit	86	No	40.2
1968	Zandvoort	Wet	2	5	+3	4	Pass	97	No	93.93
1968	Nürburgring	Wet	3	6	+5	1	Pass	100	Yes	243.2
1969	Kyalami	Dry	2	4	+3	1	Pass	100	Yes	18.8
1969	Montjuïc	Dry	2	4	-2	57	Inherit	38	No	2 laps
1969	Monza	Dry	2	3	+2	38	Pass	85	No	0.08
1971	Montjuïc	Dry	2	4	+2	6	Pass	93	No	3.4
1972	Clermont-Ferrand	Dry	2	3	0	20	Inherit	50	No	27.7
1972	Mosport Park	Dry	2	5	+3	4	Pass	96	Yes	48.2
1973	Kyalami	Dry	7	16	+6	7	Pass	92	No	24.55
1973	Zolder	Dry	3	6	-2	25	Pass	66	No	31.84

win'. True serial winners will all enjoy a slice of luck from time to time, but most of the time they make their own luck by pressuring the opposition into error or failure, and being in the right place to pick up the pieces. In any case, luck works both ways: where there is good luck, there is always bad luck to even things out.

So despite his modest pole position record, this case history points towards Stewart being a racer and a dominator, far more in harmony with the winning characteristics of his compatriot, Clark, than might first meet the eye. This similarity, or more accurately the dissimilarity with Prost's highly individual approach to winning races, is brought into even sharper focus in the following section, which compares even more extensively the differing styles of winning employed by the magnificent seven.

German Grand Prix, the Nürburgring, 1968. In terrible weather, Jackie Stewart won by more than four minutes.

Winning in style

For some, style is as important as results: it's not what you do, it's the way that you do it. For the competitively charged magnificent seven, winning came above everything: if not, they could never have reached such heady heights. Although style was not their motivation, differentiating between the manner in which each went about the process of winning is still highly compelling.

Frequency of winning was the way each held on to his status as the man to beat, but race domination was the means to that end, a sort of 'catch me if you can' mentality. And the best way to dominate a motor race is from the front – leading and going away from the opposition.

Graphic 9.6 illustrates the 'leading' part of it. There are three bars for each driver. The first gives the percentage of races led over their career. So Fangio heads the rest with a formidable 75 percent and Prost brings up the tail with 42 percent. The third bar is the career percentage of race distance led, in Fangio's case 41 percent. The bar in the middle is the ratio between the two, Fangio's 55 index being higher than Prost's 50 – the higher the index, the more distance completed per races led. Clark's index of 62 stands out from the crowd, and this specific graphic begins to add authenticity to the reputations these great drivers established: why Clark was known as the Flying Scotsman, Fangio as the Maestro and, for that matter, why Prost was called the Professor. But there's more!

Thirty-two percent of Clark's wins were by a margin of one minute or more (Graphic 9.7) and, across all of them combined, his winning margin averaged 50sec, exceeded only by Moss's 63sec (which is exaggerated from 46 by Hawthorn's five minute lap-time at Porto in 1958).

Then Graphic 9.8 adds another layer to the myth of Clark's magic, because 52 percent of his victories were flag-to-flag runaways. To repeat: the best way to dominate a motor race is from the front – leading and going away from the opposition. Clark was the great dominator, but not in that intense, brooding way that Senna needed to dominate. Clark's domination contained a certain *joie de vivre* because his superiority was so effortless. His race domination had no intent to destroy others, he did it because he simply couldn't help it… he was that good. He revelled in driving a car exceedingly quickly because it was his innate comfort zone, his natural environment. He was doing what he did best and taking pleasure from it.

An expression of that pleasure – the vitality Clark brought to winning – can be seen from another figure from Graphic 9.8. In 72 percent of his winning races, he posted the fastest lap of the race, not because he had to, but because he was in his element: driving a Formula One racing car very fast with a silky deftness of touch which was the epitome of winning in style.

To complete Clark's 'victory profile', it might even be said that he lost in style, too, because many of his non-finishes occurred when he was out there in front. Graphic 9.9 shows that, in 13 percent of the races he started, he retired his Lotus from the lead. Team Lotus was renowned for fast but fragile cars, and Clark would have had to accept the rough with the smooth. That said, if the races in which he dropped out while leading were to be added to his record of wins, his strike rate would rise to 47 percent, right up there with Fangio.

Insulating himself from the July Silverstone chill with a heavy-knit sweater is hardly stylish, but inside the car Jim Clark simply radiated style. His fourth British Grand Prix win, in 1965, produced the headline 'Can't go (Clark with engine problems) beats can't stop (Hill with failing brakes)'.

9.6 **Race dominance index** Percent distance led percentaged on percent races led

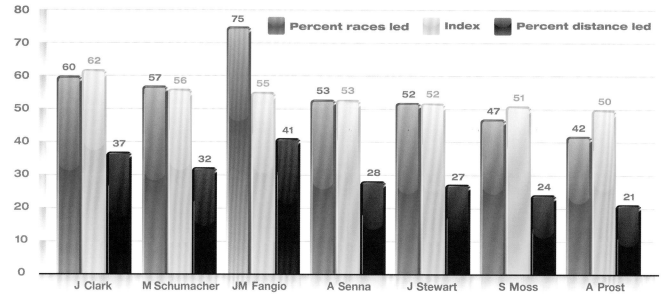

Chart legend: **Percent races led** · **Index** · **Percent distance led**

Data by driver:
- J Clark: 60, 62, 37
- M Schumacher: 57, 56, 32
- JM Fangio: 75, 55, 41
- A Senna: 53, 53, 28
- J Stewart: 52, 52, 27
- S Moss: 47, 51, 24
- A Prost: 42, 50, 21

9.7 **Winning margin**

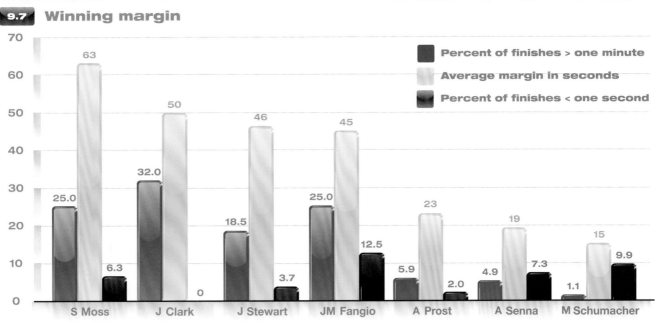

	Percent of finishes > one minute
	Average margin in seconds
	Percent of finishes < one second

	S Moss	J Clark	J Stewart	JM Fangio	A Prost	A Senna	M Schumacher
Percent of finishes > one minute	25.0	32.0	18.5	25.0	5.9	4.9	1.1
Average margin in seconds	63	50	46	45	23	19	15
Percent of finishes < one second	6.3	0	3.7	12.5	2.0	7.3	9.9

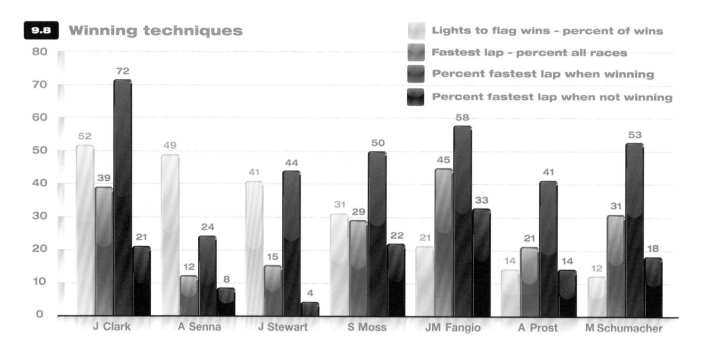

Winning techniques

- Lights to flag wins – percent of wins
- Fastest lap – percent all races
- Percent fastest lap when winning
- Percent fastest lap when not winning

J Clark: 52, 39, 72, 21
A Senna: 49, 12, 24, 8
J Stewart: 41, 15, 44, 4
S Moss: 31, 29, 50, 22
JM Fangio: 21, 45, 58, 33
A Prost: 14, 21, 41, 14
M Schumacher: 12, 31, 53, 18

Monaco, 1959. Jean Behra's Ferrari Dino 246 dwarfs Moss's pole-sitting Cooper T51. On the 81st of 100 laps, Stirling retired from the lead with transmission failure.

Moss also suffered inordinately from the slings and arrows of outrageous fortune, with appreciably the worst finishing record of any of the seven (Graphic 9.9). Moss created considerable frustration among his followers, frequently dropping out from the lead or when well placed with 'gearbox trouble', and then resuming to post the fastest race lap, his statement of what might have been. There was even press speculation that Moss was too heavy-handed with his gearbox, in other words an instrument of his own destruction. His apparently 'relaxed' driving style – steering wheel at arm's length, head back – makes such an allegation hard to accept, but only Alf Francis knows the truth!

And finally, in a section entitled 'Winning in Style', how do the grand slams and triple crowns – the ultimate expressions of superiority over or contempt for the opposition – compare? Here, a 'triple crown' is to win from pole and post the fastest lap, and a 'grand slam' is to record a triple crown and also lead every lap of the race.

In Graphic 9.10, based on percentages of wins, Clark's 32 percent for grand slams towers above the rest, a quite extraordinary statistic. Although it is assisted by the fact that Clark raced at a time when pitstops were not a feature of the racing, surely this figure, and how it compares with the other six great drivers, is highly telling in the search for ultimate greatness?

9.9 **Luck... or judgement?**

- Percent retirements from lead
- Percent other non-finishes

9.10 **Grand slams & triple crowns**

- Percent grand slams
- Percent triple crowns

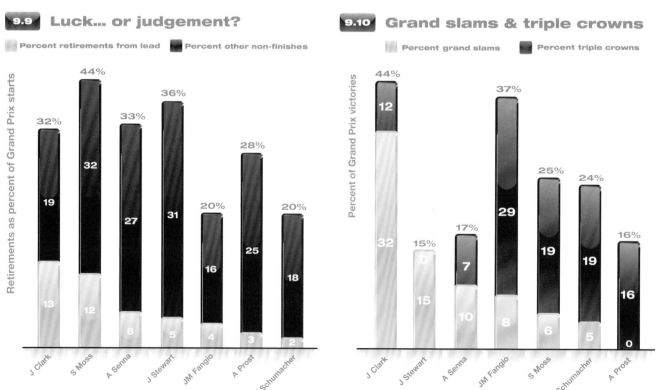

Retirements as percent of Grand Prix starts

J Clark: 32% (19, 13)
S Moss: 44% (32, 12)
A Senna: 33% (27, 6)
J Stewart: 36% (31, 5)
JM Fangio: 20% (16, 4)
A Prost: 28% (25, 3)
M Schumacher: 20% (18, 2)

Percent of Grand Prix victories

J Clark: 44% (12, 32)
J Stewart: 15% (0, 15)
A Senna: 17% (7, 10)
JM Fangio: 37% (29, 8)
S Moss: 25% (19, 6)
M Schumacher: 24% (19, 5)
A Prost: 16% (16, 0)

Victory profiles

By now, a portrait is emerging for each of the magnificent seven, but it is still blurred, not fully defined. Sharper focus and clarity comes from Graphic 9.11, which consolidates seven of the measurements for each driver used in the earlier sections of this chapter.

Using a radar chart to present these statistics creates a geometric shape which can be called a driver's 'victory profile'. As the identical scale has been used for all seven drivers, direct comparison between each profile is possible.

The profiles each include three sets of figures. First, there are the seven profile measurements (gold zone). Next, the profile rankings (purple heptagon), which attribute the number 1 to 7 to each profile measurement in descending order for each driver. For example, Fangio has the highest wins profile (47 percent) and receives ranking number 1, Schumacher is second (37 percent) and is ranked 2, and so on. Finally, the blue disk in the centre is the average of the profile rankings, Clark averaging 1.9 at one extreme and Prost 4.9 at the other.

The size and shape of each profile and this central average ranking number tell the story. Fangio and Clark have appreciably the largest profile and the lowest average ranking. Clark's profile shape is the most rounded,

9.11 Victory profiles

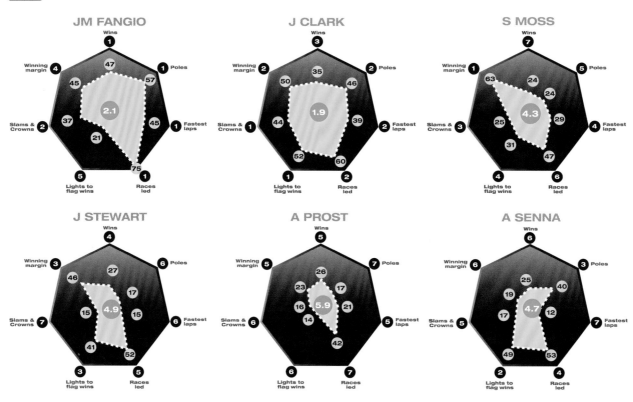

Profile rankings

Profile measurements

Average profile rankings

Wins; Poles; Fastest laps; Races led = % of starts

Lights to flag wins; Slams & Crowns = % of wins

Winning margin = seconds

ranking highest in his speciality of leading all the way. Fangio features more strongly with poles and leading races, his weakest ranking being lights-to-flag wins. Does Fangio's less rounded profile suggest that Clark was the more complete driver?

Four drivers have an average ranking of 'four-point something': Schumacher, Moss, Senna and Stewart.

Like Fangio, Schumacher is more strongly ranked down the right-hand side of his victory profile, whereas Moss's best rankings are perhaps tilted more to the left. Senna and Stewart have profiles of rather similar size and shape, except that Stewart kicks to the left with a strong win margin, and Senna to the right to reflect his pole positions speciality. For Senna, the most unexpected feature of his profile is the low figure for fastest laps – a mere 12 percent and ranking last of the seven. This suggests, perhaps, that he did not see this as part of his victory armoury in the way the others did.

Finally, Prost's profile is quite well rounded but rather small, all his rankings being 5, 6 or 7. For sure, his approach differed from the others. Does an average of 5.9 confirm his status as last among his peers?

Of course not! The victory profiles (Graphic 9.11) are an amusing, even interesting way to try to understand and appreciate measurable differences and distinctions between the seven greatest Grand Prix winners the World Championship has yet seen. But as a method to ascertain who between them was the greatest winner, the proposition is seriously flawed. For example, some of the characteristics evident in the profiles of the individuals are a reflection of the prevailing characteristics of the times, most obviously win margins. Also, the choice of criteria can make an inordinate difference. If winning from behind the front row, or the conversion of poles to wins, was given precedence, Prost, ranked first in both of these, would do significantly better overall.

No, the contents of Graphic 9.11 may at least offer an improvement over the obtuse conclusion: 'Schumacher is the greatest because he won more races than anyone else.' But to crown one of the seven as the greatest, it will take the application of more appropriate measurements and more scientific techniques. It is important not to rush to judgement too soon, and simply allow victory profiles to add some light and shade to the more significant overall conclusions which follow in the final chapter.

The 2006 Chinese Grand Prix at Shanghai was Michael Schumacher's 91st and final victory.

A contentious title for a controversial closing chapter? Perhaps, but not with the intention of being deliberately provocative. It is contentious only in a sense of encouraging debate.

The greatest? It is a topic that is the province of every sport, not least Formula One. Whether in the pit-lane or the pub, all those afflicted by Formula One fever are habitually prepared to give sway to their opinion and join the chattering classes when this topic arises.

This chapter is the culmination of a lifetime ambition that has involved a three-year journey. Although what is being attempted here may well prove to be contentious, the sheer endeavour of this project stands as a testament to the sincerity of the study. It is, after all, a labour of love in appreciation of a passion which has lasted 50 years, a love affair with the greatest sport in the universe, the first stirrings having been inspired in 1957 by the heroics of Stirling Moss, Tony Brooks and Vanwall.

The hope remains that, in another 50 years, and well into the next century, the 2007 Formula One World Championship may invoke the same sentiments inspired, perhaps, by the deeds of Lewis Hamilton, Fernando Alonso and the McLaren team.

It may seem bizarre, but the entry point to Chapter 10 happens to focus on… heavyweight boxing.

His cup floweth over. Flanked by Tony Brooks and Stirling Moss, Tony Vandervell raises the victor's trophy at Aintree in 1957 to celebrate the first World Championship Grand Prix win by a British car, his delight heightened by the fact that it was with British drivers at the British Grand Prix.

Greatness

That great boxing icon, Muhammad Ali, takes credit for providing some of the inspiration for this book. Anyone alive to the sporting scene of the 1960s and 1970s would not be oblivious to the extraordinary career of the 'Louisville Lip', in and out of the ring. In 1970, there was a televised simulation broadcast to decide the greatest heavyweight champion of all time. The subjects were Ali and Rocky Marciano. In 1956, 'The Rock' had retired as the one and only undefeated heavyweight World Champion with an astonishing 88 percent knockout rate.

Ali was the self-proclaimed 'greatest' but had authenticated his claim by winning the crown as Cassius Clay, from Sonny Liston in 1964. After a triumphant rematch, he then followed up with a succession of successful title defences, dismissing opponents with typical, yet endearing, disdain. "A bum a month", he called them. At the time the authorities stripped him of his title, in 1967 for refusing military service (and most likely a drafting to Vietnam), he remained undefeated.

The Marciano versus Ali 'super fight', as it was branded, may well have been stage-managed, but it was compulsive viewing just the same. Apparently, neither contender knew what the outcome would be when they had agreed to play a role in the event. They

"I am the greatest". That was Muhammad Ali's mantra. But when 'matched' against former undefeated champion Rocky Marciano, his claim proved hollow.

had sparred together over 70 to 75 rounds, enacting various scenarios, but, at the final bell, a computer would judge the outcome. A multitude of statistics about these two great careers – from different eras – had been programmed to establish the likely run of events. Punch-by-punch details of each boxer's records during their prime were entered: strengths, weaknesses, fighting styles and many other factors – all converted into algorithms.

In the projected 15-round bout, Marciano was declared the winner, having stopped Ali in round 13. The computer decided that Marciano's crouching, relentless aggression and unremitting stamina, coupled with his huge strength and the power of those round-armed, bone-jarring body punches, would ultimately have overcome Ali. Ali boxed and jabbed and danced and taunted and landed those devastating combinations, showing his own remarkable strength and stamina – of the mind as much as the body – but it was not quite enough. Marciano was the champion of champions.

Was I happy with the result of this great showdown? Absolutely yes. A genuine and most plausible attempt had been made to answer a question which fascinates any lover of sport.

Who is the greatest of them all?

Would Perry have beaten Sampras? How good would Stanley Matthews be by today's standards? Tiger Woods versus Jack Nicklaus? What about Warne bowling to Bradman?

Clearly some sports by their nature lend themselves to the debate more than others. Those which produce a World Champion, where one individual emerges periodically to be claimed as 'the best', are likely to feature more frequently in such debate. Another ingredient has to be that the sporting arena concerned must be regarded as the pinnacle of that sporting discipline. In 1970, heavyweight boxing certainly had all these facets.

Despite the shortcomings of the heavyweight division today, a worthy heavyweight champion is still a personality of world renown. There is an interest far beyond just the immediate sporting one. It is a primeval curiosity which harks back even further than Greek and Roman gladiatorial combat more than 2000 years ago. Great interest and appeal is sustained because the process, the very human endeavour of becoming the heavyweight World Champion, renders up from time to time an individual who is extraordinary in the true sense of the word, and so the legend perpetuates.

The greatness of Marciano and Ali is carried forward and enhanced by those who follow, who may also touch greatness. Time will place Mike Tyson and Lennox Lewis in their true perspective, but their exploits have kept the great names of the past fully alive. To be discussed long after your time, or even your lifetime, as 'the best of the best' – that truly is the mark of greatness.

But is greatness measurable?

In Formula One a swift surf on the internet reveals numerous approaches to ranking drivers. These originate from all parts of the world, Russia included, but inevitably it is only the French ones, such as *Statistiques des Pilotes*, which do not provide an English translation! Some may be rapidly dismissed as having little merit – when, for example, González is ranked ahead of Clark, or Montoya above Lauda! Many others are obviously based on the World Championship points system or a points system derived from race placings, fastest laps and so forth, where inevitably some driver records show up more favourably than others.

Nothing wrong with that, but it depends on the goal. What specific driver virtues is one setting out to assess? The fastest, the most successful, the most gifted, the most complete, the greatest racer, and so on? Some of these driver qualities can only be measured empirically, whereas a ratings system of any consequence must be fact-based. So the objective is always constrained by what is factually measurable.

Chapter 2 ('Serial Winners') set out to establish that the winning of races is an appropriate and effective factual measure on which to assess driver performance. Winning is the be-all and end-all of the Grand Prix motor race. Everything else is incidental – except occasionally, very occasionally, when the strong promise of championship points has made a driver decide that discretion is the better part of valour.

To clinch his second World Championship title in 1983, and leading the final round at Kyalami, Nelson Piquet turned down his turbo 'boost' pressure, and along with it the opportunity to win the race, on receiving news that his sole remaining rival for the title, Alain Prost, had retired from the race. Piquet knew that a comparatively safe third place, or even a fourth, would be enough. But such behaviour is the exception, not the rule. Even with today's inequitable points system, faced with a genuine opportunity for Grand Prix glory, few can resist the challenge of going for victories despite the attendant risk of losing everything. (Lewis Hamilton please note.) And whether they come easy or hard, it is the winning that matters, not the way they are accomplished. Whether from pole position or after driving the fastest lap, whether by overtaking on the track or during a pitstop, whether on merit or as the result of another's mistake or failure – however victories are earned – they all count.

Chapter 2 moreover verified that percent strike rate is a simple yet elegant way to compare race winners across different eras. Strike rate therefore provides a sound foundation on which to build a ratings system because, by extension, the greatest Grand Prix winner is more than probably the greatest Grand Prix driver.

The function of the ratings system, therefore, is to adjust strike rate by the prevailing circumstances of each victory, so that it accurately reflects true performance – one driver relative to another – regardless of a winner's epoch.

Chapter 2 also identified that only seven drivers have attained a strike rate of more than 20 percent and, also, have been victorious over a sustained period of time (at least five years). These seven – our Magnificent Seven – are:

	STRIKE RATE	STRIKE RATE INDEX
Juan Manuel Fangio	47%	100
Michael Schumacher	37%	79
Jim Clark	35%	74
Jackie Stewart	27%	57
Alain Prost	26%	55
Ayrton Senna	25%	53
Stirling Moss	24%	51

A few years ago, respected Grand Prix reporter and columnist Mark Hughes wrote on this subject in *Autosport*. At the time, Michael Schumacher's win tally stood at 83 from 204 starts, with his still-rising strike rate registering over 40 percent. Hughes began by making a simple linear extrapolation based on percent strike rate which revealed that: "Only two post-war Grand Prix stars, Fangio and Ascari, would beat Schumacher's extrapolated win tally." Hughes then took the proposition further: "What if we now incorporate a loosely scientific measure of the competitiveness of the cars everyone drove throughout their careers." And later: "If we combine this with the calculated wins based on 204 starts each, we get a machinery-adjusted/start-adjusted list that should, in theory, be fairly representative of merit, and it looks like this:

Schumacher	83 wins
Ascari	73 wins
Fangio	68 wins
Clark	58 wins
Stewart	52 wins
Senna	47 wins
Prost	45 wins
Moss	41 wins

"Doh, Michael is on top again!"

Although amusing, the (Simpsons-punctuated) tag-line with which Hughes chose to end his piece was a trifle anti-Schumacher in sentiment. This could probably be excused due to 'dominance fatigue'. Hughes had begun his article: "Almost every time Michael Schumacher stepped into the car last year, he broke an all-time record – usually his own." For Formula One followers the world over, the 2004 season had amounted to watching a Ferrari/Schumacher/Bridgestone steamroller at work: remarkable, but not riveting racing action.

Nevertheless, the article pinpointed the key issue that needs to be addressed in any valid comparison between Grand Prix winners past and present: how much the car, how much the driver? Chicken or egg?

Chicken or egg?

rank Williams never had the slightest doubt. It is known that he regards drivers as employees, a remunerated member of staff at WilliamsF1. The company's previous name was Williams Grand Prix Engineering and it seemed to convey that, in his and Patrick Head's opinion, engineering lies at the heart of winning races. The driver, of course, is an essential and important element towards ultimate success, but secondary to the requirement of producing superior machinery to beat the opposition.

This notion follows along the lines that a good driver can rarely win with a dog of a car. But produce a great car, and a driver of modest ability can succeed. Even the great drivers have had to come to terms with this reality, not least Schumacher in his bleak 2005 season. Ayrton Senna recognised it when, during the 1992 season, he offered to drive the 1993 Williams FW15C without recompense, such was the magnitude of its latent technological superiority.

With championship success at stake, the relationship between team owner and driver is a fundamental and thrilling tension at the very soul of the sport. On the one side, powerful, self-made men with supreme entrepreneurial and leadership skills. On the other, highly talented virtuosos with prodigious personal ambition. On both sides, massive egos at stake. The mix can often lead to the development of a type of love-hate relationship.

Most recently, regard the relationship between Ron Dennis, Fernando Alonso and Lewis Hamilton that ebbed and flowed during 2007, each aware that any two could destroy the ambition of the third.

This is not to say that Williams and Dennis do not recognise the worth of a 'superstar' driver. A good driver/car combination can win races, but a great driver in a great car can win championships. This also accounts for a certain inevitability that the best drivers normally migrate to the best cars, so as to perpetuate their mutual success. Despite the shared success of Williams, Renault and Nigel Mansell in 1991–92, Frank Williams did not hesitate, when the opportunity arose, to add Alain Prost to his driving line-up for the 1993 season, even though it resulted in the loss to the team of his then reigning World Champion, Mansell.

To make progress on the chicken–egg poser, the starting point is the identification of irrefutable occurrences when cars have displayed high levels of dominance, demonstrably surpassing the influence of the driver ingredient. For this purpose, it is worth revisiting a graphic from Chapter 6, repeated here as Graphic 10.1. It shows the teams that have dominated a season, listing the occasions when a single marque has claimed over 50 percent of the wins.

Of the 31 seasons listed, which accounts for about half of all the World Championships to date, seven seasons

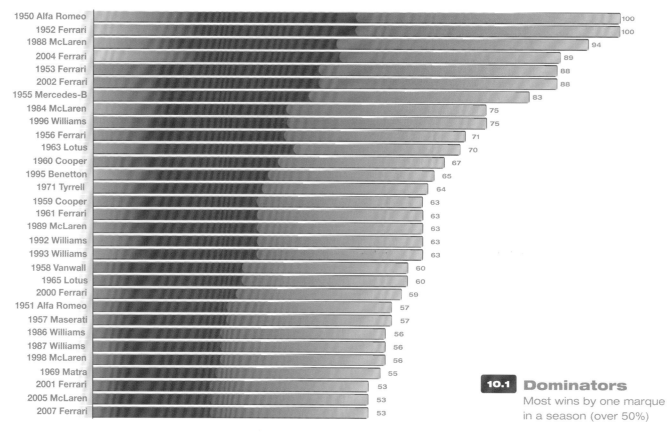

Year/Team	Value
1950 Alfa Romeo	100
1952 Ferrari	100
1988 McLaren	94
2004 Ferrari	89
1953 Ferrari	88
2002 Ferrari	88
1955 Mercedes-B	83
1984 McLaren	75
1996 Williams	75
1956 Ferrari	71
1963 Lotus	70
1960 Cooper	67
1995 Benetton	65
1971 Tyrrell	64
1959 Cooper	63
1961 Ferrari	63
1989 McLaren	63
1992 Williams	63
1993 Williams	63
1958 Vanwall	60
1965 Lotus	60
2000 Ferrari	59
1951 Alfa Romeo	57
1957 Maserati	57
1986 Williams	56
1987 Williams	56
1998 McLaren	56
1969 Matra	55
2001 Ferrari	53
2005 McLaren	53
2007 Ferrari	53

10.1 Dominators
Most wins by one marque in a season (over 50%)

tower above the rest: a pair of 100 percent clean sweeps by Alfa Romeo in 1950 and Ferrari in 1952; the 94 percent achieved by McLaren-Honda in 1988; Ferrari once more with 88 percent in 1953 and again in 2002; and finally the 83 percent attained by Mercedes-Benz in the bitter-sweet 1955 season, a figure equalled by Ferrari in 2004.

In each of these seven notable seasons, much of the winning was accomplished by one or more of the magnificent seven who, along with Alberto Ascari in 1952 and 1953, are already acknowledged to be superlative winners: Juan Manuel Fangio, Stirling Moss, Alain Prost, Ayrton Senna and Michael Schumacher. The challenge, therefore, is to deduce what fact-based information can be enlisted to separate out whether these outstanding winning sequences had more to do with the car than with their outstanding driving skills – or vice versa.

One clue towards the type of information that can produce irrefutable evidence of car superiority is 'the old one–two'. When not just one but both team cars cross the line ahead of allcomers, not only does it signify a pulverising defeat for the opposition, but it also sends the clear message that the car had more to do with the winning than the driver. In other words, if the winner had faltered during the race, another car from the same stable would still have claimed victory. By the same token, when the lead driver in a successful season does falter, for whatever reason, a win by the second driver is another sure sign that car performance has a greater influence on success than the dominant driver per se. The marque, or team, has still been capable of winning even when the more successful team driver is unable personally to deliver that victory.

The absolute share of wins, and the incidences of 1–2s and second-driver wins, can begin to fuse a series of overlapping indicators which highlight car superiority. But that is not all. In addition to absolute share, another strong measure is relative share. Compare two of the three teams at the bottom of the list of dominators (Graphic 10.1), each with an absolute share of 53 percent – an impressive team strike rate. Were Ferrari in 2001 and McLaren in 2005 equally dominant, therefore?

On the face of it, yes. But not when the share of the second most successful team that season is related. In 2005, this was Renault with a win share of 42 percent, a comparison that suggests that McLaren was rather less dominant than its 53 percent absolute share of wins may suggest in isolation. As is known, apart from Schumacher's bizarre and unrepresentative Bridgestone-shod US Grand Prix win, between them McLaren and Renault won everything in 2005 and were closely matched. Compare that with Ferrari in 2001. While McLaren in 2005 was up against a team capable of winning eight races to its 10, a relative share of 1.25, the strongest competitor to Ferrari was a team which could muster four wins against its nine, producing a much higher relative share of 2.25. Consequently, while absolute share is a strong indicator of dominance, share relative to the nearest competitor is an even sounder measure of competitive strength.

So these and other statistics – for every driver in every car in every season – must become the sort of factually based measures that comprise a ratings algorithm.

"Loosely scientific" was the expression Mark Hughes used to portray his attempt to measure the competitiveness of cars used by Grand Prix winners, and this is where our paths diverge. If a deep knowledge of Formula One is aligned with the relevant experience of dynamic measurement and ratings, a robust and substantive fact-based ratings system can be created which actually computes whether it is chicken, or whether it is egg!

In the hands of Senna and Prost, the superiority of the McLaren-Hondas in 1988 was devastating. If Senna had not tripped over Schlesser here at Monza, they would have completed a clean sweep that season.

Car superiority

Rather than launch into a detailed discussion about correlation, calibration, data granularity and deviation, the best way to understand the function of a ratings algorithm is to appreciate how it works in practice. In the case of rating car superiority, the objective of the system is to improve on the premise offered by Graphic 10.1. This is that the team with the highest percent strike rate in a given season demonstrates superiority over the next team in the pecking order – a rational yet flawed assumption.

Graphic 10.2 shows the re-ordered ranking after the ratings system has been applied, as well as the gain or loss this represents versus the order initially determined by strike rate. Strike rate being the foundation stone of the ratings system, the expectation is that changes will be subtle rather than radical, particularly at the top of the ranking. Indeed, the top four are completely unchanged. This is hardly surprising when, in those four particular seasons, every race bar two were won by the specified car and team. Such superiority could hardly be improved upon!

The gains and losses – the rankings movers – are particularly noteworthy and explain even more clearly how the ratings system operates. The largest gain is by Williams in 1991, moving up 33 places to 22nd in the rankings. In the preceding year, Williams had won both the Drivers' and the Constructors' World Championships with Alan Jones, and 1991 looked to be a continuation of the same.

Both team drivers contributed to three wins in the opening five races of the season, including two 1–2 finishes. A loss of form by Williams, due more to the competition coming back at them from many directions – Brabham, Ligier, McLaren, Ferrari and Renault were all capable of winning races that year – meant that, although Williams was usually in contention with some strong finishes, wins became much harder to come by during the balance of the season. Even so, Williams was good enough to win the final race, as it had the first, and successfully defended its Constructors' title from the diverse competition.

The ratings system indicates that, throughout the entire season, Williams had a better car than suggested by its (relatively) meagre 27 percent strike rate. The team could have expected more. Therefore, a gain in the rankings

10.2 Car superiority ranking — Strike rate ranked by ratings

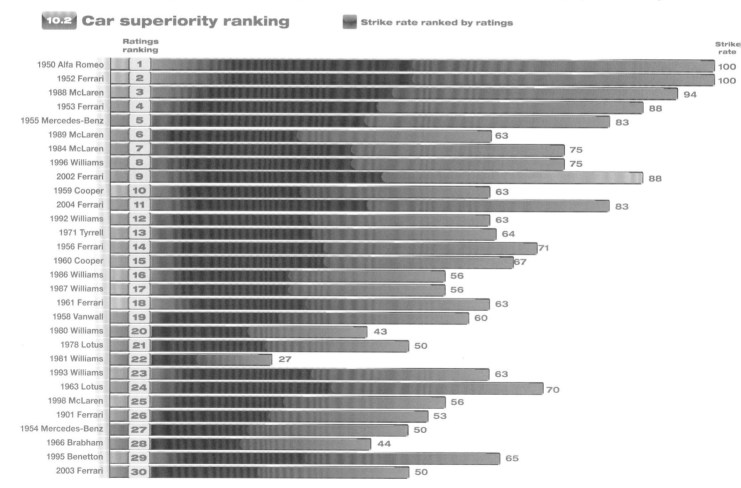

	Ratings ranking	Strike rate
1950 Alfa Romeo	1	100
1952 Ferrari	2	100
1988 McLaren	3	94
1953 Ferrari	4	88
1955 Mercedes-Benz	5	83
1989 McLaren	6	63
1984 McLaren	7	75
1996 Williams	8	75
2002 Ferrari	9	88
1959 Cooper	10	63
2004 Ferrari	11	83
1992 Williams	12	63
1971 Tyrrell	13	64
1956 Ferrari	14	71
1960 Cooper	15	67
1986 Williams	16	56
1987 Williams	17	56
1961 Ferrari	18	63
1958 Vanwall	19	60
1980 Williams	20	43
1978 Lotus	21	50
1981 Williams	22	27
1993 Williams	23	63
1963 Lotus	24	70
1998 McLaren	25	56
1901 Ferrari	26	53
1954 Mercedes-Benz	27	50
1966 Brabham	28	44
1995 Benetton	29	65
2003 Ferrari	30	50

by comparison with percent strike rate is a sign that it under-achieved in terms of wins in relation to its car superiority rating.

The four greatest teams over the decades – Ferrari, Lotus, McLaren and Williams – regularly feature in the higher echelons of the car superiority rankings (Graphic 10.2). As a team, Lotus does least well by comparison with the others. Lotus was somewhat atypical with a notoriously poor reliability record along with a frequently evident driver imbalance, the team relying heavily on the achievements of a lead driver: Jim Clark, Jochen Rindt, Emerson Fittipaldi and (by contract) Mario Andretti. This could be to the detriment of the success opportunity for the number two driver, although, with some notable exceptions, the latter were not always of the highest calibre. Despite the name, Team Lotus, the strategy was actually based less on 'team' and more on 'star driver' and/or technical innovation. Couple this with the aforementioned poor reliability, which in many ways reflected Chapman's minimalist design philosophy, and the consequential 'hit or miss' volatility of the marque is reflected in the Lotus rankings.

The highest-ranked model from Lotus is the Lotus 79, nicknamed 'Black Beauty'. Although an under-achiever, this magnificent example of Chapman's genius is more than worthy to be bracketed with each of the highest rated cars produced by the three other great teams, as listed in the table.

SEASON	MODEL	ENGINE	VICTORIES
1952–53	Ferrari 500	2.0 Ferrari in-line 4	14
1978	Lotus 79 Ford	3.0 Ford-Cosworth DFV V8	6
1988	McLaren MP4/4 Honda	1.5 Honda V6 turbo	15
1996	Williams FW15 Renault	3.0 Renault V10	12

By the same token as a gain in the rankings, a loss or drop shows that a team's results were an over-achievement in relation to the underlying competitiveness of its car. The drop of 16 places by Benetton in 1995 reflects rather well on Michael Schumacher's contribution to Benetton's success that season. It implies that a Benetton-Renault had far less of an advantage over a Williams-Renault than a 65 percent strike rate achievement might suggest. Of course, it can also reflect another dimension within the intricacies of winning. Perhaps the Williams pairing of Hill/Coulthard was not as strong as Schumacher/Herbert at Benetton?

This factor, in turn, identifies a significant limitation in the hypothesis of the ratings system to date. Would there not be something of a black hole in a system which only accounts for competitiveness between cars while ignoring competitiveness between drivers? Without question! So to build a ratings system with probity, a further dimension must be added: the strength of the driver opposition.

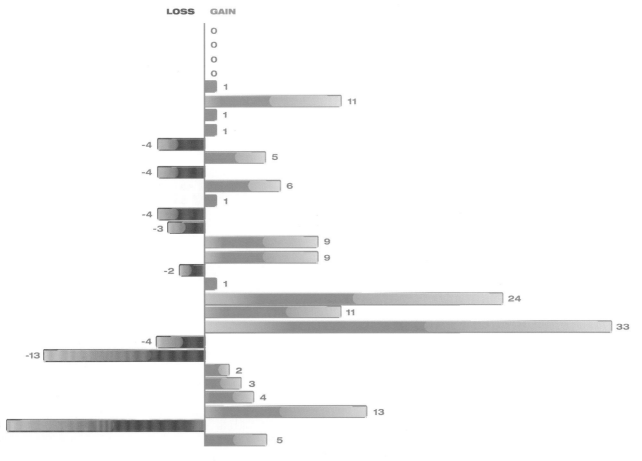

Ratings ranking v Strike rate ranking

LOSS   GAIN

0
0
0
0
1
11
1
1
-4
5
-4
6
1
-4
-3
9
9
-2
1
24
11
33
-4
-13
2
3
4
13
-16
5

The ratings model

The Venn diagram in Graphic 10.3 represents the fully fledged ratings model, designed and developed to integrate three interrelated dimensions:

Performance: A given driver's strike rate in a given season

Equipment: The car superiority rating of that driver's car

Opposition: The competitiveness rating of that driver's opposition

The opposition dimension needs to measure both the strength and the depth of driver competitiveness. For competitive strength, relative share is again one of the best measures to use. Take Senna's titanic struggle with Prost in 1988. In that season, Senna won 50 percent of the races, a statistic matched closely by Michael Schumacher in 2001 with 53 percent. Again, on the surface this might suggest that the strength of the competition they each encountered was indistinguishable, but closer inspection shows that such was not the case. Schumacher's nearest competitor was his brother, Ralf, with an 18 percent win share, whereas Senna's nearest rival, the formidable

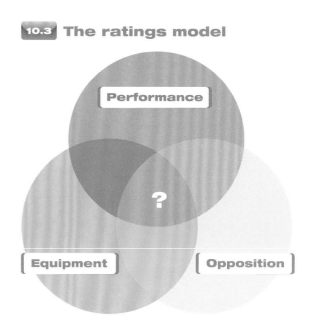

10.3 **The ratings model**

10.4 **Depth of competition** Percent wins by every driver, every season

Driver with most wins Second most Third Fourth Fifth Sixth Seventh Eighth

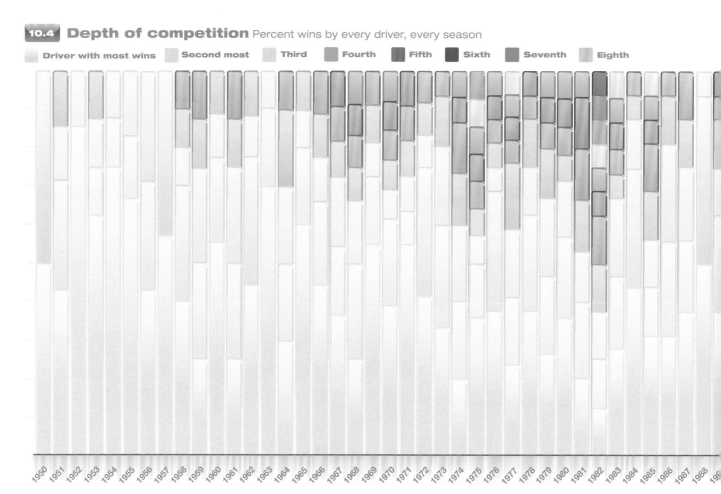

Prost, achieved 44 percent. Clearly, Alain exerted far more competitive pressure on Ayrton than Ralf on Michael. The ratings model needs to reflect this.

Competitive pressure can be exerted not only by the strength of the primary competitor but also through the depth of the secondary opposition. Graphic 10.4 separates the leading two winners each season from the rest to show how the depth of competition has varied year-to-year. In the competitive environment of the 1970s and 1980s, this competitive fragmentation is visibly a much more significant factor. So this becomes a further characteristic that needs to be incorporated into the ratings system in order accurately to balance between competitive pressure stemming from one primary source (strength), or from a multitude of potential winners (depth).

The best way to appraise how the integrated ratings model works in its entirety is by applying it to an established norm. For this purpose, the percent strike rate of the Drivers' World Champions across the 58 years of the championship provides an ideal reference point (Graphic 10.5). How does the ratings system rank the World Championships one to another? And what significant gains and losses does it introduce compared with the original strike rate pecking order, headed, as it is, by Alberto Ascari's 1952 virtuoso performance? Which championship performance surpasses Ascari's and the rest to come out on top?

Ninth   **Tenth**   **Eleventh**

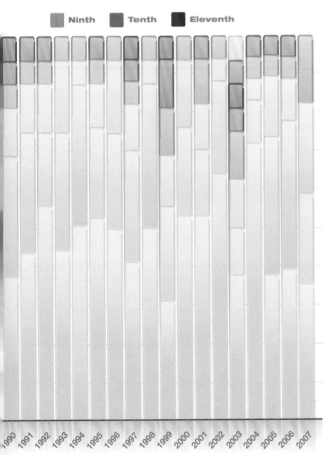

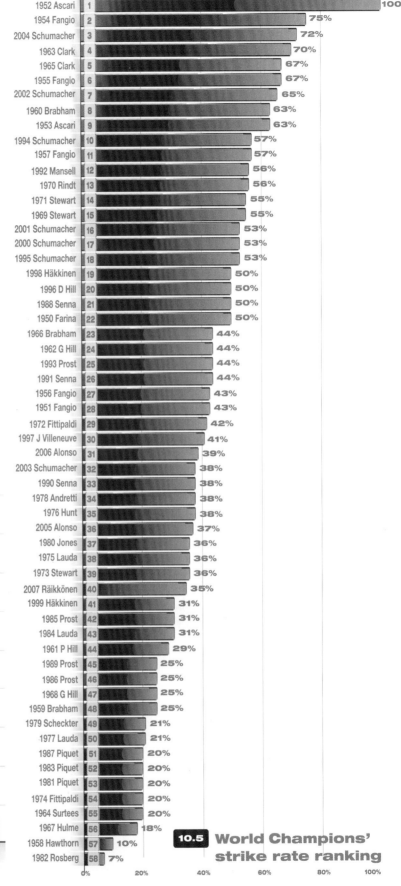

Strike rate ranking

Rank	Driver/Year	Strike rate
1	1952 Ascari	100%
2	1954 Fangio	75%
3	2004 Schumacher	72%
4	1963 Clark	70%
5	1965 Clark	67%
6	1955 Fangio	67%
7	2002 Schumacher	65%
8	1960 Brabham	63%
9	1953 Ascari	63%
10	1994 Schumacher	57%
11	1957 Fangio	57%
12	1992 Mansell	56%
13	1970 Rindt	56%
14	1971 Stewart	55%
15	1969 Stewart	55%
16	2001 Schumacher	53%
17	2000 Schumacher	53%
18	1995 Schumacher	53%
19	1998 Häkkinen	50%
20	1996 D Hill	50%
21	1988 Senna	50%
22	1950 Farina	50%
23	1966 Brabham	44%
24	1962 G Hill	44%
25	1993 Prost	44%
26	1991 Senna	44%
27	1956 Fangio	43%
28	1951 Fangio	43%
29	1972 Fittipaldi	42%
30	1997 J Villeneuve	41%
31	2006 Alonso	39%
32	2003 Schumacher	38%
33	1990 Senna	38%
34	1978 Andretti	38%
35	1976 Hunt	38%
36	2005 Alonso	37%
37	1980 Jones	36%
38	1975 Lauda	36%
39	1973 Stewart	36%
40	2007 Räikkönen	35%
41	1999 Häkkinen	31%
42	1985 Prost	31%
43	1984 Lauda	31%
44	1961 P Hill	29%
45	1989 Prost	25%
46	1986 Prost	25%
47	1968 G Hill	25%
48	1959 Brabham	25%
49	1979 Scheckter	21%
50	1977 Lauda	21%
51	1987 Piquet	20%
52	1983 Piquet	20%
53	1981 Piquet	20%
54	1974 Fittipaldi	20%
55	1964 Surtees	20%
56	1967 Hulme	18%
57	1958 Hawthorn	10%
58	1982 Rosberg	7%

10.5 **World Champions' strike rate ranking**

0%   20%   40%   60%   80%   100%

The World Championship rankings

Graphic 10.6 provides the answer to the burning question. Placed at the very top of the list of World Championships is Michael Schumacher's 1994 title with the Ford-powered Benetton. The ratings system, which rates driver performance, is proclaiming that allowing for the competitiveness of his equipment that year, and the strength and depth of the driver competition he was up against, Schumacher's achievement, with a strike rate of 57 percent, surpassed the equivalent performance of every other World Champion.

No wonder this chapter is entitled 'Contentious conclusions'!

Of all the championship years, 1994 was one of the most contentious: Ayrton Senna and Roland Ratzenberger perished at Imola. There was more than a whiff of scandal regarding the alleged illegal use of launch control and traction control. Finally, at the championship showdown in Adelaide, Schumacher snatched the title by eliminating Damon Hill in a dubious move that led to a collision.

Ironically, due to his suspension from two races due to on-track misdemeanors, Schumacher's 1994 percent strike rate is enhanced. He started in 14 Grands Prix, rather than the full 16-race series, which raised his strike rate from 50 to 57 percent. Yet despite all the hullabaloo surrounding the 1994 season, first, Schumacher was officially awarded the World Championship, and second, without question his extraordinary powers had much to do with making Ford's Cosworth HB V8 Benetton such a formidable winner that season against the Williams-Renault V10.

At number two in the rankings, Fangio's 1954 championship triumph dispels a myth. The 1954 season is often bracketed with 1955 (placed at 31) as one of two seasons of utter supremacy by the Silver Arrows. The reality is that, whereas Mercedes-Benz assisted Fangio to his third Drivers' World Championship in 1955, Fangio was instrumental in delivering a first championship to Mercedes-Benz in 1954. In that year, the Mercedes blitzkrieg began well enough with a formation finish by the streamliners on their debut at Reims but, subsequently, the Stuttgart company's results look quite ordinary if Fangio is taken out of the equation.

Various issues restricted the team's results, not

Fernando Alonso's 2006 World Championship, when he beat Michael Schumacher in a competitive Ferrari, is ranked at number 7.

least reliability. But in assessing Fangio's championship performance that season, an additional factor is that, before the belated arrival of Mercedes in the World Championships, he had already won twice with a car which subsequently won nothing and could muster only a couple of podium finishes. Nevertheless, the ratings have a neutral effect (N/C) on 1954. This suggests that, in the achievement of a magnificent 75 percent strike rate, both car and driver played significant roles, with the car, as will be seen later (Graphic 10.7), just holding the edge.

Jim Clark's pair of championships both feature in the top six, his 1965 season at number three. Neither season is appreciably altered from the established strike rate position, suggesting near-parity between driver and car inputs in what was ultimately achieved for strike rate. However, a positive for 1965 (plus three places) compared with a negative for 1963 (minus two places) indicates that the driver was a marginally greater factor in 1965, which is borne out in reality. That year, Clark was ranged against a credible team mate in Mike Spence (a lesser but worthy substitute for Pete Arundell), as well as formidable proven winners in Graham Hill, John Surtees and Jackie Stewart, all driving competitive machinery. Despite a much stiffer test than in 1963, when his number two driver had made him look especially good, results in 1965 were a virtual carbon copy. Clark and his Lotus were simply on another level. They just blew the opposition away.

10.6 WORLD CHAMPIONS RANKED BY THE RATINGS SYSTEM		plus/minus change v. strike rate ranking
1	1994 Schumacher	+10
2	1954 Fangio	N/C
3	1965 Clark	+3
4	1970 Rindt	+9
5	1957 Fangio	+5
6	1963 Clark	-2
7	2006 Alonso	+24
8	2005 Alonso	+28
9	2000 Schumacher	+8
10	1969 Stewart	+4
11	1972 Fittipaldi	+18
12	1990 Senna	+22
13	1973 Stewart	+24
14	1991 Senna	+11
15	2004 Schumacher	-12
16	1995 Schumacher	N/C
17	1960 Brabham	-8
18	1976 Hunt	+14
19	2001 Schumacher	-1
20	1962 G Hill	+3
21	2002 Schumacher	-14
22	1997 J Villeneuve	+8
23	1998 Häkkinen	-1
24	1951 Fangio	+3
25	1992 Mansell	-13
26	1986 Prost	+20
27	1966 Brabham	-3
28	1971 Stewart	-13
29	1993 Prost	-3
30	1952 Ascari	-29
31	1955 Fangio	-26
32	2007 Räikkönen	-16
33	2003 Schumacher	+3
34	1975 Lauda	+5
35	1956 Fangio	-6
36	1999 Häkkinen	+7
37	1985 Prost	+5
38	1996 D Hill	-18
39	1953 Ascari	-30
40	1978 Andretti	-6
41	1980 Jones	-1
42	1977 Lauda	+7
43	1981 Piquet	+10
44	1983 Piquet	+10
45	1968 G Hill	+1
46	1964 Surtees	+5
47	1961 P Hill	-4
48	1988 Senna	-27
49	1950 Farina	-29
50	1984 Lauda	-9
51	1979 Scheckter	-1
52	1974 Fittipaldi	N/C
53	1967 Hulme	+3
54	1959 Brabham	-9
55	1989 Prost	-7
56	1958 Hawthorn	+1
57	1987 Piquet	-2
58	1982 Rosberg	N/C

Cream rises, and ranked near the top of Graphic 10.6 are the fabled championships when drivers have delivered titles against the odds. Take Jochen Rindt at number four, defying the might of Maranello in his wretchedly curtailed 1970 season. Or Fangio at number five, in his final full season in 1957, once again seeing off the young bloods, Moss, Brooks, Collins and Hawthorn – all of them in the latest from Vanwall or Ferrari, he in a Maserati entering its fourth season and nearing the end of its competitive life.

Perception is not always reality. Working through the rankings year-by-year – relying not just on the folklore and recollection from the past, but also reflecting on the factual detail of the season – is the way to see how the ratings system re-orders the winning achievement (percent strike rate) in accord with a champion's prevailing equipment (car) and opposition (drivers).

Of equal fascination as the rankings order are the gains and losses against strike rate. Take a look at the losses indicating that the car was a greater factor than the driver in what was achieved. Inevitably, Ascari's two championships – 1952 being at the top of the strike rates – plummet around 30 places to reach a mid-point in the rankings. The ratings system detects high car superiority and low driver competitive pressure, while still acknowledging strike rates of the magnitude of 63 percent and – 100 percent.

On the positive change side, Fernando Alonso's back-to-back championships are rightly catapulted over 20 places to reach numbers seven and eight in the rankings. Extremely fast, but not always the fastest, Alonso delivered two superb titles with little better than equal equipment and in the teeth of immense competitive pressure. In

2005, Alonso stood his ground against a post-midseason onslaught from the McLarens of Kimi Räikkönen and Juan Pablo Montoya. Particularly in view of the 'mass-damper' affair, Alonso's conquest of Schumacher in 2006 must be considered an even more significant triumph.

The most graphic way concisely to review how the rankings system appraises each of the 58 World Championships is by using that wonderful analysis tool for the comparison of two variables, the Boston Matrix scatter diagram (Graphic 10.7). On the X-axis is strike rate, and on the Y-axis the ratings index, each championship being represented by a marker that is identified by season. The matrix is divided into four quadrants determined by the average for each of the X and Y variables. The top-right quadrant is tagged 'Great Driver' because here are found the symbols for the championships combining high success (percent strike rate) with high ratings (remembering that high ratings depict low car superiority and fierce competition). The bottom-right quadrant combines high success with low ratings (a superior car and/or weak competition) and therefore 'Great Car', and so on. It must be remembered that this is the assessment of the results attained by each World Champion driver in his championship year, given the equipment at his disposal and the competition he faced.

To illustrate, Nelson Piquet in 1987 and Niki Lauda in 1984 each enjoyed a great car, but neither is in the 'Great Car' quadrant because both were competitively outgunned by their team-mates with similar machinery (Nigel Mansell and Alain Prost respectively).

The distribution of the scatter diagram tells us that there is a fairly even split between driver-orientated championships

10.7 The great and the good

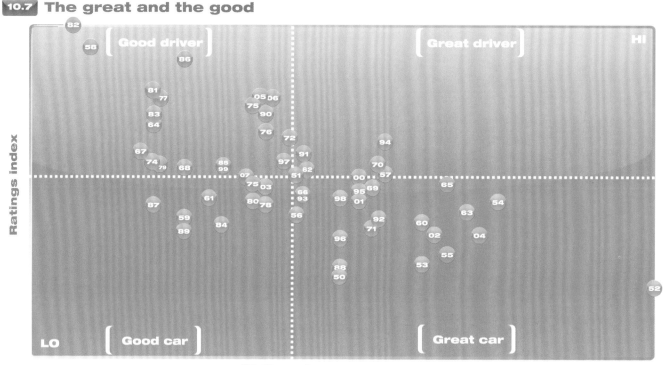

(the upper two quadrants) and car-orientated championships (the lower two quadrants). Inevitably, there is some clustering around the average where the quadrants cross, and there are three extreme outliers (1952, 1958 and 1982), each holding a position one would expect. A number of championships, including 2007, are very close to the borderline between one quadrant and another.

But of most interest are the 28 that fall into the two right-hand quadrants labelled 'Great'. These are split 21:7 in favour of 'Great Car'. The table lists them in chronological order.

Precious few arguments would be found with the results from this table which well illustrates how effectively the ratings system differentiates, bearing in mind the proviso that it is the driver that is being rated, not the car per se.

Because of the emotive expression 'Great Driver', the similar table listing the seven championships that fell into that particular quadrant may be more controversial. But bear in mind that all this list is saying is that, allowing for the champion's car superiority (or otherwise) and driver opposition, the results achieved in these championships were greater than might otherwise have been expected – the implication being that the driver made up that difference.

Love it or hate it, this very same ratings system has been used to rank the magnificent seven. The only distinction is that it has been applied to a whole career, not just a single championship season. The success in each year is weighted by the strength and depth of driver opposition and the superiority or otherwise of the machinery used.

Time to open the envelope!

YEAR	GREAT CAR	CHAMPION DRIVER
1950	Alfa Romeo	Giuseppe Farina
1952	Ferrari	Alberto Ascari
1953	Ferrari	Alberto Ascari
1954	Maserati & Mercedes-Benz	Juan Fangio
1955	Mercedes-Benz	Juan Fangio
1956	Lancia-Ferrari	Juan Fangio
1960	Cooper-Climax	Jack Brabham
1963	Lotus-Climax	Jim Clark
1965	Lotus-Climax	Jim Clark
1966	Brabham-Repco	Jack Brabham
1969	Matra-Ford	Jackie Stewart
1971	Tyrrell-Ford	Jackie Stewart
1988	McLaren-Honda	Ayrton Senna
1992	Williams-Renault	Nigel Mansell
1993	Williams-Renault	Alain Prost
1995	Benetton-Renault	Michael Schumacher
1996	Williams-Renault	Damon Hill
1998	McLaren-Mercedes-Benz	Mika Häkkinen
2001	Ferrari	Michael Schumacher
2002	Ferrari	Michael Schumacher
2004	Ferrari	Michael Schumacher

	GREAT DRIVER	CHAMPION'S CAR
1951	Juan Fangio	Alfa Romeo
1957	Juan Fangio	Maserati
1962	Graham Hill	BRM
1970	Jochen Rindt	Lotus-Ford
1991	Ayrton Senna	McLaren-Honda
1994	Michael Schumacher	Benetton-Ford
2000	Michael Schumacher	Ferrari

In 1970, the year of his tragic death at Monza, Jochen Rindt's inspired performance touched greatness. His very first victory, seen here, had only come at the end of the previous season, in the US Grand Prix at Watkins Glen.

THIRD

In third place, from Hürth-Hermühlheim in Germany, winner of more Grands Prix than any other and the greatest Formula One driver of his era, **The Red Baron** – MICHAEL SCHUMACHER!

SECOND

In second place, from Kilmany in Scotland, the most dominant Grand Prix winner of all time and the greatest Formula One driver of his era, **The Flying Scotsman** – JIM CLARK!

And in first place, from Balcarce in Argentina and taking the top step of the all-time podium, the man who won the most Grands Prix from the fewest starts – and the greatest Formula One driver of all time, **The Maestro – JUAN MANUEL FANGIO!**

The award ceremony is a thing of the past, leaving, as it so often can, contrasting emotions in its aftermath – delight or despondency, approval or annoyance. Now is the opportunity for dispassionate reflection on the results. Graphic 10.8 makes a direct comparison for the Magnificent Seven between an index based on the ratings and an index of the original strike rate order. Fangio, who topped both measures, anchors each index at 100.

As the system is founded on strike rate, it is no surprise that Fangio, with his incomparable strike rate of 47 percent, remains at the top of the ratings – but only just! Once car superiority and competitive pressure are allowed for, it becomes an extremely close call. A mere five percentage points separate the top three. The other four are clearly at a lower level by comparison although, once again, not nearly as remote of Fangio as strike rate originally placed them.

Take Moss, for example. A rating index of 79 percent against Fangio, as opposed to a strike rate index of 51 percent, is a far more suitable representation of their equivalence one to the other.

As for the order between the seven, Clark just edges ahead of Schumacher, while Senna moves in front of Prost

– and Moss ahead of both of them. This confirms, if ever there was doubt, that in the all-time rankings, Senna's rivalry did for Prost's aspirations, just as Prost did for Senna.

Naturally the cars these seven raced played indispensable parts in their illustrious careers. It is already apparent from earlier which car was the best each had at his disposal. Perhaps using the ratings to identify the car with which each won against the odds says more about their ability to wring a victory from lesser machinery (see the table below). Of the bunch, Stewart had the real dog!

YEAR	DRIVER	CAR	WINS
1953	Juan Fangio	Maserati A6GCM	1
1956	Stirling Moss	Maserati 250F	2
1966	Jim Clark	Lotus 43 BRM	1
1970	Jackie Stewart	March 701 Ford	1
1987	Alain Prost	McLaren MP4/3 TAG	3
1986	Ayrton Senna	Lotus 98T Renault	2
1992	Michael Schumacher	Benetton B192 Ford	1

10.8 **The magnificent seven revisited** Ranking the greatest grand prix drivers of all time

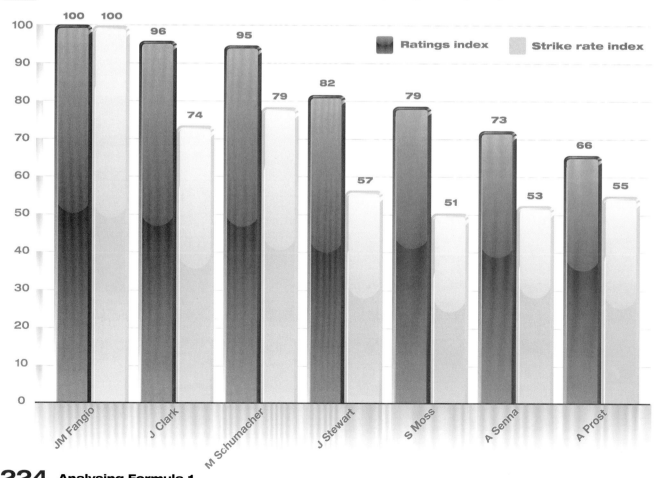

To summarise, this book has attempted to examine the history of Grand Prix racing since 1950 from a totally new perspective. With the unique use of graphical analysis, the author has tried to introduce a new level of knowledge and understanding for Grand Prix followers. The evolution of Formula One since the inception of the World Championship is tracked year-by-year over almost six decades, defining each new era and identifying the key developments and their implications. The changing Grand Prix landscape for races, circuits, drivers, cars, teams and even danger is analysed in unprecedented depth and detail.

Underpinning it all is the central theme of the study – winners and winning – and the search, fulfilled in this concluding chapter, to find a viable methodology which can differentiate and compare between the achievements of drivers across each era of the sport. It is hoped that the designation of serial winners, the Magnificent Seven and the all-time podium introduces some fresh vocabulary for Formula One and draws up a new hierarchy for Grand Prix winning. Graphic 10.9 confirms that, beyond race winners and champions – even beyond some multiple champions – there have been drivers whose winning records transcend the rest. Seven of these have truly been the masters of the sport.

Can others join them in the rarified atmosphere of greatness? Why not? There is evidence enough that two, maybe three of today's drivers are vying to turn the magnificent seven into the great eight! Whether they can dislodge those who stand astride the all-time podium is another matter. Each of those three has raised the entry barrier to staggering heights.

10.9 Hierarchy of winning

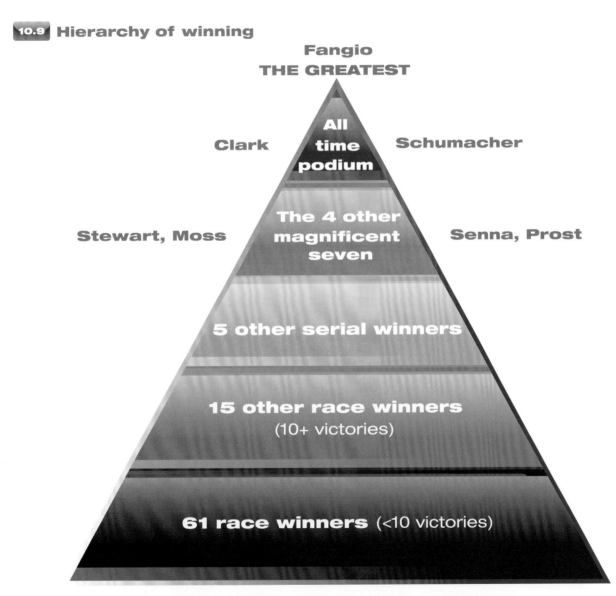

Fangio
THE GREATEST

Clark — All time podium — Schumacher

Stewart, Moss — The 4 other magnificent seven — Senna, Prost

5 other serial winners

15 other race winners (10+ victories)

61 race winners (<10 victories)

536 other Grand Prix drivers

What if?

Three drivers from highly different Grand Prix eras have emerged from the ratings process very closely matched. It is as though they are thundering across the finish-line just metres apart as the chequered flag falls on that fantasy classic, the All-Time Greats Grand Prix.

Of the three on the all-time podium, Schumacher is the only one who completed a career, beginning at the age of 22 and retiring at 37. Clark made his Grand Prix debut at 24 and died shortly before his 32nd birthday. Largely because of the intervention of the Second World War, Fangio's career was limited by age, having taken his place on the starting grid for that inaugural World Championship race in 1950 when almost 39 years old, and retiring at 47.

You can see where this is going… It was a point Mark Hughes made in his *Autosport* article: "Heroes of an earlier age couldn't have conceived of staying in one piece long enough to rack up the huge (winning) numbers he [Schumacher] has."

There are several questions to consider.

Would a more youthful Fangio have made a successful transition to rear-engined machinery, and carried on his phenomenal strike rate? Yes to the first question, only a

maybe to the second. This is not to question his continuing capacity to win races. It is simply that he might well have returned to Ferrari instead of joining one of the increasingly successful British teams, Cooper, Lotus or BRM. If that were the case, he would have had a field-day in 1961, but may not have succeeded so well before or after that season.

If, in April 1968, Clark had survived unscathed at Hockenheim, would he have maintained or would he have improved his remarkable strike rate? Yes to the first, probably to the second. If, like Schumacher, Clark had retired at 37, then with 1968 included he would have enjoyed five more seasons. Because of the intrinsic danger, in reality he may have retired sooner. Clearly in 1969 and 1971 he would have been seriously challenged by Stewart in the Matra-Ford and Tyrrell-Ford (a mouth-watering fantasy). Put another way, Stewart would have had his hands even more full! In 1968 with the Lotus 49, and in 1970 and 1972 with the Lotus 72, it would have been a Clark-fest!

Formula One represents the pinnacle of worldwide motorsport. This comprehensive investigation has concluded that, at least in the deed of winning, this spectacular racing series remains essentially unchanged. Purely stated, it

No 'what if?' discussion about Formula 1 would be complete without reference to Gilles Villeneuve, seen here in 1981 in characteristic pose at the circuit to which he gave his name.

remains: "Young men in racing cars trying to win circuit races by beating the competition without killing themselves." As chilling as the final three words may be, it is important to dwell on their implication for the sport a moment longer.

Way beyond any other change in Grand Prix racing over the years, danger is the primary ingredient that fundamentally separates past from present. Grand Prix racing remains highly dangerous but, during the 1990s, safety improved to such a level that deliberate, let alone threatened, car-on-car contact could be used to decide the outcome of a race or a championship. In this one vital way, the psyche of Grand Prix racing had changed. From 'win, but not at all costs' (a driver's skill being engaged in avoiding accidents because of the dreadful consequences), it had become 'win at all costs' (the threat or actuality of an accident, overt but unspoken).

Grand Prix racing was now no longer a blend of skill with courage. It had become a blend of skill with will; intimidatory will. For this reason, serious consideration had to be given in the building of the ratings system to account for this fundamental psychological and emotional difference between drivers of the past and the present. After much experimentation with a danger index dimension, however, this concept was shelved: it did not provide a level playing field in the assessment of modern drivers.

Of the magnificent seven, the Grand Prix careers of two others were curtailed by death or by injury, Senna at the age of 34 and Moss approaching 33. Selfish as the thought may be, Formula One was again denied two

potential rivalries of epic proportions: Moss versus Clark, Senna versus Schumacher. Such rivalries might well have blunted all the subsequent winning achievements of Clark and Schumacher. Contemplating such lost rivalries, the remaining impression is that Clark's winning record may have benefited most positively and Schumacher's most negatively. But conjecture is, after all, exactly what a fact-based ratings system has been devised to eradicate.

So, is the author as comfortable with the all-time podium of Fangio, Clark and Schumacher, as he had been in 1970 when Marciano gained the verdict over Ali? Absolutely! It is plausible, and he (for one) knows how much diligence went into building the ratings system. Even if you find the conclusions in this chapter too contentious, it is hoped that the journey the book has taken over nearly six decades has been stimulating, entertaining, and food for thought.

During more than 50 years of Formula One racing, regardless of the specific shape and form then prevailing, any driver who can achieve a strike rate of 47 percent over many seasons is an individual of very special qualities. In crowning Juan Manuel Fangio as the best of the best, what convinces me that the ratings system has produced the right result is the fact that it is endorsed by someone who drove wheel-to-wheel against Fangio.

Sir Stirling Moss – no longer simply the best driver never to win the World Championship, but now rightfully on a pedestal as one of only seven all-time greats – has always contended that Fangio was supreme: "In Formula One, he was the best."

Enough said.

Two weeks after the 1994 double tragedy at Imola, the drivers gathered on the grid at Monte Carlo to pay tribute to Ayrton Senna and Roland Ratzenberger.

Everyone knows that the gestation period of an elephant is lengthy – typically 18–22 months. But that's nothing compared with the nascent development of this book. From conception to birth at least twice... And I'm talking years here, not months!

Two aspects of my life triggered this enduring mission: a passion for Formula One from boyhood, and a zeal for numbers from my business activities.

What the latter has shown me time and again is that, if you know where to look and how to use it, there is information below the surface of simple numbers which can provide rich insights way beyond the bald statistics themselves. This knowledge and belief, together with a fascination for sporting endeavour, kept alive a goal – almost a quest.

What are the ingredients of true greatness in sport? How can greatness be measured? Can the greats of yesteryear be compared with the young lions of today? Can valid comparisons ever be drawn across the generations to measure greatness? If so, what criteria can be used? Can such thinking be applied to Grand Prix motor racing?

Take telemetry – an essential tool in Grand Prix racing today. When applied through intelligent analysis, interpretation and understanding, it speaks volumes about car and driver performance. But in the end, telemetry is merely the process of remotely monitoring a time series of factual information. By today's technology standards, the collection of the data itself is not that remarkable. The organisation and presentation of that data, to generate usable information for analysis – that is the true art form of the science.

Any genuine motor racing enthusiast will have his collection of books to enhance and stimulate his or her pleasure in the sport. The bookshelf will include one of those wonderful publications that compile and present Formula One statistics in minute detail. I devour these with as much relish as the biographies and autobiographies although, I have to admit, they always stop just at the point when I begin to get really interested.

On the final three to five pages, after cataloguing every conceivable detail on the previous 100 plus, there will be a list of starters and winners, pole positions and fastest laps. For what purpose? To provide a record? A reference to assist our dimming memories? For trivia questions at the local pub quiz?

At Silverstone in 1987, on the 63rd lap of 65, Nigel Mansell passed Williams team-mate Nelson Piquet at Stowe to take the lead. It was the greatest Grand Prix moment I ever witnessed!

Whatever the purpose of these statistics, such books occupy an important place on my shelf. If they did not exist, I would compile one myself. But once in possession of such rich 'telemetry', why not use it to draw some deeper conclusions? I became convinced that lurking beneath the surface of these statistical masterpieces could be found an even richer seam of information. I wanted to explore the 'telemetry' of the Grand Prix drivers – the factual footprints they have each bequeathed over the last five, nearly six decades. And I wanted to develop an analytical process to uncover, beyond any reasonable doubt, who has been the greatest Grand Prix winner since the inception of the FIA World Championship of Drivers. And then, based on this study and its findings, to write an informative and enjoyable book with appeal to a wide audience, to the connoisseur as well as the more casual Formula One follower.

The first step was to create or acquire a highly detailed and accurate database of the results from all 785 Grand Prix races (including 11 Indy 500s) over 58 years that could be interrogated electronically. After casting around the usual suspects, I was fortunate to opt for the superb database that was developed by David Hayhoe and David Holland for their premier reference work, *Grand Prix Data Book*, which I now regard as a companion volume to this book. The extent of their meticulous efforts to maintain the absolute accuracy of this comprehensive Formula One database is greatly to their credit, as is the help and encouragement they have given me in my quest.

The database was first accessible to me in the summer of 2004. I initially utilised it to conduct a preliminary study to test and evaluate that the ultimate project goal was, indeed, feasible. Positive results led to the development of an A–Z plan that would produce both a book and a ratings methodology, the work on the first culminating in the second. By following the steps (or chapters), additional knowledge and understanding would accrue to enhance, develop and refine the preliminary ratings methodology, which would form the basis of the concluding chapter.

The next major step was to secure a publisher, and I am most grateful to Haynes Publishing, and most especially to Mark Hughes for his faith in this project.

Then the really hard work began. Over three years, an enormous amount of study, investigation, research, analysis and evaluation has gone into the completion of Chapters 1–9. This has involved the interrogation of the database to produce analyses and establish findings; reference to numerous other sources of quantitative and qualitative information to substantiate, check and develop findings, as listed in the bibliography; creating graphics to clearly illustrate the findings and to provide the graphical content of the book; and writing explanatory or descriptive commentary which draws conclusions from the findings, completes each chapter, and moves the process forward towards the project goal.

The key learning from working through Chapters 1–9 is that Formula One remains fundamentally unchanged. It quintessentially continues to be: "Young men in racing

cars trying to win circuit races by beating the competition without killing themselves."

It was on this premise that the ratings model used in Chapter 10 was founded. The operative words in the above definition are: 'men'; 'cars'; 'win'; 'competition'.

The ratings model, therefore, comprises three dimensions – performance (men + win), equipment (cars), opposition (competition) – all of which are consistently relevant over time, and all of which can be consistently measured over time.

The final three words of the definition – 'without killing themselves' – single out the fundamental ingredient above any other that separates Grand Prix racing past from Grand Prix racing present. The fact that three of the 'magnificent seven' died or suffered career-ending injury at the wheel of racing cars attests to the ramification of danger in the sport. But the same shocking fact also stands as testimony to the outstanding work that has been conducted in the quest of safety, particularly within the context of a sport in which average speeds rose by more than one-third over 58 years. Despite the elimination of driver fatalities since 1994, one great danger still exists in Grand Prix racing today… complacency.

But at least, race after race, drivers no longer have to put their lives on the line to compete in their chosen sport – a factor for which the ratings system rightly made no allowance. If it had, something that has long been widely suspected, but up to now always needed to be whispered with a caveat, could be stated with even greater authority:

Juan Manuel Fangio is the greatest Grand Prix driver of all time.

Why is my lucky number 17? Because it was the race number Graham Hill carried on his stackpipe BRM P57 to win his first Grand Prix at Zandvoort in 1962. As a fan, following Hill was a rollercoaster of high peaks but very deep troughs!

Bibliography

The principal source of information used in Analysing Formula 1 was Grand Prix Data Book, by David Hayhoe and David Holland, published by Haynes Publishing in 2006. Additional material and research included:

Magazines and annuals
Autocourse
Autosport
Motocourse
Motor Sport

Websites
FORIX on Autosport.com
CRASH .net

DVD/Videos
Official FIA season reviews

Books
Alain Prost (Corgi Books 1993) Christopher Hilton

Ayrton Senna – The hard edge of genius (Haynes, 1995) Christopher Hilton

Beyond the Limit (Macmillan 2001) Professor Sid Watkins

British Grand Prix (PRC/Bookmart 1992) Maurice Hamilton

BRM (Pan Books, 1964) Raymond Mays/Peter Roberts

Bruce McLaren – The man and his racing team (Eyre & Spottiswoode 1971) Eoin Young

Chasing the Title (Haynes Publishing 1999) Nigel Roebuck

Damon Hill (Parragon 1996) David Tremayne

Fangio – A Pirelli Album (Pavilion Books 1991) Stirling Moss/Doug Nye

Ferrari – All the cars (Haynes Publishing 2005) Arnoldo Mondadori/Giorgio Nada

Ferrari – The Grand Prix cars (Hazleton Publishing 1984) Alan Henry

From Brands Hatch to Indianapolis (Hamlyn Publishing 1974) Tommaso Tommasi

Gilles Villeneuve – The life of the legendary racing driver (Virgin Books 2003) Gerald Donaldson

Grand Prix Men (André Deutsch 1998) Ted Macauley

Grand Prix Who's Who (Travel Publishing Ltd 2000) Steve Small

Grand Prix! – Volume 1 – 1950–1965 (Haynes Publishing 1981) Mike Lang

Grand Prix! – Volume 2 – 1966–1973 (Haynes Publishing 1982) Mike Lang

Grand Prix! – Volume 3 – 1974–1980 (Haynes Publishing 1983) Mike Lang

Grand Prix! – Volume 4 – 1981–1984 (Haynes Publishing 1992) Mike Lang

History of the Grand Prix car – 1966–85 (Hazleton Publishing 1986) Doug Nye

Hunt v Lauda (Beaverbrook Newspapers 1976) David Benson

Inside the mind of the Grand Prix driver (Haynes Publishing 2001) Christopher Hilton

The International Motor Racing Guide (David Bull Publishing 2003) Peter Higham

It was fun! (Patrick Stephens Ltd 1993) Tony Rudd

Jackie Stewart – A restless life (Virgin Books 2004) Timothy Collings/Stuart Sykes

James Hunt (Collins Willow 1994) Gerald Donaldson

Jim Clark – Portrait of a great driver (Hamlyn Publishing 1968) Graham Gauld

Jochen Rindt – The Story of a World Champion (William Kimber 1973) Heinz Prüller

Ken Tyrrell (Collins Willow 2002) Maurice Hamilton

Kings of the Nürburgring (Transport Bookman Publications 2005) Chris Nixon

Life at the Limit (William Kimber 1969) Graham Hill

Mario Andretti (David Bull Publishing 2001) Gordon Kirby

McLaren – The Grand Prix, Can-Am and Indy cars (Hazleton Publishing 1988) Doug Nye

Michael Schumacher – The quest for redemption (Transworld Publishers 1999) James Allen

Mon Ami Mate (Transport Bookman Publications 1991) Chris Nixon

Nelson Piquet (Hazleton Publishing 1991) *Mike Doodson*

Nigel Mansell – My Autobiography (Collins Willow 1995) Nigel Mansell/James Allen

Niki Lauda Formula 1 (William Kimber 1979) Niki Lauda

Stirling Moss (Cassell & Co 2001) Robert Edwards

Stirling Moss (Patrick Stephens Ltd 1997) Karl Ludvigsen

The Great Encyclopaedia of Formula 1 (Constable & Robinson Ltd 2000) Pierre Ménard

The Life of Senna (BusinessF1 Books 2004) Tom Rubython

The Maserati 250F (Aston Publications 1985) Anthony Pritchard

The Piranha Club (Virgin Books 2002) Timothy Collings

The Unofficial Formula One Encyclopaedia (Anness Publishing 2004) Mark Hughes

Theme Lotus 1956–1986 – From Chapman to Ducarouge (Motor Racing Publications 1986) Doug Nye

Vanwall (Haynes Publishing 1990) Ian Bamsey

When the Flag Drops (William Kimber 1971) Jack Brabham

Williams – Formula 1 Racing Team (Haynes Publications 1998) Alan Henry